FASCINATING LITTLE-KNOWN FACTS FROM AROUND THE WORLD

FASCINATING LITTLE-KNOWN FACTS FROM AROUND THE WORLD

A HANDBOOK
FIRST EDITION

HADARA CAROL

FASCINATING LITTLE-KNOWN FACTS FROM AROUND THE WORLD

iUniverse books may be ordered through booksellers or by contacting:

iUniverse
1663 Liberty Drive
Bloomington, IN 47403
www.iuniverse.com
844-349-9409

ISBN: 978-1-6632-3193-2 (sc)
ISBN: 978-1-6632-3207-6 (e)

Print information available on the last page.

iUniverse rev. date: 11/15/2021

I wish to thank Steve, my husband, who ended up writing a few books after his retirement, and indirectly inspired me to write this book.

To Shelli and David, my children, with love for them and their prosperity.

I wish to thank Richard Belcastro for his generous assistance in designing the beautiful cover of this book.

I also wish to thank Andrea Kessler who kept on sending me unusual and fascinating facts from around the world that inspired me to add them to this book.

Contents

Introduction ix

The origin of Civilizations & Modern Humans 1
The Middle East Past & Present 2
The Major Contributions of the Sumerian Civilization 4
The Hebrew / Israelite Civilization - Past & Present Major
        contributions 7
The Old and New Babylonian Civilizations Major Contributions ... 13
The Hittite Civilization Major Contributions 16
The Minoan & Phoenician Civilizations Major Contributions 17
The Lydian Civilization Major Contributions 19
The Ancient Egyptian Civilization Major Contributions 20
The Persian / Iranian Civilization Major Contributions 26
The Major Contributions of the Chinese Civilization 27
The Ancient Greek Civilization Major Contributions 30
The Roman Civilization Major Contributions 33
INDIA - Past and Present Civilization Major Contributions 37
Little Known Facts From The Middle Ages 39
Japan, Asia & Southeast Asia Civilizations –Past and
        Present Major Contributions 44
Health & the Human Body 48
Nutrients, Foods, Diet & Health 110
General Little-Known Facts 207
Some Bad Manners That Are Seen as Good, in Some
        Cultures Around the World 252
Unexpected Hobbies of Some U.S. Presidents 254
Little-Known Tidbits About Some Animals and Insects 255
Farming / Plants 282
Signature Dishes of the Fifty States of the US 297

Famous Personalities That Never Attended or Dropped
    Out of School/College, or Did Not Have Much Schooling ... 302
Women and Men That Deserve to be More Famous........................ 308
Unknown Little - Facts about Men & Women That Are
    Famous for Their Contributions 323

Introduction

So, you think that you know it all?
Not a chance!

There are many among us in the world that walks through life unaware that they act or follow the behavior, cultures, traditions, and ideas of past generations and cultures. Most do not question this or try to find out why it is so, but rather take it for granted.

As for myself, I question things and do not always accept the norm as is. I admit that it has been very frustrating at times to ask unusual questions and not receive satisfying answers from many people, including my teachers, parents, family members and friends. However, I am determined to never give up and to continue the quest to acquire whatever knowledge I seek.

I stumbled upon some of the answers to my questions through my long teaching career focusing on history, which spanned over more than three decades -- teaching on many levels, from junior high school to community college.

In 1991, my family and I moved from Long Island, New York to Scottsdale, Arizona, to find a better life.

As a new teacher coming from another state, I frequently received the toughest students. I am thankful that those difficult students gave me a lot of hardship through my teaching career, because they inspired me indirectly to dig deeper than usual in order to find more fascinating little-known facts that I would later share with them. I used to tell my students that if I did not need to spend time to discipline them, I would be able to dedicate two minutes at the end of class to tell them a cool and fascinating little-known fact.

To my surprise it actually worked well most of the time and they tended to cooperate.

In this book I intend to uncover some very fascinating little-known facts that I used to share with my students, which actually touch our lives every single day. I will present these facts and show how they are related to our life and current time.

At first while reading the book you will come across the unusual contributions of the Sumerians, Babylonians, Hittites, Phoenicians, Lydians, Egyptians, Hebrews, Persians and Indians (from India) that resonate even today. For example, you will discover why we place great importance to the "red carpet" treatment, why we have seven days in a week, and how the game of chess and terms like "check-mate" came about.

Later, you will discover the unusual contributions and ideas that came to us from the Chinese, Greeks, and Romans, for example, across various time periods spanning from the Middle Ages to the Renaissance, to the Age of Exploration and beyond. Topics of note include the origin of the word 'salary' that we use today, in addition to the origin of the "middle finger flip", why we extend the right hand as a symbol of friendship, and why men and women wear pants today.

The origin of Civilizations & Modern Humans

Civilizations tend to appear in the world when the supply of food becomes scarce during part of the year. When that happens, it forces people to get together and find ways to store the food for later times.

Most ancient civilizations began in great river valleys. In the ancient civilizations that we know about, people did not just learn how to store and preserve their food. They also developed different languages and some even learned how to read and write and develop their own alphabet in their own language. In addition, these new civilizations would also build cities, create division of labor, and foster trade with their neighbors. Furthermore, they also were able to advance in the arts and the sciences.

It is believed that modern humans originated from the continent of Africa. The scientists of today based that hypothesis on genetic surveys of human populations. They also believed that the first emigration of modern humans from Africa was eastward, toward Asia, and not northward through the eastern Mediterranean.

Did you know? Great empires such as the Persians, the Trojans, the Egyptians, the Greeks, the Romans, and later on the British, all rose and perished within 240 years. They were not only conquered by external enemies, but also rotted from within. America now, in the year 2021, has passed that 240-year mark, and the rot is starting to be visible and accelerating like never before. So, are we going to learn from the failures of other great empires, or are we going to be destined for the same fate?

The Middle East Past & Present

Did you know why the Middle East region has such importance throughout history to the present day? The Middle East is the cradle to many civilizations including the Akkadians, Sumerians, Phoenicians, Hebrews, Babylonians, and Egyptians. In addition, the region is the birthplace of the three major monotheistic faiths: Judaism, Christianity and Islam. The Middle East has immense geographic importance being the land bridge to three continents-Europe, Asia and Africa. This region contains water routes of immense importance. These include the Nile, Tigris, and Euphrates rivers as well as the Shatt al-Arab -- the 12-mile confluence of the Tigris and Euphrates that flows into the Persian Gulf. Five of the most important straits in the world are located in the region too. These are the Dardanelles, the Bosporus, Tiran, the Bab el-Mandeb and Hormuz. In addition, one of the great man-made maritime highways, the Suez Canal, is situated in the area too. Furthermore, one can also find in the region vast reserves of petroleum (Middle East Rules of Thumb p.1, iUniverse, Inc.).

Did you Know what Middle East countries were artificially created by Great Britain, France and Italy? With the exception of Israel, the countries of Libya, Sudan, Jordan, Syria, Lebanon, and Iraq all were 'created' by Great Britain, France, and Italy. Saudi Arabia was 'created' by force, by one man, King Abd al-'Aziz ibn Abdur Rahman Al-Feisal Al Sa'ud (commonly known as ibn Saud) in 1932. Israel, in contrast, was re-established as a sovereign nation in the very land where two previous Jewish sovereign nations had existed before they were conquered by outside aggressors (Middle East Rules of Thumb p.3, iUniverse, Inc.).

Did you know? King Fahd International Airport in Dammam, Saudi Arabia is so massive that it is built on 192,000 acers of land, which is bigger than the entire city of Mumbai in India.

***Did you know that* the Koran, the holy book of Islam, allows Muslims to own slaves?** Most black slaves were castrated. The name Abdallah is popular name in Islam, and it actually stands for Ab means slave, and Abid means slaves. Allah is the name given in Islam to the Universal God. So, Abdallah means the slave of Allah, the slave of God.

The Major Contributions of the Sumerian Civilization

Did you know that the Sumerians were the first civilization in the world? That is why their culture is called a Parent Culture – a culture followed by other civilizations in the past and present time. They had an organized government & religion, division of labor, class structure, system of writing and recording events, and they lived in cities. It is thought that the first metropolitan city was 'Ur' located in Mesopotamia.

Did you know? The farmers in Sumer invented some of the first irrigation systems. They also created levees to hold back the floods from their fields and cut canals to channel river water to the fields.

Did you know? The Sumerians were the first ancient people who invented a method of how to make bronze by combining copper & tin together at high temperatures. It is because of the discovery of bronze, that they were the first civilization to invent the metal plow. This was unlike the Egyptians who were the first to invent a plow made of wood, which tended to be weak and break often.

Did you ever wonder why we use wheels today?

The Sumerian civilization was the first to invent wheels for their wagons. These wheels did not look much like the wheels of today. Though they were made from wood, this great invention changed and made life better for all the generations to come, including ours. They also invented the potter's wheel that we use today to make pots, jars, and dishes.

Did you ever question why we have seven-day week? The Sumerians chose to have seven days in a week because they were able to see seven planets in the sky with their naked eye. They were able to see Mercury, Venus, Mars, Jupiter, Saturn and two stars that they thought were planets.

Did you know? We can sail today, and people also sailed in the past, because the Sumerians invented the first sailboats.

Did you know? The Sumerian invented the first 'alphabet' called Cuneiform. It was made up of wedge-shaped symbols that were carved into clay tablets. It included about 300 symbols representing the syllables of words. The writing of today developed from Cuneiform and varies from hand-writing and mechanical printing to computer generated images and text.

Did you realize that a circle can have as many degrees as you want it to have? So how come circles today have 360 degrees? The Sumerians for some unknown reason favored the use of the number 60. They decided arbitrarily that a circle should have 360 (60x6) degrees more than 6,000 years ago. Furthermore, they introduced the lunar calendar. This calendar is based on the phases of the moon, and it is also used today in many countries around the world. The reason had to do with the fact that in Sumer most of the time the sky was not covered with clouds, and it did not rain much, so they could clearly see all the phases of the moon.

Did you ever wonder who invented the umbrella? The climate in Sumer was such that most of the year it was very hot and sunny, and people needed some kind of protection from the scorching sun, so someone there invented the parasol – it looks like an umbrella and will shade you from the sun. Since it was expensive to buy, only the rich people then were able to afford to purchase it. The Romans, thousands of years later, came across the parasol idea in their conquest, and improved it a bit by rubbing oil on the parasols to make it waterproof. Why? They did this because Rome's climate is rainy most of the year, and the Romans needed some protection from the rain outside their houses. In addition, the Sumerians made the straight pins from iron and bone. (The Book of Amazing Curiosities p.10).

Did you ever wonder who introduced to the world arches in architecture? It was the Sumerians. It was not easy as it looks, it involved a lot of accurate calculations that requires knowledge of mathematics.

Did you know who invented first he perfume in Mesopotamia? It was first invented by a woman chemist called Tapputi around 1200 B.C.E. She had a powerful role in the government and religion of Babylon in Mesopotamia. Her role was to be the overseer of the Mesopotamian Royal Palace. These facts were found written in 1200 B.C.E. on a Cuneiform tablet.

Did you know? Based on cosmetic cases found at archaeological sites dating back to Circa 3500 B.C.E., it is thought that the ancient Sumerian Queen Schub-ad of ancient Ur and the upper classes there, were the first to wear lipstick. It was made by mixing crushed red gemstones with oil and waxes as well as white lead. From there the knowledge of how to make it spread to the neighboring Assyrians and then to the ancient Egyptians who also wore red lipstick as an indicator of high social status. However, the Egyptian red lipstick was made from crushed bugs - an ingredient that is still appears in many lipsticks today. From there it made its way to ancient Greece, where only prostitutes were required by law to put it on. The Ancient Greek lipstick was made from a combination of red dye, sheep sweat, and crocodile droppings. In 16th century England, Queen Elizabeth revived the red lipstick's popularity. At that time, the red lipstick was made from beeswax and red plant-based dye and was worn only by upper class women. However, by the 1700s, red lipstick was outlawed in England on the basis that women were using it to seduce men into marriage. The charge? Witchcraft! Similar laws prevailed in the United States, where a marriage could be annulled if it were found that women had been wearing red lipstick during courtship (axiologybeauty.com).

The Hebrew / Israelite Civilization - Past & Present Major contributions

Did you know? Archeologist were able to find landfills of trash that contained the ashes, shells, ceramic shards, olive pits, and wine jars, because of the arid Negev desert in Israel. The Carbon dating of the trash is links to an ancient town's sudden collapse at the time of the mini–Ice Age that was brought about by the nearby volcanic eruption.

Did you know how the word Jerusalem came about? The word Jerusalem comes from two Babylonian words. Uru means "city" and Salim, the "god of peace". Together, they are Urusalim, or "city of peace." Over the centuries, Urusalim became Jerusalem.

Did you ever wonder who introduced monotheism to the world, the origin of the Star of David and the laws ordering the merciful killing of animals for food consumption? The ancient Hebrews /Israelites introduced these all to the world. Monotheism is the belief in one universal G-d, while most of the ancient peoples at that time believed in polytheism, the belief in many gods. They also introduced the Old Testament to the world. They are the ones who followed the Ten Commandments as well as the Golden Rule, written 1,000 years before Christ, that state "love thy neighbor as thyself" Leviticus 19:18. It actually commands people to treat others as they themselves would like to be treated. The Hebrew / Israelites monotheistic religion influenced and brought about newer monotheistic religions such as, Christianity and Islam to the world.

Did you know? The Ancient Israelites were the first to introduce mercy killing of animals for food consumption to the world. The idea of Kosher meats is greatly based on the fact that the animals should not be tortured as they were being killed, nor should one eat a sick animal. In ancient times it was found that animals that were tortured while being killed had a much softer flesh than those who were not. Furthermore, in ancient times they used to cook calves in their mother's milk. The ancient Israelites considered it to be a very cruel practice. That is why today religious Jews do not eat meat and milk together at the same time. If you look carefully today you will see that many, but not all food items, have a small symbol that tells whether it contains dairy or not. If the small sign on a certain food items is 'K/D' it means to those who need to know it that it is kosher, but it has milk product in it and should be eaten with other milk product only. In addition, Kosher foods also include animals and seafood that do not consume one another. Kosher meat includes animals that eat plants and no other animals. Kosher fish includes fish that do not eat other fish and have scales. Land animals that chew their cud and have cloven hooves are also kosher. Since pigs eat everything, and in ancient times were the garbage eaters, they are not considered to be kosher. Even though pigs have cloven hooves, they do not chew their cud, and therefore are not to be eaten in Judaism and Islam. In addition, clams, crabs and other sea creatures that eat from the bottom of the ocean, are also not considered to be kosher to eat. These laws were very practical and follow a lot of common sense. The laws made sure that the people would eat only healthy food and not get sick, and that the animals will be killed fast and humanely so they will not suffer too much pain.

Did you know that Commandment #5 "Thou shall not Kill" is translated wrong from Hebrew? It supposed to be "Thou shall not murder". Murder is a killing with a premeditated plan to kill somebody in the future. The meaning of' 'to kill' actually means to protect yourself immediately on the spot when somebody wants to harm you, and there is no planning involved.

Did you know? The Ten Commandments and other elements of the Hebrew law provided a major source for the development of Western legal system and democracy (The Bill of Rights in Action, Fall 2000 Volume 16 Number 4 p.1).

Did you know that the U.S. Founding fathers were inspired by the Old Testament? They came up with the three branches of our government based on the Old Testament. The first branch "For the Lord (G-D) is our Judge" - they founded the Judicial Branch -in the Supreme Court. The second branch "The Lord (G-D) is our Law giver"- they founded the Legislative Branch – Congress, and the third branch "The Lord (G-D) is our king ... He will save us" – the Executive Branch – the President -- Isaiah 33:22

Did you know? The Star of David originated from the base of the pomegranate that has, in most cases, a six-pointed star.

Did you know? In ancient Israel, the pomegranate stood for prosperity and long life

Did you know? Jewish law influenced Roman law, English law, the U.S. Declaration of Independence and the Constitution.

Did you know? The Hebrews, like all other ancient people, were permitted to have slavery. In many cases, some persons ended up bonding themselves into slavery in order to pay their debts. Others were thieves that were ordered by the court into slavery if they could not otherwise give back what they took from their victims. By the end of their servitude term, masters had to release slaves after six years, and give them a gift to help them start a new life. Since Jewish law placed so many restrictions on slavery, it almost disappeared by the Middle Ages (The Bill of Rights in Action, Fall 2000 Volume 16 Number 4, p.4).

Did you know? Hebrew kings were never considered to be gods or high priests with the power to interpret G-d's will. Like everyone else, they had to obey the Ten Commandments and the law of the

Torah. The written Torah, not the whims of king, was considered the law of the land (The Bill of Rights in Action, Fall 2000 Volume 16 Number 4, p.4).

Did you know? The early Hebrews placed the wedding ring on the right index finger, while in India it was worn on the thumb. Later on, it became a custom to place the ring on the 4th finger-'ring finger' because physicians of long ago believed that a 'vein of love' ran from the ring finger straight to the heart. So, it was perfectly logical to wear a ring on that finger. The Romans copied this practice and did not question it. The ring finger also became the Roman physician's 'healing finger'.

Did you know? The tradition of eating hard boiled eggs in the Jewish holiday Passover was adopted from the early pagan festivals that celebrated spring and the beginning of new life. This custom was adopted later on by Christianity too to symbolize, in this case, the moment in the New Testament when Jesus was resurrected after his crucifixion (eggs.com).

Did you know that the Dead Sea is not dead? The Dead Sea is a land locked Salt Lake between Israel and Jordan. Its name goes back to about 323 B.C.E. The Dead Sea is the world's saltiest body of water. While no fish can survive in very salty waters, the Dead Sea is not in fact 'dead,' but contains salt-loving microorganism that thrive in this environment. The shore of the Dead Seas is also the lowest point on the Earth's land surface at about 1,300 feet below sea level. Salt and other minerals are extracted from it in vast quantities for use in the chemical industries. If you don't know how to swim, no worry, you will not be able to drown there, but rather float because of the body's increased buoyancy in the high salt content water present there.

Did you know that Michelangelo's famous statue of David depicts horns on top of his head? Humans obviously do not have horns. The reason for this depiction has to do with the fact that Michelangelo relied on the wrong translation of the Old Testament (he had no clue about it and neither did others at that time). The Hebrew language is very concise and limited because it was not spoken for many centuries. Why? because the Romans conquered the Holy Land and pushed many of the Jews out of there. So, the wrong translation stated that Moses had horns (animal horns) of light. The correct translation should rather be rays of light. However, Hebrew does not have a word for 'rays' of light. So, it uses two words that together will mean rays of light. Therefore, in the Middle Ages, the reason Jewish men were believed to wear hats on their heads was to cover their 'horns' and were laughed at and ridiculed by many in the Middle Ages in Europe. That is what happens when people lack knowledge.

Did you know? Israel is 60 percent desert and has truly little fresh water for usage. Therefore, its scientists ended up inventing how to desalinate water from the Mediterranean Sea soon after Israel was re-established. In addition, in 2020 they invented the Watergen, which is a machine that is able to produce fresh water by pulling the humidity from the air. Furthermore, Israel has over 200 million trees, and it is one of the only nations in the world that entered the 21st Century with more trees than it had 100 years ago.

Did you know? Ben-Gurion University of the Negev in Israel announced in 2021 the formation of Israel's first school of Sustainability and Climate Change, an interdisciplinary research and innovation initiative to tackle the world's most pressing environmental issues.

Ben-Gurion Prof. Sigal Abramovich is a member of the Department of Earth and Environmental Science, as well as the head of its Laboratory for Foraminiferal Research. She has been studying the effects of desalination pollution, like heavy metals on the marine environment. As she was studying the tiny shells known as foraminifera, she found out that they contained heavy metals due to the brine discharge from desalination plants across the

Mediterranean coast of Israel. She also on a mission to find a way to biodegrade plastic – polyethylene (PET) by bacteria – a more environmentally friendly way to break down and recycle the most common type of plastic in food and beverage packaging as well as in textile products (www.aabgu.org).

The Old and New Babylonian Civilizations Major Contributions

Did you ever wonder why we have 60 seconds in a minute and 60 minutes in an hour and 24 hours in a day? Won't it be much simpler to divide the minutes and seconds by the number 100? We owe it to the Babylonians, who adopted it from the Sumerians. However, it is still a mystery as to why they chose the number 60. They also came up with the idea that there are 24 hours in a day. In addition, the Babylonians introduced the Zodiac wheel with twelve signs, one for each month.

Did you know that their greatest King, Hammurabi, introduced for the first time ever in history a written code of laws known as the Code of Hammurabi?

It was a great move because when laws are written down justice can be fairer to the people, no matter as to their race, class, or gender. Furthermore, this code of laws stressed proper punishment for any crime committed. One can find its influence in the Old Testament and in countries around the world today. In addition, the Babylonians came up with hanging gardens, such as the Hanging Garden of Babylon. They figured out how to bring water with clay pipes to a higher ground. Today many shopping malls have such gardens, and our scientists learned from them the technique of how-to bring water to higher dwellings.

Did you ever wonder why do we use the word honeymoon? In Babylon 4,000 years ago for a month after a wedding, the bride's father would supply his new son-in-law with all the mead he could drink. Mead is an alcoholic drink made from fermented honey. Also, their calendar was lunar (Moon based), and this period was called the honey month, which we know today as the honeymoon.

Did you know that consumers have been frustrated by unacceptable customer service since ancient times? Archeologists found one of the earliest recorded complaints written on a clay tablet in 1750 B.C.E. by a Babylonian man. The man demanded a refund from a merchant who sent him inferior copper ingots. This is what was written to the merchant: "what do you take me for, that you treat somebody like me with such contempt?" (Consumer Reports On Health, Jan. 2020, p.26).

Did you ever wonder when humans first started to use the zero? For centuries there was no symbol for the number zero. Instead, various cultures used just an empty space. It is believed that the Babylonians were the first to use a place holder for zero in their numbering system in 350 B.C. However, it was not a real zero. The real symbol zero may have been invented around 32 B.C. in Central America by Meso Americans. We are still not sure if the Olmecs or the Mayans were the first to introduce it into their system of calculation. The Mayans invented it independently around 4 A.D. It was later devised in India in the middle of the 5th Century, spread to Cambodia near the end of the Seventh Century, and into China and the Islamic countries at the end of the 8th Century. Zero reached Western Europe in the 12th Century. Around 130 A.D. the Greek mathematicians and astronomer Ptolemy, influenced mainly by the Babylonians, started to use the symbol that represent zero as a number, not just to hold a place. However, the symbol for zero, an open oval standing on one end would take several centuries to become accepted as a universal number in the World. In addition, the zero is the only number that cannot be represented by the Roman numerals. The zero as a number is actually representing zero angles. (The Book of Amazing Curiosities p.292).

Did you know that the oldest surviving world map depicts the worldview of the Babylonians around 600 B.C.? It was carved on a 5-inch stone tablet, whereby the city of Babylon appears to be in the center of their known world. Babylon probably at that time was the world's most populated city and had trade with other cities around it. The map was more a political map used to champion the city than being based on scientific knowledge per say. (Popular Mechanics, July/August 2020 p.32).

The Hittite Civilization
Major Contributions

Did you know who were the first people that figure out how to make iron weapons? They were the Hittites. The Hittites were ancient people who settled in the area were Turkey is located today, at around 1600 BC. At that time, the weapons that existed were made of bronze. Bronze was made by combining copper and tin together under high temperatures, and it is a softer metal in comparison to iron. So, the ancient people who possessed bronze weapons did not have a chance to win in battle facing those who used iron weapons. Eventually, the Hittites helped to spread the knowledge of how to use iron. Today, iron is used to make steel products – such as cars, building materials, and utensils etc. In addition, the Hittites improved the Sumerian invention of the wheel. How? They realized that wooden solid wheels were very heavy, especially when they had to drive their war chariots fast in battle. So, they invented the spoked wheels that were lighter and gave them the speed they required to move fast in battle. Today we still use their invention by having spoked wheels mounted on bicycles, motorcycles, and cars to make them light and fast.

The Minoan & Phoenician Civilizations Major Contributions

Did you know that the alphabet that we use today, 26-letter alphabet, evolved from the Phoenician alphabet? They actually adopted and improved the alphabet of the ancient Sumerians and spread it all around the Mediterranean region. Their alphabet contained 22 symbols standing for consonant sounds, written in vertical columns from right to left.

Did you wonder why in the past, as well as today, we place great importance to the "red carpet" treatment? We used to believe that the Phoenicians were the first to discover how to produce purple-red dye.

However, today in the year 2020 scholars agree that they probably were not the first to come up with it. Instead, evidence increasingly points to the island of Crete in modern Greece as its place of origin, and the Minoan Civilization was the first to figure out how to produce it. Today, archaeologists found out that from about 3000 B.C. until the mid-fifteenth century B.C., the Minoans actually established extensive maritime trade networks around the Aegean Sea. Ancient tablets from the Minoan palace at Knossos refer to the royal use of purple textiles, going as far back as 1800 B.C. So, for at least 300 years before the rise of the Phoenicians, the people in Crete already were coloring their textile using 'Murex" dye, which is a strong, purple-red dye, Tyrian purple, was produced by extracting the mucus from the hypobranchial gland of two snail species commonly known as "Murex", Murex-Brandaris and the Hexaplex-Trunculu, that gave them the purple-red dye, Tyrian purple. In order to produce one pound of this dye they needed slave labor to harvest 60,000 snail glands. So, it became very expensive to produce and buy the purple–red dyed clothing. Therefore, only the rich could afford to have it, thus purple-red dye was associated with the upper-class way of dressing. The Phoenicians, eventually learned of the Murex dyeing technique through trade relations, and later on they improved upon it as well as expanded the dye's reach. By the 8th Century B.C., they had the monopoly on this industry. Down the road as the dye became more widely available, various Roman rulers, starting with Julius Caesar (r.46-44 B.C.), attempted to maintain its exclusive status by restricting its use to their society's elite. The emperor Nero (r. A.D. 54-68) is known to have fined those who wore certain shades of Murex-based purple clothing without permission and fined those who sold it to commoners. In the 3rd Century A.D. the *Historia Augusta*, a collection of Roman emperors' biographies, records that the industry had become tightly controlled by the Roman government at that time (Archaeology, November /December 2020 pp.59-64).

Did you know why today's number system is known as "Arabic" number system (1,2,3,4,10)? Originally it was invented by the Phoenicians. Each number represents the number of angles. So, 1 has one angle, 2 has two angles 3 has three angles, 4 has 4 angles etc. In addition, they built ships with advances such as a steering oar and sails. However, the number 0 was not in use yet, and instead they left an empty space for calculations. The reason why it is called today "Arabic "number system is due to the fact that the Arabs adopted it from the Phoenicians and spread it around their conquered territories.

The Lydian Civilization
Major Contributions

Did you know who invented the idea of having coins as money instead of bartering, (exchanging goods for goods)? The Lydians did. They were located in west Anatolia, where Turkey is today. Herodotus, a famous Greek historian, was the one to report it. The early coins were made of electrum, an alloy, or natural mix, of gold and silver. The image on the coin showed its value. Coins replaced the barter system, leading to the money market economy in the ancient world. This is a practice that is continuing to this day with the additional inventions of paper money, plastic credit cards, and electronic transfers.

The Ancient Egyptian Civilization Major Contributions

Did you know? Since Egypt had an arid desert climate, archaeologists were able to discover 500,000 preserved papyrus fragments. They contained receipts, tax forms, medical texts, horoscopes, and forgotten works of Sappho and Sophocles that illuminate what residents owned, who they married, and which novels they read most.

Did you know? The ancient Egyptians were very advanced in their knowledge of medicine, and they figured out how to battle diseases and relieve pain. Homer, the famous Greek author of *the Iliad* and *the Odyssey*, wrote in *the Odyssey* in c.800 BC, that Egyptian men were more skilled in medicine than any other in humankind. Additionally, later on, the revered Greek historian, Herodotus, who visited Egypt around 440 BC, also testified in his writings about the advanced medicinal knowledge and practice of the ancient Egyptians. Only after 1822, when the Rosetta-Stone (a granite stone engraved in 196 BC - with Egyptian Hieroglyphics translated into Greek and Demotic text) was discovered did historians start to read and learn more about the extensive ancient Egyptian medical documents, that were written on scrolls of papyrus around 4000 years ago. They found out that the ancient Egyptian doctors used activated charcoal to improve the life of their patients and the rest of the population in general. In addition, they had knowledge of how to treat problems with urinary, blood, hair, skin, and eye health. Furthermore, the scholars also stumbled upon the major key to healing and health. What they discovered was remarkable. The Oxford scientists found out that one ingredient - **CARBON** (also known as activated charcoal) was the **SINGLE** thing that tied all the ancient Egyptian medical texts, writings, and artifacts together.

Today, French pharmaceutical scientists adopted the Egyptian idea of using activated charcoal to heal people. They developed a new supplement called **Renaitre**, that includes activated charcoal, and was clinically proven to eliminate every toxin from our bodies, as well as bring about cellular rejuvenation. Renaitre is so effective that a 50-gram dose of its activated charcoal has the surface area of 10 football fields. It also encourages bowel movements, so it helps to rid the body of toxins quickly and efficiently.

Did you know that the Egyptians were the first ancient people to adopt and practice preventive medicine? Archaeologist in Egypt found papyrus scrolls and ostraca at Deir el-Medina, an old village that contained workers who built the pharaohs' tombs in the Valley of the Kings. This village is located near ancient Thebes (modern day Luxor, Egypt). The papari and ostraca that were found dated from the second millennia B.C., during Egypt's New Kingdom. They revealed to us that ancient Egypt had a government run healthcare system and that these workers received variety of healthcare benefits, including paid sick days and free visit to physicians. We also found out that there were three types of medical providers: physician and scorpion charmer, who were paid by the state and a wise woman who was paid privately by the patient. The physician treated his patients with ointments and prescriptions. The scorpion charmer treated poisonous bites and stings, but he also serves as an intermediary between his patients and the deities by practicing forms of preventive medicine, such as making amulets and charms for his patients. The wise woman, a kind of folk practitioner, helped diagnose the divine causes of illnesses. She would help her patients determine which god or goddess needed to be worshiped in order to cure a particular illness. In addition, the ancient Egyptians also invented the first toothbrush that did not resemble much of what we have today. It was actually a chewed stick. Furthermore, they also invented a form of a toothpaste. Unfortunately, it took many thousands of years until the idea took roots first in 1498 and later at the beginning of the 20th Century in Europe and the rest of the world (Biblical Archaeology Review Magazine July/August 2015 p.24).

Did you ever wonder why our number system is based on the number ten, and that we study geometry in school? The ancient Egyptians adopted the Phoenicians' number system and invented geometry in order to have accuracy when building the pyramids –tombs for the pharaohs.

Did you know? The Egyptians introduced cosmetics to the world. They were also the first ancient people to invent paper made of the papyrus plants, while other ancient people at that time were still writing on stones or metal. In addition, in order to write on this kind of paper they had to invent the pen and the ink. They also invented games that we still play today, such as the bowling game and King Tut to name a few.

Did you know what an important tool the Egyptians invented in agriculture, that we still use today? It is the plow. They came up with the wooden plow. They had no knowledge at that time of how to produce iron. This knowledge, of how to make for the first time, iron tools and weapons, will be revealed to the Hittites, ancient people who settled in the area were today Turkey is located, around 1600 BC.

Did you know? When iron making was introduced to the world, the ancient Egyptians believed it was a sacred metal of the sky.

Did you know what food does not spoil for hundreds of years, if not for thousands, and can be found in sealed jars in Ancient Egypt? It is honey. Why it is so, because of its acidity, lack of water and the hydrogen peroxide that it contains (Smithsonian.com). Honey has been used not only as food but also as medicinal remedy because of its properties for centuries. It creates a perfect barrier against infection for wounds. The Ancient Egyptians physicians used honey for medical needs on a regular basis. It was all due to its thickness as well as other properties. They used it as a natural medicine and bandages to cure wounds because nothing could grow on it. The Sumerian clay tablets revealed that the Sumerians physicians used honey in 30% of their cases. We found out through the years that minute amount of the hydrogen peroxide in honey is the right amount that promotes healing. In ancient Rome, honey was as precious as money, that is why it was used to pay with it taxes to the government. Today, Derma Sciences, a medical device company, came up with Medihoney, which are bandages covered in honey that we use today in hospitals around the world, and in private use, to heal wounds.

Did you know that about 4,800 years ago, the first recorded exchange of wedding rings took place in ancient Egypt? The groom placed a ring on his bride's finger, to demonstrate his confidence in her ability to take care of their household. Since then, it had long been a common practice to wear a wedding ring on the third finger of the left hand. However, this tradition became official practice after the son of King Henry VIII put it in writing in The Book of Common Prayer. (The Book of Curiosities p.529).

Did you know that one of the oldest board games in the world is checkers? The Egyptians invented the checkers game around 1,600 B.C.E. and it remained extremely popular in the Western World for centuries up to now. The game is played by two people with 24 playing pieces on a board with 64 light and dark squares. There is even a reference to a checkers-like game in Homer's *Odyssey* (Homer was a famous ancient Greek scholar). The modern version of checkers arrived in the 12th Century A.D. with the adoption of the 64 square board. In the 16th Century A.D. the rule of capture was added, giving us the contemporary version of the game. The earliest checkers book was published in Spain in 154. In England and Scotland checkers is called "draughts".

Did you know that the Sahara Desert, that is located in North Africa, is not the world's largest? Antarctica is. Antarctica is almost 5.5 million square miles, and the Sahara Desert is only 3.3 million square miles.

Did you know that one of the most famous queens of Egypt was Nefertiti? Her name means "the beautiful one" Some scholars believe that she may have not been Egyptian at all. Nobody knows for sure as to her origin. At 15 she married Amenhotep IV, who later became king of Egypt. Nefertiti and her husband, Amenhotep IV, were responsible for bringing monotheism to ancient Egypt. They worshiped the Sun god Aten. Later in his honor Amenhotep IV changed his name to Akhenaten and Nefertiti changed her name to Neferneferuaten-Nefertiti. Fourteen years later into Akhenaten's rule Nefertiti seemed to disappear and no one knows what happened to her. Maybe she died in the plague that killed half of the population of Egypt, or perhaps there was a conflict in the royal family, and she was banished from the kingdom or murdered. It remains a mystery and no one knows for sure as to her demise.

Did you know that Egypt's most famous ruler, Cleopatra was not Egyptian at all? She was Macedonian Greek in origin. She by the way was an exceptional young woman. She started to rule Egypt at the age of 18, after her father, Ptolemy XII Auletes died. She was extremely intelligent and brilliant in business and politics. She was the first in her family to learn to speak Egyptian. In addition, she could speak nine languages. Cleopatra was the last of the Ptolemy dynasty and the last pharaoh in Egypt. Rome took over Egypt after her death (The Book of Amazing Curiosities p.226).

Did you know how we end up having a Christmas tree in Christmas? The experts today claim that the use of trees during winter holiday dates back thousands of years ago. The ancient Egyptians celebrated the winter solstice by decorating their homes with dates, and palm leaves. The Romans, on the other hand, celebrated a seasonal festival around December 25th called Saturnalia, in honor of their god Saturn. This was the predecessor of Christmas. The Romans also decorated their homes with tree branches and lights as well as exchange gifts with one another. As for how this tradition started in America, some historians believe that Hessian troops that came from Germany during the Revolutionary War brought it to America. However, others believe that it was brought by the German immigrants, who settled in Pennsylvania and the surrounding states.

Did you know that the Egyptians were the first ancient people to invent the drinking straw? They use it to drink beer that they stored in closed small clay containers that kept the beer somewhat cold. The straws were made of hollow twigs.

Did you know how the "Dead man's head" also known as Mummy color came about? They mixed one-part oil, one-part amber resin, and too many parts of *Homo sapiens* (humans). It got its brown tint from flesh, bones, and bandages of well-preserved Egyptian corpses. Fittingly, artist used it for skin tones.

Did you know that the ibis was the sacred bird of Thoth, the ancient Egyptian god of wisdom and writing? Beginning about 600 B.C. ibises were frequently mummified and given as sacrifices to the gods. About 10,000 ibises were sacrificed every year. Scholars today believe that these birds were imported from across the African continent. They concluded it after they studied the genomes of 14 mummified ibis dating back 2,500 years ago. To their surprise, they found out that these birds were genetically diverse (Archaeology May/June 2020 p.18).

Did you know? The ancient Egyptian writing system was from right to left in most cases, but it could also be written from left to right (Archaeology Magazine, Egypt 2020 p.9).

The Persian / Iranian Civilization Major Contributions

Did you know that the Persian Empire was the 1st largest empire in the ancient world? It survived for 1,000 years even though it was conquered by many invading armies. So, what was the secret to their long survival? It had a cultural elasticity, which means that they tolerated other cultures, religions, and peoples. Therefore, the invaders were able to adopt to the Persian way of life and became part of the Persian society. The Persians were the first, before the Greeks, to come up with the idea that freedom and human rights should be given to all their citizens. The Persian Empire included 23 different peoples who coexisted peacefully under a central and very efficient government. The Persians also were the first to have an efficient postal system. To keep track of what was taking place in their giant empire they ended up with a great spying system. The Persians also came up with a religion called Zoroastrianism, named after Zoroaster the priest. He introduced the belief in one mighty God, in angels, demons, saviors, good vs. evil, heaven vs. hell. So, as you can see all these ideas influenced the three monotheistic religions in the world, first Judaism, later Christianity and then Islam. To sum it up, we in the U.S. and the Western World are greatly influenced by the ancient Persians.

Did you know? The Persians did not invent the chess game, it was invented by the ancient Indians from India. However, the Persians improved the game for future generations to come.

Did you know that some English words are actually Persian words that entered the English language? For example, some English words that originate in Persian language are admiral, candy, cipher and crimson to name a few.

The Major Contributions of the Chinese Civilization

Did you know that the ancient Chinese Civilization made tremendous impact on our Western Civilization? They indirectly inspire us today to wear caps and gowns in graduation ceremonies. This tradition came to us from the ancient Chinese Emperors. They used to wear caps and gowns made of silk. Silk comes from the cocoons that small insects called silkworms make. In order to get the silk from the cocoons they used slave labor, because it required a lot of effort, and it was very time consuming. Hence, silk was awfully expensive to make so, only Emperors and the upper classes could afford to buy it and wear it. Therefore, cloth made of silk symbolized wealth and power.

Did you know that they also invented many things that we still use today? They invented the mariner compasses, paper (made from rags and wood pulp), printing (block and movable type), gun powder, the spinning wheel (to weave fabric), calligraphy, ship's rudder, civil service systems, fishing reels, the lunar calendar, porcelain, martial arts (Kung Fu), the conveyer belt, smallpox vaccine, the yo-yo, stirrups, acupuncture, suspension bridges, and the wheelbarrow to name a few. Unlike the Western wheelbarrow, the Chinese Prime Minister Zhunge Liang invented in 231AD a wheelbarrow that had a wheel in the center. This wheel formed the center of gravity and allowed one person to transport a much heavier load than the Western wheelbarrow of today, that has the wheels mounted in the front. So, it is long overdue for us to construct such a wheelbarrow.

Did you know that they were the first to cultivate tea and that tea can help fight infection? Today we know that it increases the body's defenses against infection, and it contains a substance that seems to protect us against certain diseases. A component in the tea primes the immune system to attack invading viruses, bacteria, and fungi. Five cups of tea a day may keep the doctor away. However, do not add milk to the tea, or it will neutralize the effect completely.

Did you know that they came up with a system of beliefs such as Confucianism and Taoism that we can adopt today, no matter as to what religion we follow? It is because Confucianism mainly stresses the need to respect greatly old people and Taoism mainly stresses the fact that a person can gain happiness by being good to all things (YinYang). So, as you can see it does not clash with any particular religion, including three of the monotheistic religions in the world Judaism, Christianity and Islam.

Did you know? The Chinese emperor Shen-Nung was the first person to use acupuncture as a medical treatment in 2,700 B.C.

Did you know who invented Kung Fu, the world's oldest martial art in China? A group of monks, as a method of self-defense against attacks by warlords who wanted to plunder their places of worship. It was first practiced around 1500 B.C. in China. Kung Fu's movements are based on those of the snake, tiger, lion, dragon, and crane. The disciples of Kung Fu took a vow to protect the weak and poor from the rich and greedy. That is the promise that Kung Fu students still make today.

Did you know? The construction of the Great Wall in China took over 2000 years to complete, and because it took so many years to complete it ended up not giving them the protection that they needed from the Mongols.

Did you know that the Kiwi fruit originated from China? It used to be called Chinese gooseberries and later was changed to Kiwis after New Zealanders started to grow these plants and export it to the U.S. Kiwis is a nickname used today for New Zealanders. Kiwi is considered to be a super food. One medium kiwi contains 71%

of the recommended daily intake of Vitamin C as well as Vitamin E, folate, carotenoids and polyphenols.

Did you know? Tien tsin, or Chinese red pepper, is named after the port city Tianjin. However, chili peppers did not originate in the People's Republic of China, though they are a key ingredient in many classic dishes, such as the Sichuan staple known as Kung Pao Chicken. The spicy plant is actually native to Mexico. Columbus introduced it to European traders during the Columbian exchange, and they ended up bringing it to the east part of the world during the 16th century. (Popular Science Spring 2020 p.14

The Ancient Greek Civilization
Major Contributions

Did you know? We owe our Western way of life to the ancient Greeks. They introduced democracy, philosophy (Socrates, Plato, and Aristotle to name a few) to the world, as well as the Olympic Games and the Greek theater that included dramas and comedies. The ancient Greeks also came up with the Hippocratic Oath, which is an oath that every new physician must swear to. It deals with a code of ethics that new physicians must follow such as: to treat patients to the best of their ability, to preserve patients' privacy, and to teach and pass their knowledge of medicine to the next generation of doctors. The core of this ethical belief is to 'do no harm' to the patient.

Did you know? The U.S.A. as well as other European countries, adopted the ancient Greek's style of architecture. Greek columns were used to build government buildings. For example, the United States built the Lincoln Memorial as well as the Supreme Court in that style. In addition, the Lincoln Memorial is modeled after the Greek Parthenon - a temple in Athens dedicated to Athena, the Greek goddess of wisdom.

Did you know? The ancient Greeks found a way to collect water from a pile of rocks in an arid climate 2,500 years ago. They observed and learned it from the desert mice who ended up pilling stones and small rocks in order to collect some moisture from the air. By doing so the ancient Greeks ended up collecting water as pure as rain, filtered by stones that provided clean drinking water for them. Keep in mind that condensation in general depends on the daily cycle of heating and cooling the earth by the Sun.

Did you know? The Athenians also introduced to the world the idea that government officials should get paid for their work. Thus, the poor citizens, as well as the rich could participate in running the government. They also introduced the idea of having a jury system whereby the jurors were paid, thus allowing fair trials.

Did you know? Alexander the Great, the famous king and commander of Macedonia (Greece), introduced chemical warfare, for the first time in the world. His army threw caustic lime at the enemy soldiers to distract them with burning and itching eyes, so they would not be able to continue to fight and be successful.

Did you know? the ancient Greeks are also credited for introducing the idea of wedding flowers around the 5th Century B.C. Flowers and plants, such as ivy, were used to create a crown for the bride to wear, which represented a gift of nature. The ivy stood for everlasting and unbreakable love as well as warded off evil spirits. (The Book of Amazing Curiosities p.526).

Did you know? In ancient Greece tossing an apple to a girl was a traditional proposal of marriage. Catching it meant that she accepted the gesture.

Did you know? In ancient Greece pomegranates represented long-lasting heath and fertility.

Did you know? We still do not know who came up with the birthday cake tradition. Some scholars believe that the ancient Greeks came up with it. While others believe that it was the Romans. Yet others believe that it all started in the Middle Ages in Germany.

Did you know? The origin of shaking hands is somewhat murky. We know that handshake existed for thousands of years, but historians are not sure as to who came up with it first. Archaeologists found out evidence that in the 5th Century B.C. handshake was a common custom in Greece. However, some others claim that it started in the Middle Ages in England. The shaking hands symbolized peace, as well as was a way to communicate that no one was going to use their weapons against the other.

Did you know? Today we continue to shake with our right hands, not only because most of us are right-handed. It is partly still because shaking with our right hand was the signal to foes and non-foes, that we were not going to draw our swords, and that we want to be friends with them. In addition, in some cultures including the nomads of the desert, water was scarce, so they had to adopt a system to keep themselves as clean as possible. Therefore, they ended up using their left hand to wipe their behinds, and the right hand for eating and shaking hands. Furthermore, shaking with the left hand was considered, and it is still, a great insult to others.

Did you know? The Greeks were also the first known culture to apply scientific approach to measuring and mapping the world. The philosopher Pythagoras theorized in the 6th Century B.C. that the Earth was round and not flat as it previously believed to be. The Greek scholar Eratosthenes by 200 B.C. was able to accurately estimate the planet's circumference within 1,000 miles. Ptolemy, a famous Greek-Egyptian astronomer compiled an eight-volume atlas called Geographia that formed the basis for the next 1,500 years of map making. It was completed in 150 A.D. Yet, after the fall of the Roman Empire his work disappeared and reemerged about 800 years later. His knowledge of geography and map making helped Columbus's voyage to the Americas as well as Ferdinand Magellan's expedition around the globe.

Did you know? Oregano, a highly effective medicinal herb, was used by the ancient Greeks to treat wounds, insect bites, snakebites, digestive and respiratory infection – and for good reason - oregano oil is a great natural antibiotic, antiviral as well as antifungal remedy used then and now.

The Roman Civilization
Major Contributions

Did you know? The Romans conquered the Greeks and adopted many of their ways, and the Western World ended up adopting a lot from the Romans.

Did you know? Legend has it that the city of Rome is named after Romulus. He and Remus were brothers who, the story goes, were raised by a she-wolf. However, today it is believed that it is more likely that the city's name comes from the Latin word *groma* meaning "crossroads".

Did you ever wonder why we use the word salary to pay someone for their job? First, the word salary comes from the Latin word for salt, salarium. Salt was valuable as money and hard to get in the past. Why? This was because it was needed to preserve food. In those days there was no other way to do it. The invention of electricity and refrigeration of food did not exist then. Since salt was extremely hard to come by the Roman soldiers were paid half in gold and half in salt. Today, we know that we need some salt to facilitate the transport of nutrients and oxygen, as well as allows nerves to transmit messages, and helps the muscles work efficiently. Nevertheless, salt in our diet should be reduced because we can find it in all our foods, even if we do not add it ourselves. Make sure when you add a little salt to your food that it is iodized salt. Why? Iodine prevents people from having goiter and thyroid disorders.

Did you know who came up first with the idea of some sort of a "toilet paper"? It was the ancient Romans. They used communal sponges, made of sea sponges on a stick, that were called xylospongium or tersorium, which were then replaced in a bucket of bathwater. Over the centuries different countries and cultures used leaves, hay, fruit skins and even corn cobs. The wealthiest however used rags, that were washed after every use by their slaves. Around 589AD, the Chinese were the first to use something like what we know today as toilet paper. Five hundred years later a New Yorker by the name of Joseph Gayetty introduced the first prepackaged toilet paper in 1857. It was called "The Therapeutic Paper". The company sold the paper in packs of 500 sheets at 50 cents per pack, it was an expensive price in those days. In addition, Gayetty's name was printed on every sheet.

Did you ever wonder why we have the custom of unrolling the red carpet when famous people come to visit another country, city, or a state? It originated from the Ancient Phoenicians and later it was adopted by the Romans and the rest of Humanity. The Red dye – Tyrian purple, also known as royal purple, was produced from the mucus of the hypobranchial gland of two species of Murex, Murex brandaris and Murex trunculus. In order to just produce one pound of the red-purple dye, slaves had to squeeze the smelly glands of 60,000 snails. It was indeed a very costly and labor-intensive to produce and therefore red clothing was only worn by the nobles and the rich in those days.

Did you know who came up with the name "Palestine" where today Israel is? It was the Roman emperor Hadrian in 135 CE. after suppressing the Jewish revolt that was led by Shimon Bar Kokhba. Hadrian wanted to eradicate Jewish nationhood, statehood, and any connection they had to the Land of Israel. Why? Hadrian was very mad that the Jews fought him extremely hard and were unwilling to give up the fight easily. So, he renamed the Land of Israel Palestina-after the Philistines, the worst ancient enemy of the Israelites. In addition, he also was seeking to erase the Jewish connection to Jerusalem, the holiest city of Judaism. Therefore, he razed the city and changed its name to *Aelia Capitolina.* In addition, you should also keep in mind that never in recorded history, has there ever been an independent sovereign Arab state called "Palestine" (Middle East Rules of Thumb p.33 & p.137).

Did you know that many of the wedding customs in the United States and in other countries trace their roots to the Romans? We tend to have pre-wedding banquets, gifts for the bride and groom, and the ring given as a symbol of union. Most wedding were held in June and not in August, because it was too hot and sticky in Rome that it was considered unlucky. After the ceremony, the attendees were invited to eat until they were stuffed.

Did you know that walnuts are not nuts? In ancient Rome they combined the tinted walnut sap with, ashes, leeches, and charred things to make dark hair dye. The juice was used to make walnut ink which was used by Leonardo da Vinci, Rembrandt, and Rubens to draw sketches. In addition, in 17th Century England, walnut oil was used as depilatory, thinning the eyebrows and hairlines of women when that look was in fashion (2019/Jan2020 p.43 & p.45).

Did you know that the ancient Romans believed that the walnut was a physical model of the brain? The hard shell was the skull, the papery partition the membrane, and the two pieces of the nut were the two hemispheres of the brain.

Did you ever wonder who introduced the idea of ice cream / snow cones? The Romans did, especially Emperor Nero. In the first century Emperor Nero ordered his servants to bring buckets of snow from the northern mountains to the Roman cities, where it was flavored with fruit toppings, and served to hungry Romans. (The Book of Amazing Curiosities p.20).

Did you know? In ancient Rome not only gold and silver coins were used to pay taxes, but also honey and salt. These were valuable at that time because they were hard to come by.

Did you know? Zero is the only number that cannot be represented by the Roman numerals.

Did you know? The word calendar is derived from the Latin word calendarium, meaning "interest register" or "account book" itself a derivation from calendae/Kalendae, the first day of the Roman month, the day on which future market days feasts, and other occasions were proclaimed.

Did you know how we ended up with the holiday called Halloween?

Halloween is rooted in our agricultural past, marking the end of harvesttime and the beginning of the new year. Following the triumph of the Roman Empire over Celts-occupied land in the 1ˢᵗ Century A.D.. The Romans combined many Celtic traditions, including Samhain (an ancient pagan Celtic festival that is Gaelic for "summer end," a day to bid good-bye to warmth and light) with their own. This day evolved into All Hallows' Day or Allhallowmas, "hallow" meaning "to sanctify" (The Old Farmer's Almanac, Fall & Winter, 2020 p.14).

INDIA - Past and Present Civilization Major Contributions

Did you know that English is distantly related to Sanskrit? Both languages, Sanskrit and English, are members of a large group of languages called Indo-European language family. The relationships show in the roots for some of the most basic words in these languages. In English we say mother, in Sanskrit they say 'matar' in English we say father in Sanskrit they say 'pitar' in English we say brother, in Sanskrit they say 'bratar' in English we say sister in Sanskrit they say 'svasar' in English we say daughter in Sanskrit they say 'duhitar' in English we say son in Sanskrit they say 'sunus.' In addition, we use the word punch, in Hindi it means number five. To us punch means drink made up of five-part mixture of alcohol, water, sugar, lemon, and spices. In Hindi, the word shampoo means massage. In English it means to wash our hair with soap-that we call shampoo too.

Did you know that the ancient Indians from India adopted from the Phoenicians the number system "1 to 9" and the "0" that we use today? This system of numbers is called today "Arabic Numerals" because it was introduced into Western Europe by the Arabian scholars to the world. A more accurate name for them should be Hindu-Arabic number system. The ancient Indians, as well, used the decimal system and formulated the beginning of Algebra. The Indians also knew how to plan cities with water and sewer systems. They were the first to use soap, cement, and tempered steel. They also developed the chess game that will later be adopted and improved by the Persians. Asoka, a famous Indian Emperor believed in Ahimsa, non-violence. His ideas influenced Mahatma Gandhi who later influenced Martin Luther King Jr.

Did you know that Martin Luther King Jr. was influenced by the ideas of Mahatma Gandhi from India? It all started when Asoka, a famous Indian Emperor started to follow Ahimsa, a nonviolence method dealing with the world. His ideas influenced Mahatma Gandhi who was an Indian lawyer, as well as anti-colonial nationalist, who led a nonviolent successful resistance movement for India's independent from British Rule. His actions in turn inspired Martin Luther King Jr. and movements for civil rights and freedom across the world.

Did you know? India has the most women pilots in the world.

Little Known Facts From The Middle Ages

Did you know that Latin is the source of many English words and that **the English language did not exist in Roman times?** During the Middle Ages, when English began to take shape as a separate language, new words with Latin roots have entered the vocabulary of English such as: salary, question, audio, erase, graduate, index, journey, kitchen, labor, mobile, peace, umbrella, salmon, and radius to mention a few.

Did you know how the saying "F-ck You" came about? In the Middle Ages, the English invented the 6-foot-long Longbow. It was made of strong, yet flexible wood from the Yew tree. In order to pluck the bow, they used the middle right figure. So, they used to say get ready to "pluck the Yew" which meant pluck the bow. After saying it fast and over the course of many years, people started to say it the wrong way -- so pluck the Yew became "f-ck you".

Did you know that the word "berserk" originated from the Norse language? It means "going crazy". The word came to us from the Vikings warriors who were known as the berserkers. Why? They were named berserkers because before battle they used to ingest wild mushrooms that made them go furiously violent or out of control to the point where they used to howl like wild animals and bite their shields. In addition, at times they were not able to distinguish in battle between foe or friends. Hence, the term "going berserk."

Did you know? A recent study discovered that some Icelandic people with deep roots in the country possessed mitochondrial DNA specific to Native Americans. Since mitochondrial DNA is passed down from women, it is likely that a Native American woman crossed the Atlantic Ocean with the Vikings (Blowingfacts.org).

Did you know? The phrase "second string" which today means "replacement" or "backup" originated in the Middle Ages, when an archer carried a second string in case the one on his bow broke.

Did you know from where did we get the idea to say, "good night, sleep tight"? It came to us from Shakespeare's time. In those days, mattresses were secured on bed frames by ropes. When you step into bed the mattress from your weight will make the bed firmer to sleep on. Hence the phrase "good night sleep tight".

Did you know? Shakespeare's original Globe Theatre (built in 1599) was destroyed in 1613 when a real cannon used for special effects during a production of Henry VIII set fire to the thatched roof, burning the building to the ground.

Did you know why there is a cliché' that we use "It is raining cats and dogs"? Some claim that it originated in the Middle Ages. Why? At that time most buildings had straw thatched roofs that were very weak. It was also common for dogs and cats to hide in these roofs for shelter. However, very heavy rain and wind would often cause the roofs to give way, causing pets to fall from their high ground shelters, creating the illusion that they are raining from the sky. (The Book of Amazing Curiosity p. 97).

Did you ever wonder why the barber's pole is made up of red-and white stripes? In the medieval times, doctors, as a profession, did not exist. The barber ended up being like a doctor and a barber. They did surgeries and bloodletting, as well as the trimming of hair and beards. The red color symbolizes the bloodletting and white the clean bandages. (The Book of Amazing Curiosity p. 21).

Did you know that the Bubonic Plague pandemic in the Middle Ages in the mid-1300s killed almost 200 million people, across Europe and Asia? In a matter of a few years, it killed out nearly half of Europe's population, as well as killed 60% of the population of Iceland. Today we know that it was mostly caused by fleas carried by rats. In addition, archaeologists found autopsy records from that time, that indicated that the internal organs of people dying from the Bubonic plague had almost liquified and that the blood withing the bodies had congealed. The Scientists today believe that the disease was passed merely by touching an infected person.

Did you know why it is called the Black Death? It is because those who were infected got blackened spots that swelled on their body. Death came quickly, usually within three days. Yet it took as long as a month before the symptoms appeared.

Did you know? During the Black Death (Bubonic Plague), people suspected that the plague has to do with incoming ships, so ships were forced to wait for 40 days, before they could unload their cargo. It was done to prevent possible infection from occurring. The Italian word for 40 is "quaranta". This is how the word "quarantine" entered the English language.

Did you know that the Black Plague actually started in the Himalayan Mountains of southern Asia in the 1200's? So why did it end up in Europe in the 1300s? It all had to do with trade and cargo ships that had stowed rats infested with the fleas that carry the disease. When the ships made landfall, so did the rats, and the infection began to spread all around, especially in cities.

Did you know that today scientists discovered an odd connection between the Black Death (Bubonic Plague) that took place about 700 years ago, and the Human immunodeficiency virus (HIV)? They found out that a large percentage of Europe's native population has a genetic mutation known as CCRS-delta 32 (short for mutation "32"). This mutation, they believe, took place during the Black Death in Europe. It prevents CCR5 receptors in the body's white blood cells from acting as entry ports for viruses. Thus, viruses such as HIV cannot enter the white blood cells through those receptors and replicate. So, people of only European descent are found to have the 32 mutation that partially protects them from viruses that work in this manner. This mutation was not found in people from eastern Asia or Africa, because the plague did not spread there. (The Book of Unusual Knowledge p.562).

Did you know that during the Middle Ages sandals evolved into shoes? However, there were not "right" or "left' shoes. In addition, there were only two sizes, big and bigger. Only in 1818 were shoes finally made with unique right and left sides. All shoes were made by hand until the 1900's. After that they were made in part by machines, and they came in approximately150 different sizes.

Did you know why brides stand on the left? In the old days, "marriage by capture," the groom needed to leave his right hand free. Why? In case he needed to grab his sword and fight off another suitor trying to steal his bride to be, at the last minute.

Did you know? During the Christian Crusades, clergymen were outraged by parishioners who wore shoes whose toes were so long that they were not able to kneel in church. A result the church came up with a law, that people attending services could only wear shoes with toes no longer than two inches.

Did you Know? The military salute is a motion that evolved from medieval times when knights in armor raised their visor to reveal their identity.

Did you know that Leonardo da Vinci was not only a great artist who is famous for painting the Mona Lisa, among other famous pieces, but he also was one of the most prolific inventors of all times? His inventions were precursors to inventions that we benefit from today. The most well-known of his inventions are scissors, flying machine, parachute, robotic knight, machine gun, self-propelled cart, armored tank, aerial screw helicopter, revolving bridge, scuba gear, and an ideal city.

Did you know? During the Middle Ages, in the 16th century, a health theory circulated widely among physicians in Europe that foods that resembled body parts were especially beneficial for the health of those parts. For example, they believed that ingesting fireflies could help improve night vision, that red coral could help the blood, and that walnuts could help the brain (Reader's Digest, Dec.2019/ Jan.2020 p. 42).

Japan, Asia & Southeast Asia Civilizations –Past and Present Major Contributions

Did you Know that the origin of the fortune cookie traces back to Japan and not China? Some believe that the fortune cookie was introduced to the U.S. by a Japanese immigrant named Makoto Hagiwara in 1914 in San Francisco. While others believe that it was David Jung, founder of the Hong Kong Noodle Company in 1918 in Los Angeles. Jung was genuinely concerned about the number of poor people living on the streets. So, he ended up passing out free fortune cookies to them with inspirational verses written by a presbyterian minister. His aim was to give the poor people some hope for better future.

Did you know? The Japanese game Sudoku is called that way, because in Japanese, it means "single number", and in the game you use each number 1 to 9 only once per row and per column. The game is actually based on an 18th century Swiss game, and it was adapted and released as Sudoku by the Japanese publisher in 1984.

Did you know? In Japan, unlike the U.S., they keep weird bugs as pets. And apparently, they buy them from vending machines. These exotic pets range from bats, birds (especially owls), grasshoppers, mice, lizards, to tarantulas.

Did you know? Towns in ancient Japan used to hold contests to see which person could break wind the loudest.

Did you know? In medieval Japan, any woman that was found alone in a room with a man other than her own husband was immediately put to death, no questions asked.

Did you know? Vending machines in Japan sells some of the following: men's ties, fresh eggs, ten-kilo bags of rice, umbrellas, hot popcorn, hot Ramen Noodles, fishing equipment, toilet paper, beer, fresh flowers, frequent flyer miles, dry ice, and Rhinoceros Beetles to name a few.

Did you know? The Japanese passport is the world's most powerful passport. It grants visa-free access to 190 countries out of 195.

Did you know? In Japanese schools, students do not get any exam until they reach the fourth grade. Why? It is because the goal for the first 3 years of school I not to judge the student's ability to memorize, but to establish good manners and to develop their character. Japanese scholars teach manners first and foremost.

Did you know? Judo is the most popular martial art to come from Japan. The word Judo in Japanese means "the gentle way". Unlike more aggressive martial arts, Judo emphasizes giving in to an opponent's attack until the right moment comes to strike back. The philosophy of Judo is to save energy until the opponent has used all his/her energy. Judo is less than 100 years old. Judo is a combination of ancient fighting technique that was used by samurai warriors in feudal Japan with wrestling methods.

Did you know? Karate is a mix of martial arts from several Asian countries. It originated in Okinawa, a tiny Japanese island. The word Karate in Japanese means "empty hands". Karate is a martial art in which a person kicks or strikes with the hands, elbows, knees and feet. In 1600, Japan conquered the island of Okinawa and forbade the people of the island to own any firearms. As result, the Okinawans formed secret self-defense societies that used the body as a natural weapon.

Did you know? In Okinawa, Japan more than 450 people who are living there are 100 years or older. Therefore, Okinawa is referred to as the healthiest place to live on earth (Weird World 1.pdf).

Did you know? Tempura is wheat batter, a cornerstone of Japanese cuisine. Chef's batter and deep-fry everything from shrimp to shitake mushrooms. This practice originated from the Portuguese, who ate battered green beans called *peixinhos da horta*- "little fish of the garden"-on holy days when Catholics abstained from meat. The European traders brought it to Japan in the 1540's and they left their recipes behind there (Popular Science, spring 2020 p.14).

Did you know? Mount Fuji, is the highest mountain in Japan, located on Honshu Island near Tokyo, and its last eruption took place in 1707.

Did you know? The largest cave in the world is in Vietnam and is so big that it has its own river, jungle and climate.

Did you know? North Korea and Cuba are the only places where you cannot buy Coca-Cola.

Did you know? Coca-Cola was originally green.

Did you know? Tae Kwon Do is the national pastime of South Korea. It means the art of kicking and punching. like other martial arts, and it was created by monks for their protection. Unlike the more aggressive martial arts, the goal of Tae Kwon Do is not to hurt the opponents. Instead, its goal is to concentrate on the good feeling that comes from being in control of your body.

Did you know? Genghis Khan, who was a famous and powerful Mongol leader, slept with so many women that about 1 in 200 people today are related to him.

Did you know? The name Altai comes from the Mongolian word Altain Ula, meaning "mountain of gold." In the 700 C.E. people that were located near these mountains believed that they were rich in gold and silver.

Did you know? Singapore is the largest country in the world that has no farms.

Did you know? Smithfield Farms, the largest pork producing farm in the USA, was sold to in September 2021 to China with the unanimous support of its stockholders. The same similar thing happened to some chicken farms in the USA. In addition, Star-Kist Tuna was sold to Korea and is in big conflict with the U.S. concerning quality, safety, and records, which Korea refused to produce.

Did you know? India is the most diverse country in the world, culturally, economically, climatically, ethnically, and religiously. Even in term of food preparation it is extremely diverse.

Did you know? India's "Go Air" airlines only hires female flight attendants because they are lighter, so they can save up to $500,000 per year in fuel.

Did you know? There are metro trains in China today that pass-through apartment houses.

Did you know? Taiwan is the first country in the world to offer free Wi-Fi connectivity to its citizens and to all its foreign tourists.

Did you know? There is an "Eco Bridge" in Singapore that allows animals to cross the highway easily.

Health & the Human Body

Did you know? About 15% of all organ donations each year are given by "living" donors. Each person on the organ donors list can save up to 75 lives. (Women's World 10/11/2021, p.11).

Did you know? If you woke up in the morning in the year 2020 in good health, you have more luck than at least one million people in the world, who will not live through the week.

Did you know? Climate played a role in how human noses got their shape. Wider nostrils prevent overheating in hot climates while narrow nostrils tend to retain more moisture in frigid and dry climates (Popular Science, Spring 2020, p. 106).

Did you know? Left-handed people are an oddity among humans. Only about 1 in 9 of us are using our left hands as our dominant hand. However, researchers found out that in chimpanzees and bonobos (pygmy chimpanzees) the split is more like 1 in 3. For Orangutans, 2 of 3 individuals are left-handed (Popular Science, Spring 2020, p. 111).

Did you know? Losing even 5% of your body weight can make a big difference in your health. It is never too late to start (Weill Cornell Medicine, Iris Cantor Women's Health Center, January 2021, p.1).

Did you know? Japanese researchers found out that walking outdoors in nature is so soothing that it reduces fattening stress hormones by about 15% (Woman's World Magazine, 2021).

Did you know? Researchers found out that exposure to blue light from the sun triggers the release of stored fat that lies right below our skin's surface, even when we wear sunscreen (Woman's World, 2021).

Did you know? Researchers found out that overweight and obese individual under 60 were 46% more likely to be COVID-19 positive. In addition, they found out that COVID-19 positive people who are overweight had a 113% higher risk of being hospitalized, had a 74% higher risk of being admitted to the intensive-care unit, and had a 48% higher increase of death as an outcome (Weill Cornell Medicine, Iris Cantor Women's Health Center, January 2021, p.1).

Did you know? The National Foundation of Cancer Research (NFCR) that was founded in 1973 claims that we can do simple things in order to reduce our cancer risk, such as to: avoid tobacco products and second-hand smoke, eat more fruits and vegetables, increase the amount of fiber in our diet, limit alcohol intake, wear a SPF 30 or higher sunscreen, and maintain physical activity and healthy weight (www.NFCR.org).

Did you know? Our eyes are always the same size, from birth on, but our nose and ears change size as we grow up.

Did you know? According to the estimates of the Federal Communications Commission 10,000 lives could be saved annually if emergency responders could get to 911 callers just one minute faster. It can be done by getting rid of the regional 911 call centers and replacing them with local 911 centers (Reader's Digest, February 2020, p.80).

Did you know? In today's advanced, technological age, researchers found out that contacting friends and family members by phone rather than by e-mail will give them a stronger feeling of being bonded. Feeling connected to others is essential for health as well as our well-being (Reader's Digest, March 2021 p.45).

Did you know? There are a lot of health benefits for being kind. First, we feel happy when we are kind to others because our act tends to elevate the levels of endorphins and dopamine in our body which leads to feeling good emotions. Kindness also produces oxytocin in the brain and body causing a release of nitric oxide in blood vessels.

This dilates blood vessels and reduces blood pressure. So, kindness is good for the heart. In addition, it was also discovered that oxytocin reduces levels of free-radicals and inflammation in the cardiovascular system, slowing the aging process as well. Kindness also improves relationships, tightens emotional bonds, and reduces stress on the body. Kindness also tends to be contagious, thereby inspiring others to be kind too (*The Five Side Effects of Kindness* by David Hamilton, Ph.D. 2017).

Did you know? Our body has 75,000 miles of veins, capillaries, and arteries. Therefore, a healthy circulatory system is the secret to a healthier body. Make sure that plaque does not build up in your arteries, because it tends to cause blockages in your circulatory system and leads to the reduction in oxygen and nutrient delivery to your cells (New Health Revelations p.10).

Did you know? Being active at any size is good for your health, but it is not as effective as losing weight (Tufts University, Health &Nutrition Letter, June 2021 p.2).

Did you know? Just losing as few as 2.2 pounds can lower your blood pressure. In addition, a higher intake of dietary calcium, especially from plants, helps to regulate blood pressure. The key foods to keep in mind are greens and beans including Swiss Chard, broccoli, brussels sprouts, tofu, hummus and baked beans, to mention a few (AARP, February/March 2021, p.26).

Did you know? In order to lower your blood pressure, you need to follow Janet Brill PhD's advice and lose weight by eating lots of fruits & vegetables, limiting sodium (less than 2,300 mg per day), exercising and restricting alcohol consumption to one drink a day for women, and two a day for men (Newsmax Magazine, July 2021, p.84).

Did you know? There are more than about 5.8 million adults in the United States today (2021) mainly seniors, that are living with Alzheimer's disease as well as related disorders (ADRD) that includes vascular dementia and Lewy body disease. However, we still do not know whether vascular disease contributes to Alzheimer's disease or interact with it (Iris Cantor Women's Health Center, Volume 25 /Number 10, October p. 8).

Did you Know? Professor Bruno Dubois, the director of the Institute of Memory and Alzheimer's Disease (IMMA) in Paris, France claims that those who complain about memory-loss actually do not have Alzheimer. Why? Those who suffer from it actually are unaware that it is happening to them. In general, people over 60 and older can have some moments of forgetfulness, which is very normal for their age-group to experience (www.thealternativedaily.com).

Did you know? Aluminum foil is not inert and therefore when exposed to certain foods that are acidic or contain spices aluminum tends to leach a portion of its metallic element to food. So, every time you use aluminum foil in the kitchen, it can seriously harm your health. We know today that there is a direct link between aluminum ingestion and Alzheimer's Disease, which is a debilitating neurological disorder. It was also discovered that aluminum either directly or indirectly impacts osteoblast production, which in turn leads to bone wasting. In addition, aluminum when inhaled as a fine powder can promote pulmonary fibrosis, a form of lung disease (https://www.thealternativedaily. com/3-scary-reasons-ditch-aluminum-foil/?).

Did you know? People who stay active and increase the number of steps they take in a day, from 1,000 to 3,000 can reduce their mortality risk by 12% as well as reduce their risk for Alzheimer's disease and experience less cognitive decline. Those who hit 10,000 steps a day cut their risk by 46%. In addition, a new study in 2020 shows that higher aerobic fitness is linked to a greater improvement of cognitive function. Furthermore, even a little physical activity was found to also reduce the risk of Alzheimer's Disease in older people (Tufts University Health & Nutrition Letter December 2020, p.4 & Healthy Aging, Icahn School of Medicine at Mount Sinai, May 2021 p.3).

Did you know? Our bones and our muscles work as a unit. They get stronger as a unit and tend to get weaker as a unit. Therefore, it is important to incorporate muscle-strengthening exercise into our daily routine. according to Bess Dawsom-Hughes, lead scientist in the Bone Metabolism Lab at Jean Mayer USDA Human Nutrition Research Center on Aging at Tufts University (AARP Bulletin, September2021, p.24).

Did you know? High levels of thyroid hormone can interfere with the formation of new bone mass. Therefore, it is important that doctors find the correct thyroid hormone dose to satisfy the body's metabolism needs, but not to over treat, which can lead to bone loss according to Kendall Moseley, M.D., medical director of the Johns Hopkins Metabolic Bones & Osteoporosis Center. Keep also in mind that systemic inflammation can increase the rate of bone loss according to Stuart Weinerman, MD., an endocrinologist and assistant professor of medicine at the Zucker School of Medicine at Hofstra/Northwell (AARP Bulletin, September 2021, p.24).

Did you know? The brain's overall size begins to shrink when you are in your 30's or 40's and the rate of shrinkage increases once you reach the age of 60.Brin shrinkage does not happen to all areas of the brain at once. Some areas tend to shrink more and faster than others.

Did you know? In order to support our brain health as we age we need to do the following: first, get physically active every day, second, follow a heart-healthy diet, third, stay mentally active, fourth, stay social, fifth, keep an eye on cardiovascular diseases that can cause you to have high blood pressure, high cholesterol and diabetes, sixth, quit smoking, seventh, incorporate all the B vitamins to your diet, eight, make sure that your diet is also rich in vitamin D and calcium too (https://www.mayoclinic.org).

Did you know? Brain cells connect with each other at points called synapses. In Alzheimer's Disease, abnormal proteins build up between the synapses, preventing communication between brain cells and brain regions (Icahn School of Medicine at Mount Sinai, Focus on Healthy Aging, July 2021 p.3).

Did you know? Women make up about two-thirds of family caregivers for people with AD (Alzheimer's Disease), and there is evidence that people who are caring for a loved one with AD may be more likely to develop the condition themselves later on. This all has to do with the stress of the job of being a caregiver that may lead to reduction in their cardiovascular health, and that in turn may reduce their blood flow to the brain. In general, high levels of stress, depression, and poor sleep are all associated with being a caregiver and can severely impact one's life (Healthy Aging, Icahn School of Medicine at Mount Sinai, May 2021 p.3).

Did you know? Cardiovascular disease is the number one killer of women, causing 1 in 3 deaths each year. That is approximately one women every minute. Therefore, women should not only take care of their family members but also of themselves (Health Magazine, September 2021, p.35).

Did you know? Most hospitals make money by selling the umbilical cords cut from women who gave birth. They are used in vein transplant surgery.

Did you know? In order to slow the onset of Alzheimer Disease, reduce anxiety, reduce risk of depression, improve sleep, lower risk of heart disease and stroke, lower risk of hypertension, reduce weight gain, lower risk of fall-related injuries, lower risk of cancers and lower risk of early death it is advised to **first** have a healthy diet and keep a person's alcohol intake to no more than one drink per day or avoid it all together. **Second**, you need to get plenty of exercise, at minimum 30 minutes of moderate physical activity per day. **Third**, manage your morbidities such as high blood pressure, cholesterol, blood sugar, and seek help for depression. **Fourth**, avoid smoking. **Fifth**, socialize online with others or limit your contact in person, since COVID-19 is still a risk (Healthy Aging, Icahn School of Medicine at Mount Sinai, May 2021 p.3 & Nutrition Action, October 2021, p. 5).

Did you know? According to the World Health Organization lack of physical activity is the fourth leading cause of death in the world (Nutrition Action (October 2021, p.7).

Did you know? People who have lost cognitive ability and long-term memory can still sing, word for word, the songs of their youth. The reason for this phenomenon is not well understood yet (AARP, February/March 2021 p.4).

Did you know? A new study found out that people who did eight basic strength moves- including squats with weights, bicep curls, and abdominal crunches, twice a week, felt about 20% less tension after two months (Better Homes & Gardens, March 2021 p.112).

Did you know? Falls can cause fractures, but most often people do not hear about the fact that they can also lead to pneumonia, brain injuries, muscle breakdown, permanent disability and even death (Harvard Health Letter, Harvard Medical School, Volume 46, Number 5 March 20, p.1).

Did you know? On February 9, 2021, Dr. Oz on his television show, taught his viewers how to keep their brains healthy and avoid having Alzheimer's diseases in the future, even if they could inherit it in their DNA from their parents. The first thing that he suggested to do is follow the "SHIELD" acronym. This stands for the following:

S - sleep for 7-8 hours per night, H - handle stress properly, I - interact with people, in person or on the Web, E - exercise regularly, L - learn new things, D - have a healthy diet.

Did you know? There are six harmful habits that can affect a person's brain and they are: not getting enough sleep, using electronic devices, including smartphones and tablets before going to bed, consuming too much sugar, smoking, overeating and spending too much time sitting down (Iris Cantor Women's Health Center, Women's Health Advisor, Volume 25 / Number 10, October 2021 p.6).

Did you know? It was recently discovered by researchers that a regular afternoon nap was associated with better language use and memory in older adults. However, it is also important for older adults to continue to stay physically active and keep socializing with their friends (Consumer Reports On Health, May 2021 p.3).

Did you know? Researchers discovered that stretching tends to reduce blood pressure more than just walking and or other exercises (Journal of Physical Activity and Health, Dec. 2020).

Did you know? Recent studies show that smoking can shrink the brain and can increase the risk of age-related memory degradation, not to mention other health conditions.

Did you know? Overeating leads to weight gain, but what many of us did not know is that excess fat in the body actually play a role in reducing our brain size too.

Did you know? Diet and memory supplements may prevent or even reverse Alzheimer's Disease, according to a recent study done in 2020. However, not all supplements function similarly. So, it's important to make sure that it contains the following essential ingredients: Huperzine A, Phosphatidylserine 20%, Choline Bitartrate, and DHA Omega 3 as well as Amino Acids. Huperzine A enhances general cognitive function, specifically memory, cognition and behavioral functions. Phosphatidylserine is essential for brain neuron support, to maintain memory function and improved neuroplasticity. Choline Bitartrate boosts levels of choline, increasing acetylcholine production to raise nerve membrane fluidity. DHA Omega-3 Amino Acids promote better blood flow for improved cognition, function and memory boosting.

Did you know? Researchers found out that sniffing rosemary can increase memory by 75% (www.healthhouseinfo.com).

Did you know? Hearing loss is an inevitable result

of aging and living. In order to protect one's hearing as much as possible they have to first, stay away from loud noises. Secondly, taking a 200 mg dose of magnesium each day to strengthen our ears is also helpful. Vitamin A, E & D can even reverse some hearing loss in some cases. It is also recommended to take fish oil, omega-3 fatty acids and folic acids, to help sustain long-term hearing health. Beware of NSAID drugs, alcohol, aspirin and acetaminophen. All of these have been linked to increased rates of hearing loss. Alcohol, in particular, had been strongly linked to permanent and sudden hearing loss. Keep in mind that most hearing loss is irreversible. It can happen instantly if a person makes a poor choice doesn't protect their ears in high-risk situations, such gunfire in a shooting range, attending rock concerts or working in a place that produce loud noises. So, in order to have the best protection from hearing loss, people should try to have a healthy diet, exercise regularly and make sure to stay away as much as possible form very loud noises (https://healthscameexosed.com).

Did you know? Several studies have found out that people who use acetaminophen (*Tylenol* or *Paracetamol*) or ibuprofen (*Advil*) at least twice a week, are up to 24% more likely to develop hearing loss than people who take them less frequently. The good news is that this type of hearing loss tends to be reversible up to a certain point. However, continuing to use these medications at high doses can result in permanent hearing loss or tinnitus (ringing in the ears) (Consumer Reports On Health, 2021, p.10).

Did you know? Thyroid function tests can be affected by your meds. Take in consideration the following meds: prednisone

(Rayos, Sterapred), amiodarone (Cordarone, Pacerone), and tamoxifen (Nolvadex). If you take levothyroxine, keep your doctor informed about the other drugs you take and ask your doctor if you should discontinue them before taking thyroid function tests (Icahn School of Medicine at Mount Sinai, Focus on Healthy Aging, July 2021 p.3).

Did you know? Decreased thyroid function can force fat gain especially around the abdomen. This can occur because the thyroid is like a "metabolic gas pedal" so, when it slows down it is like slamming on the "metabolic breaks." In order to speed up metabolism and reduce fat accumulation around the midsection, one needs to eat thyroid-healing foods that include iodine and selenium. The foods that are best for healthy thyroid include kelp, nori, wakame, salted nuts such as Brazil nuts, macadamia nuts, hazelnuts, pine nuts and peanuts to mention a few. In addition, it is advised to also eat soy foods such as tofu, tempeh and edamame. It is also recommended to eat certain vegetables such as cabbage, broccoli, kale, cauliflower and spinach. As for fruits, it is advised to eat starchy plants such as sweet potatoes, cassava root and also to consume peaches and strawberries. (support@transformationsinsider.com).

Did you know? Low thyroid can cause elevated cholesterol in your body (Health Magazine May 2021, p.39).

Did you know? When our core body temperature is low it slows the metabolism and increases our weight.

Did you know? When you buy new clothes that are water and stain resistant, they tend to contain chemicals known as

PFAS – polyfluoroalkyl substance, that can be problematic for your thyroid. They can actually disrupt the normal function of the thyroid hormones. So, by simply washing the new clothes twice before wearing them will get rid of at least 50% of the harmful chemicals. Alternatively, you can wash the clothes by adding 1 tablespoon of Borax per gallon of water (*First for Women,* February 1, 2021, p.42).

Did you know? Store receipts contain chemicals that can affect the thyroid too. These are called BPA – bisphenol-A, which rubs off onto cash and your hands. Studies show that compounds in hand sanitizer make the BPA on your hands absorb through the skin and it then enters the bloodstream. So, in order to keep yourself safe, it is recommended that you wash your hands thoroughly with soap and water when you get home from shopping. This issue can also be eliminated by paying with a credit card and asking for an e-receipt *(First for Women,* February 1, 2021, p.42).

Did you know? The air in your house can end up be even more polluted than the air in the world's most polluted cities. It all has to do with the fact that people use things like hair spray, or burn candles, -- or even things like smoke from a woodstove or a fireplace, or fumes from the nonstick coating on the cookware that you use every day contribute to the overall quality of the air in the home. When it all mixed together in a house with closed windows it can become dangerous to one's health and raise the inflammation level in the body as well as a person's blood pressure as well as also hardening arteries causing damage to the body's circulatory system. To reduce the pollution level in the house, it is a good idea to open windows often and use fans to circulate the air. (Reader's Digest, February 1, 2021, p.64).

Did you know? Scientists in the past, suspected that blood pressure medicine could increase the cancer risk in people. However, today, based on 31 trials involving a total of 260,000 people around the world, it was found that blood pressure medicines do not raise the risk of cancer in people. In addition, the researchers found out that these medications actually help prevent heart attacks and strokes in people with high blood pressure. Furthermore, if you do not have a pet or cannot care for one, researchers found out that watching adorable animals on a screen can trigger a similar effect to actually being with a live pet, by lowering your stress level and blood pressure, as well as improving your general wellbeing (Reader's Digest, March 2021, pp.45-46).

Did you know? Gardening tends to reduce stress, helps you relax, and can provide you with a great workout, as taxing as lawnmowing, raking, digging, pruning and hedge trimming. All these activities will help you burn as much energy and calories as walking, cycling, swimming and aerobics. However, you need to take precautions not to get dehydrated or end up with a bad sunburn. Therefore, you need wear sunscreen and wide-brimmed hat, and drink plenty of fluids to stay hydrated in sunny, hot locations. In addition, avoid overtaxing yourself by splitting large projects into 20- or 30-minute sessions. In between these sessions, switch to a different task that requires a different body position and different muscles to reduce stress on the body (Healthy Aging, Icahn School of Medicine, at Mount Sinai, May 2021, p.5).

Did you know? Farmers in the USA and elsewhere sometimes use Chlorpyrifos, which is a brain-harming pesticide. In 2021 California outlawed nearly all uses of this chemical and that in turn is beginning to influence other states to do the same (NRDC- Natural Resources Defense Council).

Did you know? Spending more than 2 hours a day talking on a cellphone raises blood indicators of underactive thyroid by about 39%. It has to do with EMFs -electromagnetic radiation waves emitted by wireless technology. Try to keep cellphones as far away from your head as possible. Thusly, it is a good idea to talk on speakerphone or use a non-Bluetooth headset that plugs into the phone (*First for Women*, February 1, 2021, p.42).

Did you know? There is a difference between MSG and glutamate. Glutamate is an amino acid found naturally in protein-rich foods like beef. On the other hand, MSG- Monosodium Glutamate, is an additive made by humans when glutamate and sodium are combined. In addition, exposure to MSG early in life can result in lifelong insulin resistance that leads to Type 2 diabetes (*First for Women*, February2, 2021 p.28 & Newsmax Magazine Natural Cures 2021, p. 47).

Did you know? Our bodies can handle the glutamate it gets from food. Glutamate is an important neurotransmitter present in over 90% of all brain synapses and is naturally occurring molecule that nerve cells use to send signals to other cells in the central nervous system. However, when we eat processed food that contains artificially made MSG in large quantities, the body tends to be overwhelmed, and that can end up causing headaches, nausea, sweating and heart palpitations (*First for Women*, February 1, 2021, p.28).

Did you know? Processed "junk" food is cheap, quick, and is easy to get, make and eat but is incredibly bad for general consumption. Many people have difficulty figuring out what is considered processed food and what is not. Lately, nutrition experts and scientists have come up with a system that can help us figure out what is what. According to these experts, unprocessed or minimally processed food includes the edible parts of plants, herbs, fungi, seeds, roots, nuts and algae. In addition, for these foods to be considered unprocessed they should have been treated with NO additives, whatsoever - no salt, oil, or preservatives (logan@ bloodsugarfit.com).

Did you know? Bacon, cold cuts, ham, hot dogs' sausages, and other processed meats can cause colorectal cancer. In addition, researchers found out that people who ate processed meats at least five times a week had 67% higher risk of getting dementia than those who ate those meats less than once a week. Eating processed meats even once a week was linked to a 13% higher risk of getting it (Nutrition Action Health Letter, May 2021, p.7).

Did you know? Scientists call the "fifth taste" 'umami.' Umami itself is often described as a deep, meaty flavor. Some foods that have a strong umami flavor are beef, tomatoes and mushrooms to mention a few, and are rich in the naturally occurring amino acid glutamate. This amino acid is necessary for nearly every bodily process, including regulating metabolism (*First for Women,* February 1, 2021, pp. 28-29).

Did you know? Glutamate is required for making specialized immune cells. It is also necessary for the creation of Gamma Aminobutyric Acid (GABA), a key mood-boosting, brain chemical. As result, by increasing the intake of umami foods, one can reduce their risk of feeling anxious and cranky. It also tends to reduce the severity of allergy symptoms and joint pain (*First for Women,* February 1, 2021, p.29).

Did you know? Glutamate-rich umami foods flips a switch in the brain that tells the body when it is full. It also ends cravings for fatty, high-calorie foods (*First for Women,* February 1, p.29).

Did you know? In the 21st Century, Computer Vision Syndrome, also known as CVS, is becoming a major health problems among office workers as well as others including children who use computers for long hours of the day. The result is eyestrain and fatigue from constant refocusing, burning sensation, headaches, vision distortions, and neck and back pain as well. In order to guard against CVS, one needs to get computer glasses, or blink purposely about 22 times per minute. Most people, when they are staring at a screen only blink seven times, so their eyes get dry. In addition, people should use soothing eye drops, avoid glare, and position their monitor properly. It should be positioned about 20 to 25 inches from their faces and 10 to 20 degrees below their line of vision (FC&A Medical Publishing, pp.36 -38).

Did you know? The average computer user blinks 7 times a minute.

Did you know? The color which we see when we close our eyes is called 'Eigengrau' which is different from black.

Did you know? Staying positive can have a great impact on our health. Georgetown researchers found out that doing a small act of kindness each day reduces premature aging by about 60%. Why? Helping others spurs the release of compounds that help the brain, heart, and the immune system function at peak (*First for women,* December 2020, p.44).

Did you know? According to researchers about 75-98 percent of illnesses that we encounter today are directly the result of our thought life. So, what we actually think about affects us both physically and emotionally. In fact, just fear alone triggers more than about 1,400 known physical and chemical responses in our bodies as well as activating more than 30 different hormones (Switch On Your Brain, by Dr. Caroline Leaf, Baker Books, 2013).

Did you know? Brain function in humans is improved through sleep. Humans tend to sleep anywhere from about 6 to 8 hours per day. However, sleeping more than 8 hours a day can affect your health in a bad way (Health, May 2021, p.74).

Did you know? Researchers in the Journal of Happiness Studies found out that showing gratitude, not only helps us focus on the good in life, but also increases our mental health in the long run (*First for women,* December 21, p.48).

Did you know? Scientists studying people 18 years old and older, found that gaming improved mental health. Perhaps this is because of the social aspect of playing games with others. Research also suggests that video games can relieve stress in adults and children. However, overdoing it can lead to problems too. (Better Homes & Gardens, May 2021, p.112).

Did you know that in Latin, "virus" means poison? Not all viruses deserve a bad rap. Researchers from the University of Florida found out in 2017 that while some viruses are capable of causing severe or fatal diseases, others can lead to cures for cancer and help to correct genetic disorders (*Renew* by UnitedHealthcare, 2021, p.28).

Did you know? Bone marrow produces many types of blood cells among them white blood cells, which target invading viruses.

Did you know? An epidemic is when a disease affects a large number of people within a population or region.

Did you Know? A pandemic is when a disease spread over a very wide area, such as across several countries or across the globe.

Did you know? Herd Immunity is when a large portion of a community becomes immune to a particular disease, making future spread unlikely. According to Mayo Clinic it can be achieved by vaccinating the population against a particular disease or by people recovering from a disease on their own and producing antibodies that will protect them from future infection (*Renew* by UnitedHealthcare, 2021, p.29).

Did you know? In order to have effective Herd Immunity, 90% of the population either had the disease or were vaccinated for it. Since usually it is not the case, most people need to get the particular vaccination. Keep in mind that the flu and Corona Viruses are very contagious (Reader's Digest, November 2020, p.85).

Did you know that viruses can only survive inside a living cell? They cannot survive indefinitely on a doorknob or countertop, and they cannot move or reproduce without the help of a living host cell (*Renew* UnitedHealthcare, 2021, pp. 28-29).

Did you know that viruses have been found everywhere on earth? They are all around us and they are diverse. In fact, there are more types of individual viruses than stars in the Galaxy (*Renew* UnitedHealthcare, 2021, p. 28).

Did you know that viruses can spread in lots of ways? Mosquitoes, for example, can spread viruses among the people they bite. Eating virus contaminated food can cause foodborne derived illnesses such as gastroenteritis and hepatitis. Sneezes and coughs from an infected person can transmit viruses that cause the common cold. Other viruses, such as Ebola, spread from contact with infected blood, feces or vomit (*Renew* UnitedHealthcare, 2021, p.28).

Did you know? When you sneeze, all bodily functions stop, even your heart!

Did you know? When your body first detects a virus, your immune system goes into overdrive to keep you healthy. However, in some cases, the immune system gets stuck in overdrive. If the immune system fails to switch off it can lead to an inflammatory event called a Cytokine Storm that can lead to the fatal shutdown of multiple organs. In fact, Cytokine Storms are thought to explain the devastating effects of the 1918 Spanish flu epidemic (Bottom Line, Health Breakthroughs 2021, p.2).

Did you know? There are common sense habits that may prevent you from getting the flu, viruses or other diseases. One needs to wear a mask in public (keep in mind that not all masks are alike) and maintain social distancing. Beyond getting a flu shot every year, ask your doctor about vaccinations before traveling internationally. Wash your hands often with soap and water or with alcohol-based sanitizer. When coughing or sneezing do it into the inside of your elbow or into a tissue. Try not to touch your eyes, nose or mouth. Also, add vitamin D to your body. You can do this by increasing your exposure to sunlight, or by eating fish, egg yolks, beef liver, or mushrooms that were exposed to UVB light, which contain a lot of vitamin D. Taking supplements can also be quite effective. In addition, try to stay hydrated which can boost the immune system, and allow it to defend your body from viruses. Furthermore, have a healthy diet rich in fruits and vegetables, since they will provide your body's immune system with the nutrients it needs to function properly (Dr. Stephanie Seitz, ND. M. Southwest College of Naturopathic Medicine & Health Science, Scottsdale North News, February 2021 Vol. 3 No. 5 p.18, & *Renew* UnitedHealthcare, 2021, p.29).

Did you know? Vitamin D is essential for your health because it regulates many functions in the body, including hormone balance, metabolism, blood pressure, bone density, immune function as well as help you fight cancer. Low levels of Vitamin D are associated with upper and lower respiratory infections, heart disease, asthma, cancer, diabetes, multiple sclerosis, HIV, hypertension, inflammatory bowel disease, Alzheimer's disease as well as other autoimmune diseases.

Did you know? Vitamin D deficiency is a worldwide, public health problem in both developed and developing countries. People tend to get more colds and flu in the winter because in winter sunshine is less available in different parts of the world and therefore people tend to be deficient in this vitamin.

Did you know? As vitamin D levels decline with age, the risk of Parkinson's Alzheimer's, and cognitive impairment rises. This vitamin also helps in the absorption of calcium in the body. So, it is important to add Vitamin D supplement to your diet on a daily basis (AARP Bulletin, June 2021, p.32).

Did you know? 1 in 4 people in the U.S. have inadequate blood levels of vitamin D. This affects the elderly, females more than males, those who live far north or south of the equator, people with dark skin pigmentation, those who work and stay inside during the day, and people with poor dietary habits (AARP Bulletin, June 2021, p.32).

Did you know? Vitamin D-3 or cholecalciferol supplements are easily utilized by the body more so than Vitamins D-2. When you take Vitamins D-3 as a supplement, make sure to take it with the fat-soluble vitamins A and K2 because they work synergistically with vitamin D to protect you against toxic effects in case you have excess amount of vitamin D that accumulated in your system. In addition, sufficient levels of potassium and magnesium can also help protect you against vitamin D toxicity. If you are planning to take vitamin D supplements you will need to make sure to check your blood vitamin D level from time to time because if it is too high, it can be toxic to your kidneys. Keep in mind that you cannot overdose on Vitamin D from just eating food that contains it, but you can overdose by taking too much Vitamin D as supplements.

Did you know? Healthy foods that contain Vitamin D include egg yolks, salmon, mackerel, organ meats, and some types of mushrooms that were exposed to the Sun. Keep in mind that sunlight has far more benefits for our health than just increasing our Vitamin D levels naturally when compared to artificial sources. A recent (2021)

20-Year study found out that individuals that avoided sun exposure were twice as likely to die from all causes (thenutritionwatchdog.co).

Did you know? If you want to get vitamin D only from the Sun you need to expose enough skin for 20-40 minutes per day, without sunscreen at the strongest time of day, between the hours of 10:00 am - 2:00 pm.

Did you know? Researchers found out that sunscreens with the active ingredient oxybenzone 5% can disrupt the endocrine system in the body. Instead, it is recommended to use sunscreens that contain Titanium Dioxide and Zinc Oxide since they are safe and effective. In addition, higher SPF is not necessarily better, and just using sunscreen with 30 SPF protection is sufficient. However, sunscreen needs to be stored in a cool place below 85 F, storing it in high temperatures will destroy its effectiveness, and it should be applied 30 minutes before exposure to the Sun (AZ Family 5/4/2021 10:00 PM -11:00 PM Channels 3 & 5).

Did you know? If you have asthma, you should stay clear from household disinfectants because they may worsen your condition. Instead, consider a safer alternative, such as a solution containing vinegar, water, and a drop of dish detergent. In addition, it is a good idea to have more ventilation when using cleaning products, so open doors and windows, and turn on exhaust fans if you must use a disinfectant (Consumer Reports On Health, May2021 p.3).

Did you know? Hypothyroidism, underactive thyroid or low thyroid, occurs when the thyroid gland does not produce enough thyroid hormone. It is 10 times more frequently occurring in women than in men and is usually diagnosed when a person is middle aged. So, one needs to make sure to ask their doctor to check and make sure that their thyroid gland is working properly. This condition can cause depression, poor ability to tolerate cold, feeling tired all the time and having muscle weakness (FC&A Medical publishing p.21).

Did you know? Hepatitis C is liver infection that often goes undetected for years, until serious complications such as liver scarring arise. Therefore, it is recommended that Hepatitis C screening be given to everyone ages 18 to79.

Did you know? Acetaminophen (found in Tylenol) and NSAIDs such as ibuprofen (found in Advil) are great for occasional aches and pains. However, relying on them heavily for years may raise the risk for kidney damage, stomach ulcers, and heart attacks and it may even adversely affect the inner ear.

Did you know? A recent review in the Annals of Oncology, in May 2020 reveled that aspirin may reduce the risk of developing several cancers of the digestive tract, including some that are usually fatal, such as cancers of the pancreas and liver. It also tends to reduce the risk of getting colorectal, esophageal and stomach cancers (Healthy Aging, Icahn School of Medicine at Mount Sinai, October 2020, p.1).

Did you know? Antibiotics are not effective against viruses, but vaccines can be. Antibiotics, on the other hand, will kill bacteria. So, you should not ask your doctor for antibiotics when you have the flu, because the flu is a viral infection. There are other medications designed to help with the flu such as for example Tamiflu, but those medications are usually most effective if used early on in the course of the illness. In addition, researchers found out that up to one third of all antibiotic prescriptions are not necessary and yet doctors prescribed them because of pressure from patients to do so. Furthermore, you should also keep in mind that antibacterial cleaners are ineffective against viruses and can lead to antibiotic resistance. Instead of antibacterial cleansers, use those with the active ingredient of hydrogen peroxide, ammonia, or other disinfectant products to clean items that may be contaminated with a virus or bacteria. Also keep in mind that as we age, we are more likely to contract infectious diseases and more likely to die from them. This is possibly because infection-fighting cells in the bloodstream called T-cells decrease as we get older. This is why we need to get the flu vaccine as soon as possible when the flu season is about to begin, because it takes about two weeks to develop protection after a vaccination is administered (Journal of the Royal Society of Medicine & Reader's Digest, November 2020 pp.83-84 & *Renew* by UnitedHealthcare 2021, p.29)

Did you know? It is important to get a flu shot every year for number of reasons. First, it will reduce your likelihood of contracting it, being hospitalized for, or dying from influenza. In addition, if you do get sick with the flu

after being vaccinated, the vaccine can reduce the severity of your illness (Harvard Women's Health Watch, November 2020, p.2).

Did you know? Soap and water are the best and most effective defense against viruses and bacteria. A drop of soap diluted in water literally destroy viruses and bacteria and make them useless. However, make sure to wash your hands for 20 seconds, and dry them with a clean towel. Avoid public restrooms' air hand dryers, since they just blow contaminants all over the place (Reader's Digest, November 2020, p.84).

Did you know? The FDA has warned that some hand sanitizers that contain methanol, or wood alcohol can be toxic or even deadly if ingested. On the other hand, other sanitizers that contain less than 60% ethanol or isopropanol are not potent enough to kill many germs. Therefore, it is advised to use soap and water instead whenever possible, because it is still the best available protection (Reader's Digest, December 2020 /January 2021, p.40).

Did you know? Prior to antibiotics, silver was the go-to treatment for eliminating bacteria, and it is still widely used in the medical field for wound and burn care.

Did you know? Our immune system is a complex network made up of the thymus, spleen, lymph nodes, bone marrow, white blood cells, antibodies, and skin. It shields us from infection, fights off diseases and helps us heal from illness and wounds. However, if the immune system is too strong or weak, we can be more vulnerable to illnesses and ailments (Health, January/February 2021, pp.41-42).

Did you know? 70% to 80% of our body's immune cells are located in our digestive biome - our gut. It is a fact that our immunity to viruses may well be dependent upon the health of our gut microbiome. As we age, the gut microbiome naturally deteriorates. The deterioration is worse in those who suffer from diabetes, heart disease and other elderly afflictions. This is why older people fall prey to illnesses much more easily and those with underlying health issues are most at risk (Cellular and Molecular Immunology journal & Bottom Line's Health Breakthroughs 2021, pp.2-3).

Did you know? Deep breathing stimulates the Vagus Nerve, which is the longest and most complex of the 12 pairs of cranial nerves. When stimulated, it triggers the release of various chemicals that can induce calm throughout the body (UCLA Health, Healthy Years 2020 p.3).

Did you know? Stress can cause the body to produce more than regular amount of the hormone cortisol. While cortisol tends to help fight stress, it can also slow your metabolism down. So, it is a good idea to find ways to de-stress on a regular basis when possible (FC&A Medical Publishing p.21).

Did you know? Stress is known to exacerbate many health problems and allergies appear to be among them. However, according to the study done by MD Amber Patterson, alleviating stress will not cure allergies, but it may help to decrease the episodes of intense symptoms. In addition, stress will also triple the risk of restless sleep. According to UCLA researchers, an evening dose of simple carbs will signal your brain to shut down production of an alertness-triggering neurotransmitter called orexin and thereby allow you to sleep the night without interruptions *(First for Women,* 12/21/2020, p.33).

Did you know? About 32 million Americans have food allergies, which constitutes about nearly 10% of the population. It is about 10 times the amount that was reported just three decades ago. However, there is new hope since in January 2021 the Food and Drug Administration approved a new drug called Palforzia, the first drug that is designed to desensitize patients to an allergenic foodstuff, specifically to peanuts. Clinical trials found it to work for about two-thirds of patients. It is indeed a big step forward, but it will not be able to help those who suffer from multiple food allergies. Furthermore, over the past five years or so, scientists are trying to understand the basic mechanism of these disorders and they have found out growing evidence that food allergies tend to result from imbalances in the gut microbiome due to complex influences that include the environment, lifestyle, dietary and genetic makeup (Discover, January/February 2021, p.47).

Did you know? People often do not start taking their allergy medications until their symptoms get unbearable, and then their allergies become much harder to treat. They should rather watch the local news for pollen counts, and as soon as it starts to rise, they should taking their medications for their allergies.

Did you know? Researchers have identified more than 80 distinct autoimmune disorders. All share the common underlying issue of the body's immune system attacking itself. In 2020, it is estimated that 24 million Americans have an autoimmune disease, and that the number will increase in the future. Inflammation tends to hinder our immune system's ability to fight against the flu and viruses like the Corona Virus (AARP Bulletin, September 2020, p.13).

Did you know? A 2015 study in *the Lancet* found out that people who work more than 55 hours a week have a 33% higher risk of strokes and 13% greater risk of heart diseases than those who work 35 to 40 hours. Why? Because people who are clocking long hours at work tend to have less time to eat healthy meals, relax, or exercise, all of which can cause heart problems (Health, October 2020, p.48).

Did you know? In recent years researchers found out that people need to get enough sleep regularly. A lack of enough sleep causes many problems including affecting the short and long- term memory, causing depression and anxiety as well as can lead to psychiatric disorders and affect the way we even look. In addition, lack of sleep can shorten our life by a few years even if we keep eating healthy food and staying active. It also will reduce the effectiveness of our immune system, increase our chances of developing high blood pressure, cause weight gain, and even cause us to have higher risk of getting diabetes and heart disease. https://longlifeandhealth. org/how-sleep-extends-your-life/).

Did you know? To get to sleep faster, we need to turn off all electronics at least a half-hour before going to bed. We also need to make sure that our bedroom is dark as well as we need to turn the thermostat down. In addition, six hours before bedtime we need to avoid caffeine and alcohol (https://longlifeandhealth.org/how-sleep-extends-your-life/).

Did you know? As people get older, their sleep patterns change. These changes affect the circadian rhythm and metabolism, both believed to be responsible for the length of human lifespan. People that tend to live longer were found to enjoy longer sleep patterns (https://longlifeandhealth.org/how-sleep-extends-your-life/).

Did you know? It is important to maintain a routine sleep schedule. A solid six to eight hours of sleep nightly is critical for heart health. A recent study published in the Journal of the American College of Cardiology found out that those with the most irregular sleep hours had twice the risk of heart attack or stroke or dying from CVD - cardiovascular disease (Health, September 2020 p.50 and Better Homes & Gardens, March 2021, p.112).

Did you know? The body makes germ-killing antibodies while we sleep. So, if someone is sick, getting rest cuts the recovery time by about 55% (*First for women*, April 5, 2021, p. 31).

Did you know? If you have a cold and it lingers for too long, it is advised by some University of Wisconsin researchers to drink four mugs of sugar free black, green or oolong tea daily. According to their research, the tea will reduce the symptoms by 32%, speed recovery by 35% and reduce the risk of complications (like sinus infections and bronchitis) by as much as 75%. The reason is due to the fact that these teas contain EGCG and *theaflavins* that block the growth and spread of viruses, plus tamp down symptom-triggering inflammation. In addition, a study in the journal *Phytomedicine* reveals that tea will also hinder the growth of the virus that causes COVID-19 (*First for women*, April 2021, p.31).

Did you know? A Swedish trial recently found out that weighted blankets of about 15 pounds or so, created comfort and calm as well as a grounding effect for people. That in turn caused people to improve their sleep and mental health issues such as depression and anxiety (Reader's Digest, March 2021, p.44).

Did you know? Simple exercising for just 15 minutes a day is shown to enhance energy and deepen sleep (Woman's World, 2021).

Did you know? A 2019 study found out that participants who regularly slept for too many hours at night, about nine or more hours, actually had a 34% higher incidence of heart disease. Sleeping for that long duration may signify an underlying condition such as sleep apnea, which may increase the risk of cardiovascular disease – CVD. However, a study in 2021 found out that sleeping only for 6-8 hours nightly will increase a person daytime energy and activity and will make he/she burn more calories (AARP, February/March 2021, p.25 & Woman's World, 2021).

Did you know? Among Americans aged 65 or older, 47% have prediabetes, and another 27% have diabetes. The death toll from diabetes is truly mind-boggling. High blood sugar kills about 3.2 million people every single year in the U.S. (Nutrition Action Health Letter, July/August 2020 p.5) & Bottom lines Health Breakthroughs 2021, p.2).

Did you know? Diabetes is the leading cause of new cases of blindness among adults ages 20-74. In addition, it kills more Americans every year than breast cancer and AIDS combined. Furthermore, people with diabetes are about 8 times more likely than others to have a lower leg amputation (research confirmed by Mayo Clinic, Harvard Health and the American Diabetes Association, Fall 2020).

Did you know? A massive new study conducted in 2020 by researchers from Brigham and Women's Hospital as well as the VA Boston Healthcare System suggest that taking statins led to significant reduction in cardiovascular deaths as well as deaths from all causes for those over 75 years old (AARP Bulletin, September 2020 /Vol.61/No.7 p.4).

Did you know? In general, our body requires cholesterol for building cell walls, digestive fat, and controlling certain hormone. Our bloodstream contains two types of cholesterol. One is low density lipoprotein known as LDL "bad" cholesterol and the other is high density lipoprotein known as HDL "good" cholesterol. Our liver produces all the cholesterol the body needs to carry out the body vital functions. It is especially important to keep these two in the right balance to maintain cardiovascular health. Too much of LDL cholesterol can raise our risk of heart attack because it causes buildup of plaque on the inner lining of our arteries. This in turn will eventually lead to narrowing of our arteries and cause them to loose flexibility - a condition called atherosclerosis. In worse cases the plaques can rupture and form clots that can travel through the bloodstream to the heart or brain, causing a heart attack or stroke. HDL is known as the "good" cholesterol because it scavenges and transports LDL the "bad" cholesterol to the liver where it converts it to bile or be eliminated in stools.

You should aim to have your LDL level to be below 100 milligrams per deciliter (mg/dL) and your HDL level to be 50 mg/dL or hither (Healthy Aging, Icahn School of Medicine at Mount Sinai, December 2020, p.6 & Iris Cantor Women's Health Center, Women's Health Advisor, Volume 25/Number10, October 2021, p.1).

Did you know? Cholesterol is made up of lipids, which are a type of fatty substance found in blood and tissue. Lipids tend to stabilize cell membranes, and it is a key building block for vital hormones, as well as the main constituent of bile, which is needed to digest fats and fat-soluble vitamins such as: A,D,E, and K. Cholesterol also helps nerve function by helping nerve cells to communicate and helps the skin synthesize vitamin D with exposure to the sunlight (Healthy Aging, Icahn School of Medicine at Mount Sinai, December 2020, p.1).

Did you know? If you have high triglycerides, a low HDL "good" cholesterol and high blood pressure, it is almost always an indication that you suffer from insulin resistance. That occurs when the insulin the body produces is no longer efficiently lowering your blood sugar by admitting sugar into cells, and that leads to diabetes of one kind or another (Nutrition Action Health Letter, July/August 2020, p.3).

Did you know? Some research suggests that the ratio of total cholesterol to the HDL (good cholesterol) level may be a better predicter for cardiovascular risk than individual values. One can calculate the ratio by dividing their total cholesterol by the HDL level. The optimal ratio should be 3.5 or less (Healthy Aging, Icahn School of Medicine at Mount Sinai, December 2020, p.1).

Did you know? In 2020, researchers believe that genetics plays a role in how much LDL, bad cholesterol, your liver produces. So, if your parents had high LDL there is a good chance that you will have it too. In addition, some blood pressure medications and antidepressants drugs as well as Rheumatoid Arthritis can also increase your LDL to some degree. So, you need to check it with your doctor and pharmacist to weigh the benefits verses the risk (Healthy Aging, Icahn School of Medicine at Mount Sinai, December 2020, p.1).

Did you know? Cholesterol levels tend to rise with age. So, for example, post-menopausal women tend to have an increase in their LDL "bad" cholesterol and a decrease in their HDL "good" cholesterol (Healthy Aging, Icahn School of Medicine at Mount Sinai December 2020, p.6).

Did you know? Genetics also play a role in how much cholesterol the liver will produce. In the case of Asian Americans, African American and Hispanic it was found that all tend to have high LDL "bad" cholesterol levels in their bodies during their entire life span (Healthy Aging, Icahn School of Medicine at Mount Sinai, December 2020, p.6).

Did you know? Medical conditions, known also as comorbidities, can contribute to high LDL ("bad") cholesterol. They include diabetes, sleep apnea, hypothyroidism (underactive thyroid) and kidney disease (Healthy Aging, Icahn School of Medicine at Mount Sinai, December 2020, p.6).

Did you know? The tooth is the only part of the human body that cannot heal itself.

Did you know? Besides refined sugar, grains can also cause cavities in your teeth.

Did you know? Cavities in prehistoric times were not common until humans started to add refined sugar and flour to their diet. It all has to do with a specific oral bacteria.

This bacteria digest the residue of carbs that are left behind on your teeth after eating, and when it mixes with your saliva it forms plaque that eats away at your tooth enamel.

Did you know? Phytic acid is the primary reason why grains cause cavities and gum disease in humans. The rate of cavity-causing oral bacteria increased as humans began to farm grains 10,000 years ago. Phytic acid helps plants store phosphorus, a mineral that allows them to grow and survive, but the effect on humans is quite different. The phytic acid is actually binds in the human's digestive system with essential nutrients, which prevent humans from absorbing zinc, iron, magnesium, calcium and Vitamin D, all of which are needed in order for the body to absorb calcium. Calcium and Vitamin D are essential vitamins that help to prevent tooth decay and gum disease.

Did you know? Gum disease increases the risk for many health problem such as: tooth loss, heart disease, cancer of the stomach as well as the esophagus (Harvard Health Letter, October 2020, p.8 & Harvard Women's Health Watch, October 2020, p.8).

Did you know? Today we know that the health of teeth has a symbiotic connection to heart health. We know that an adult human has 32 teeth in his/her mouth. In the Hebrew language the number 32 in the alphabet is equal to the word 'LEV' in Hebrew which translates to 'heart,' spelled Lamed and Bet. The letter Lamed in Hebrew is representing the number 30, and the letter Bet is equal to the number 2. So, number 32 in the Hebrew letters forms the word 'Lev.' 'Lev' in Hebrew means heart.

Did you know? It is essential that you brush your teeth two or three times a day in order to protect your heart. Scientists have found out that brushing your teeth will lower your risk of a heart failure by 12 percent, as well as lower levels of gum disease too. In addition, it is believed that inflamed gums lead to increased overall inflammation in the body, which can damage the heart as well as other organs. If you cannot do the full teeth cleaning routine after eating because you are at work, at list rinse your mouth with water at the very least, and try to floss your teeth (AARP, February/March 2021, p. 28).

Did you know? Aloe vera gel is not only good for treating sunburn, but it is also used to promote oral health. Aloe is a common and safe ingredient found in many natural toothpastes. The National Institute of Health notes that aloe vera gel is also helpful in fighting off gingivitis, as well as the swelling of the gums (*Renew* by UnitedHealthcare, 2021, pp. 5-6).

Did you know? Bad breath is another aspect of oral health, and it is not a surprise that what you eat affect your breath. It is not just garlic and onions that can give you bad breath. Foods and beverages that reduce saliva can also contribute to bad breath. Saliva acts as a cleanser, removing bacteria and other causes of bad breath. That is why you get "morning breath" because the saliva production slows down overnight while you sleep. Keep in mind also that being hungry or dehydrated reduces saliva production too. You can combat bad breath by eating more fruits and vegetables and less meat and fatty foods (Weill Cornell Medicine, Iris Cantor Women's Health Center, January 2021, p.2).

Did you know? Many people are unaware that they are brushing their teeth too hard or too long (you need to keep it under two minutes or less) and causing damage while doing so. Using the wrong toothbrush and incorrect brushing technique are the real cause behind why dentists are seeing an increase in gum abrasion, gum recession and periodontal disease (FC&A, Medical Publishing p.35).

Did you know? Dentists have recommended that a toothbrush be kept at least six (6) feet away from a toilet to avoid airborne particles resulting from the flush.

Did you know? Anna Peterson, who is a dentist, warns that using mouthwash after brushing our teeth does more harm than good. Why? A typical toothpaste has around 1450 parts per million Fluoride, while a mouthwash has only 220 parts per million Fluoride. So, we actually rinse off all the high concentration of Fluoride, for a low concentration of Fluoride. However, it is a good idea to use mouthwash after meals and in between brushing our teeth. In addition, it is not a good idea to scrub our teeth with toothpaste because it will cause us to have tooth decay. Also, it is advised that after brushing our teeth we should limit rinsing our mouth, as to not rinse away much of the Fluoride (Http://teach1776.Ning.com).

Did you know? The researchers at the University of Washington found out that people who experience bleeding gums despite regular brushing and flossing, were deficient in Vitamin C. When they started to consume Vitamin C, their gums stopped bleeding in a matter of weeks. The reason has to do with the fact that Vitamin C aids in the process of keeping blood vessel cell walls healthy and strong. One can add to their diet food that contains Vitamin C such as oranges, strawberries, kale, peppers and kiwis. However, it you do not like these foods, you can take vitamin C supplements every day. However, keep in mind that not all vitamin C supplements are alike. The best once absorbed slowly in the body. Today one can find in the supermarkets a very good vitamin C supplement called Ester-C (500mg. or 100mg etc.) 24 Hour Immune Support manufactured by NatureSmart LLC, Bohemia, NY. Keep in mind that just 500 mg of it will go a long way. Do not take too much of it. Consuming too much vitamin C can lead to overdose. Keep in mind that **lack of vitamins C** in the body or **too much of vitamin C** in the body (taking 3,000 mg. or more per day) **can cause scurvy**. *(First for women* June 7, 2021, p.33).

Did you know? Dentists recommend using soft toothbrushes, but not all brushes labeled soft are actually soft. So, in order for you to buy the correct toothbrush it is recommended that you go to and buy a super soft, ultra-soft, or sensitive toothbrush (AC&A, Medical Publishing p.3).

Did you know? Today, researchers found out that antimicrobial silver technology reduces bacteria buildup on toothbrush bristles to keep them clean. Today you can buy a toothbrush on the internet by going to Mouthwatcher.com and get Doctor Plotka's toothbrush that is incredibly soft and has flossing bristles that are infused with silver to naturally eliminate 99.9% of bacteria on the bristles within six hours. These bristles are made of polyester, and they are long-lasting than the traditional nylon bristles. The outer bristles are as thin as a human hair, that can gently brush away food and plaque that other brushes miss. The thicker inner bristles will clean your teeth and gums the best a toothbrush can do.

Did you know? Your gum and teeth health can impact your breast cancer risk too in a big way (Ultimate Women's Guide to Beating Disease, p.38).

Did you know? People who follow the Paleo diet typically do not experience teeth and gum problems. Paleo diet typically includes lean meats, eggs, fish, seeds, nuts, fruits, vegetables and healthy fats and oil such avocado oil and olive oil. Healthy people who follow this diet tend to avoid processed foods, grains and sugar.

Did you know? Researchers today claim that there is no scientific basis to back up claims that coconut oil is good for our health. Coconut oil is rich in saturated fat and therefore it can actually raise our unhealthy LDL cholesterol and contribute to heart disease. According to the USDA Nutrient Data Laboratory, one tablespoon of coconut oil contains about 11.7 milligrams of saturated fat and 117 calories that our body must burn off to avoid gaining weight (Health & Nutrition Letter, Tufts University 2021, p. 5).

Did you know? Our digestive system can make us have energy or it can make us fat. It all depends on what kind of foods we ingest. It is important to keep in mind that we need to stay away from foods that contain High Fructose Corn Syrup as well as Olestra, also known today as Olean, because our bodies store them as fat.

Did you know? Researchers found out that a low-fat diet can contribute to the onset of cavities. It is because low-fat diets increase the risk of fat-soluble vitamins deficiencies such as: A, E, D and K. Therefore, it is important to remember that fat-soluble vitamins need some healthy fats in order to be absorbed in the body. Vitamins A, E & D provide cell protection, and they are vital for the immune system. They help cells fight off infection. Vitamin A helps keep mucous membranes in the mouth healthy, which can help prevent gum disease and cancer. Vitamin D helps calcium and phosphate to be absorbed in the body, in order to keep bones and teeth in the body healthy and strong. Vitamin K acts as a saliva buffer against sugar and other oral bacterial acids that break down bones and cause tooth decay.

Did you know? Periodontitis, advanced gum disease, is caused by bacterial infection that damages the soft tissue and bone that supports the teeth and may be linked to higher risk of certain cancers, such as lung cancer, colorectal cancer and colon cancer according to a new study published in the *Journal of the National Cancer Institute*. The study was conducted for 15 years on 7,500 people. Therefore, it is especially important for people to see a dentist regularly to keep their teeth and gums healthy as much as possible (Health & Nutrition Letter, Tufts University, December 2018-VOL.36, NO.12 p.2).

Did you know? Scientists in Taiwan found out that living with gingivitis for more than ten years increases the risk of Alzheimer's by as much as 70%. Their advice is to floss the teeth often (Reader's Digest, October 2020, p.33).

Did you know? Researchers found out that patients with Rheumatoid Arthritis and gum disease who had their tartar beneath their gums scaped away, had significantly less joint pain, stiffness and swelling after about six weeks from the time of the procedure. Reducing oral bacteria may ease inflammation elsewhere in the body (Bottom Line's Ageless Health, Ageless Beauty, p.7).

Did you know? Korean researchers found out that people who brushed their teeth three to four times a day had a 10% lower risk of atrial fibrillation (an irregular heartbeat that can lead to blood clots, stroke, and heart failure) and a 12% lower risk of heart failure. So, brushing actually removes the plaque that causes gum disease, and gum disease is associated with inflammation that causes atrial fibrillation (Health, September 2020, p.50).

Did you know? Just brushing the teeth alone misses about 35% of the tooth surface, so there is also a need to floss it.

Did you know? Plaque is formed from hardened bacteria which can enter the bloodstream through the gums and can lead to heart disease, heart attack, and stroke.

Did you know? New cancer therapy that cures oral cancer was discovered in 2020 that is better than radiation treatment. This therapy is uses cowpea mosaic virus or CPMV that can be found on the leaves of infected cowpea plants, the source of black-eyed peas. These cancer-fighting viruses are relatively cheap to make because they are self-replicating, and they do not need outside intervention once they are injected into the tumor. This therapy does not let the cancer cells trick the immune system into thinking that nothing is wrong. Instead, it warns the body that there are cancer cells so it can start to fight back.

Did you know? COPD (Chronic Obstructive Pulmonary Disease) is known as emphysema and chronic bronchitis. It is the third leading killer disease in the US. So, it is important to catch it early even though the symptoms tend to be virtually invisible. The key symptom to watch out for is shortness of breath, particularly during exercise or any other type of exertion (Ultimate Women's Guide to Beating Disease 2018, p.65).

Did you know? People who increase the number of steps they take in a day from 1,000 to 3,000 may reduce their mortality risk by 12%. Those who hit 10,000 steps per day cut their risk by about 46%. In addition, if one is to step up their activity level by exercising longer and harder can lower their risk of heart failure up to 35% (Health & Nutrition Letter p.4).

Did you know? A new study shows that higher aerobic fitness is linked to improved cognitive function among adults (Health & Nutrition Letter p.4). Other studies from the Universities of Basel, Switzerland and Tsukuba in Japan have found that coordinated and challenging sports with players such as tennis or soccer, have a greater effect on cognitive abilities than solo fitness activities (Health, September 2020, p.57).

Did you know? In a recent study of middle-aged men, it was found that those who exercised intensely for more than 450 minutes a week were 27% more likely to develop calcium buildups in their coronary arteries (AARP, February/March 2021, p. 25).

Did you know? A new study found out that leg muscles are more active during squatting than siting, and that squatting increases the production of an enzyme that breaks down triglycerides (the bad cholesterol) to use for fuel for the body (Health, September 2020, p.48).

Did you know? You can ease sore muscles and sports injuries by preparing your own cold pack that molds to your body. In order to do so mix rubbing alcohol with water in a zip-top plastic bag and pop it in the freezer. The alcohol keeps the pack slushy so you can very easily shape it to fit anywhere that ache in your body. It is also much cheaper to prepare it at home as well as be more comfortable than what you can find on the market (Supermarket Super Remedies, by Jerry Baker p.233).

Did you know? It is important to manage anger, because anger tend to trigger the production of adrenaline and cortisol in the body, which increase clotting, constrict the blood vessels, and cause the heart rate and blood pressor to go up. As result, it will raise heart attack risk in people. So, when it happens it is a good idea to take a walk or do jumping jacks, because movement helps the body to metabolize the hormonal surge according to C. Noel Bairey Merz, M.D., director of the Barbara Streisand Women's Hearth Center at Cedars-Sinai in Los Angeles (Health September 2020, p.50).

Did you know? The brain does not finish developing until age 25 or so. Basically, "the brain develops the gas first and brakes later" so said John Draper, PhD in his article that was published in Newsmax Magazine in July 2021, p.84.

Did you know? People who keep their minds active have slower declines in memory and thinking. They build a cognitive reserve, which helps the brain to continue to function. Researchers found out that playing old-fashioned games such as cards, bingo, and chess, or keeping up with arts and crafts such as sewing, woodworking and painting, several times a week are all linked to sharper thinking and memory skills. However, they advised us to stay focused on something that we love to do and get passionate about it, rather than constantly switching our attention from one thing to another. Furthermore, meditation, or Hatha yoga done ten minutes a day or more may calm the stress circuits in the brain that link up areas involved with memory and thinking. In addition, a recent study showed that African Americans with coronary disease who meditate for 20 minutes twice a day had 48% fewer heart attacks than those who did not meditate on a regular basis (Reader's Digest, Sept. 2020 p.72 & AARP Bulletin, March 2019, p.18).

Did you know? Research now shows that yoga can help lower blood pressure, reduce harmful cholesterol levels, improve blood glucose levels, boost brainpower, help lose weight and ease pain, and increase your flexibility too (www.health.harvard.edu/yoga).

Did you know? Lower levels of estrogen have been linked to lower glucose metabolism by the brain. This may reduce Adenosine Triphosphate (ATP), a compound that provides energy for cells. About three quarters of the ATP is generated in the brain and used as fuel to communicate between brain cells (Healthy Aging, Icahn School of Medicine at Mount Sinai, May 2021, p.3).

Did you know? In 2015, researchers at Harvard University found out that runners had a higher concentration of bacteria called Vellonella, than those who do not run, which help break down the lactic acid that forms in muscles (Reader's Digest, October 2020, p.32).

Did you know? The Heart Foundation concluded that sitting for prolong periods of time is as bad as smoking for our health. Sitting for long periods of time slows down more than just our metabolism. It actually launches a catalytic chain of events that can lead to harmful health outcomes. It actually can increase our chance of getting diabetes by 112% and heart attack or stroke by 147%, as well as shorten our lifespan. In 2016 a study by *the Lancet*, an independent medical journal, concluded that one hour of moderate exercise a day may have a positive effect on people who sat for eight hours a day. So, it appears with sitting, as with all things, that moderation is the key to keep us healthy (https://longlifeandhealth. org/what-is-sitting-disease/).

Did you know? A study reported by the American Journal of Epidemiology claims that sitting for six or more hours per day increases the risk of death from Diabetes, kidney disease, suicide, Chronic Obstructive Pulmonary Disease, liver and other digestive diseases, Parkinson's disease, Alzheimer's disease, and muscle-skeletal disorders, in addition to cardiovascular disease and cancer. The study also found out that people who already have diabetes are in greatest risk of dying from lack of activity (Health & Nutrition Letter Tuft University December 2018, VOL.36, NO.12 p.2).

Did you know? We take about 8 million breaths a year and it effects every system in our body.

Did you know why humans have many shades of skin color? It all has to do with human adaptation to climates. Large amounts of Melanin help to protect skin from the Sun and improves vision in bright sunlight. So, people will have dark colored skin and dark eyes in hot, sunny climates. However, in cloudy climates and long winters, dark skin may interfere with the production of Vitamin D in the body. Therefore, people living in this climate will have light skin and light-colored eyes.

However, today because of advancements in transportation, people tend to move all over the world and therefore you can find many different shades of skin and different eye color people everywhere on planet earth.

Did you know? The Incidence of skin cancer is continuing to rise in the US, including basal cell carcinoma and squamous cell carcinoma. Melanoma is rarer but is much more deadly if not caught early. The Mohs- Micrographic Surgery, was pioneered by Dr. Frederic E. Mohs in the 1930s, tend to successfully treat today (2021) many skin cancers (Wellness Letter, University of California, Berkeley p.5).

Did you know? Babies are born naturally without kneecaps, and they do not appear until the child reaches 2 to 6 years of age.

Did you know? Your heart is one of the most important organs in your body that does not develop cancer. Keeping it healthy is a key part of having a long and happy life.

Did you know? As many as 10 percent of all heart attacks strike people younger than 45 (Reader's Digest, February 2021, How to Keep Your Heart Young p.58).

Did you know? Around the age of 50 human being heart muscle start to stiffen, making it tougher for it to pump blood efficiently throughout the body. The medical term for it is Diastolic Dysfunction, where the muscle is not able to relax after each beat, increasing wear and tear on the heart (Reader's Digest, February 2021, p.69).

Did you know? Researchers at Taiwan University found out that a full bladder causes your heart to beat faster and it also puts stress on your coronary arteries. That in turn can lead to a heart attack in some people. So, empty your bladder when you have the urge, as soon as possible (Reader's Digest, February 1, 2021, p.68).

Did you know? The American Heart Association (AHA) claims that an adult person with type 2 diabetes has a four-time greater risk of dying from a heart disease. However, today one can find a multitude of medications that can improve diabetes type two and at the same time reduce the likelihood of a heart attack, stroke, heart failure and even kidney disease. The following are some of the medicines that give this kind of multiple benefit: empagliflozin (Jardiance), dulaglutide (Trulicity), and semaglutide (Ozempic) to mention a few (Reader's Digest, February 2021, p.62).

Did you know? Most women can hear better than men, while most men can read smaller print than women.

Did you know? Women typically blink nearly twice as often as men.

Did you know? A Dutch study found out that pregnant women who spontaneously gave birth before 37 weeks may have a greater risk of coronary artery disease, 71 percent higher risk of a stroke, and more than double the risk of overall heart disease. They believe that these women may have issues with inflammation in their body that is linked to preterm delivery and is common among heart disease patients (Reader's Digest, February 2021, p.63).

Did you know? Researchers at the University of Alabama Birmingham found that women who enter menopause early (before age 46) may have double their risk for a heart attack or stroke. They suspect that when ovulation stop prematurely it can be a sign of blood vessel disease (Woman's Day & Reader's Digest, February 20021, p.63).

Did you know? Hormone replacement therapy with estrogen, which many women turn to during menopause, may offer more than just relief from hot flashes. It seems to also protect nerve cells and improve thinking ability (*First for women*, April 5, 2021, p.40).

Did you know? Postmenopausal women who took 75mg. of Resveratrol twice a day found out that it helped them process information faster and improved their working memory (*First for women,* April 26, 2021, p.92).

Did you know? Estrogen is essential for the maintenance of many of the body's systems. It is not only responsible for the reproductive health in the body but is also responsible for bone development, mood management and heart health. When estrogen levels decline, women often develop stiffening of the heart muscle. A regular moderate exercise and a balanced diet can help greatly (Reader's Digest, February 1, 2021, p.63 & p.69).

Did you know? Pound for pound human bones tend to be stronger than steel (Reader's Digest, June 2021, p.117).

Did you know? Human thigh bones are stronger than concrete.

Did you know? Stress, depression and other health issues can affect your memory. In addition, it was discovered that many drugs may cause memory loss too, as a side effect. The common drugs that can cause these symptoms include those for allergies (antihistamines), anxiety, cholesterol lowering (statins), depression, high blood pressure, incontinence, insomnia, pain (narcotics), Parkinson's and seizure medicines (*First for women,* April 26, 2021, p.92 & Newsmax Magazine, Natural Cures 2021, p.43).

Did you know? People who regularly worry about the future and dwell on the past all the time tend to have a larger drop in cognitive ability and had more harmful brain proteins than those who did not. In addition, researchers also found a link between anxiety and depression that leads to higher incidence of Alzheimer and other types of dementia (Harvard Women's Health Watch, October 2020, p.1).

Did you know? Smell loss could be an early warning sign of Alzheimer's disease, Schizophrenia, or autoimmune disease such as Lupus. In addition, it can also be a leading indicator of contracting COVID-19 (Reader's Digest, June 2021, pp. 44-45).

Did you know? Pregnant women have especially sensitive noses. It is believed that it is due to the fact that increased sensitivity during pregnancy reduces the likelihood of the mother ingesting toxins (Reader's Digest, June 2021, p.45).

Did you know? Our sense of smell naturally declines as we age. A third of people in their 80s cannot smell at all. Smoking dulls the sense too. Our sense of smell is strongest when we are hungry (Reader's Digest, June 2021, p.45).

Did you know? Your lifestyle and habits influence your brain health. While younger brains excel at noticing details, older brains take in the big picture and utilize lessons learned from past experiences. In addition, researchers found out that our cognitive abilities actually improve over time. In addition, our brain, as we age, tends to improve its ability to pick up on others' feelings. Since it is really hard to do so, it takes time to learn this skill. Researchers from Duke University and the National Institute of Mental Health as well as Montefiore Einstein Center for the Aging Brain found out in 2017 that the brain, as we get older, builds resilience and adapts to changes in our lives, as well as continues to improve our vocabulary well into our 70s (Health, January/February 2021, p.58).

Did you know? Researchers found out that simply looking at beautiful travel photos tend to release oxytocin in the brain that help us feel calm, focused and energized. In a way it is a mini vacation for our brain (Women's World, 10/11/2021, p.45).

Did you know? A large portion of the brain is made of fat.

Did you know? The estimated human brain capacity, in terabytes, is about 1,000 terabytes, while the total size of the collections in the Library of Congress, in terabytes, is only approximately 50 terabytes.

Did you know? The brain requires more than 25% of the oxygen that is used by the human body.

Did you know? It will take a human brain between three and six minutes without oxygen to die (Reader's Digest, February 2020, p.75).

Did you know? Neurons in the brain makes enough electricity each day to run a light bulb of 20 watts.

Did you know? Our brain works faster than the world's greatest computer. The information going to our brain from our arms and legs travels at 150 miles per hour.

Did you know? There is no such thing as a "left" or "right" brained person. In order to carry out most tasks successfully, the two hemispheres of the brain need to interact.

Did you know? The longest-living cells in the body are brain cells, which can live for as long as a human does. However, as we age, we tend to lose brain cells and that tends to impact every aspect of our lives, as to how we think and how we feel. Recently, scientists discovered how to produce a protein called "Apoaequorin" that can support healthy brain function. This protein belongs to the same family of proteins as those found in humans. However, it was originally discovered in jellyfish. Today one can buy Prevagen, that contains this important protein in most pharmacies or supermarkets.

Did you know? In the past 5 to 10 years, a growing body of research has established that stuttering is biological in nature. Specifically, it looks like a neurodevelopmental disorder. In most of the more than 70 million people worldwide who shutter, the condition appears early in life. Researchers found out that people who suffer from it have differences in neutral connectivity, and they also have changes in how their speech and motor systems are integrated. In addition, they also have alterations in the activity of crucial neurotransmitters such as Dopamine. Furthermore, there is also a genetic component to it. Today researchers identified four genes that dramatically increase the likelihood of this speech problem. The neuroscientists call the problem "a system-level problem" in the brain. Some aspect of stuttering remains a puzzle. The condition affects about 1% of adults and roughly 5% of children, up to 80 % of whom recover and end up having a fluent speech. Some famous people who had to overcome stuttering include King George VI of England, U.S. President Joe Biden, actors Samuel L. Jackson,

Marilyn Monroe, James Earl Jones and Emily Blunt, to mention a few (Scientific American, August 2021, p.59).

Did you know? Researchers have found out that patients that suffer from Schizophrenia, depression, and addiction have less gray matter in their brain than healthy individuals. Researchers are now exploring the possibility that these disorders could have similar causes and treatments.

Did you know? Helmets do not prevent concussions according to Weill Cornell Concussion and Brain Injury Clinic. A helmet does not stop the brain from banging around inside the skull, which is the cause of a concussion. So, what is the point of wearing a helmet? Helmets prevent skull fractures, which can also injure the brain.

Did you know? In order to remove a splinter easily, one need to apply a paste of baking soda and water to the area and wait for several minutes for the splinter to pop out of the skin (1000LifeHacks.com).

Did you know? Smelling rubbing alcohol can relieve nausea almost instantly for some people (1000LifeHacks.com).

Did you know? Compression pants can bump up a person's metabolism by about 15% if we wear them while we are active. Why? Because they support our circulatory system and speed up oxygen transport through the body and that maximizes the fat loss (Woman's World August 2021).

Did you know? Only about 25 people in the world are known to have Hyperthymesia. -- a condition that allows them to remember every details of their lives.

Did you know? Your kidneys are among the most industrious organs in your body with plenty of work capacity. Each kidney contains 1 million tiny filters that work together to filter an average of 2.2 pints (1.3liters) of blood every minute, that is 3168 pints (1872 liters) every single day, despite each kidney only being the size of a fist. They also expel an average of 2.5pints(1.4 liters) of urine from your body every day too. In addition, they remove excess fluid and waste material from the body by filtering between 30 to 50 gallons of blood every day. In each kidney there are about a million nephrons, a tiny filtering units, that make sure that the body will have just the right amounts of salt, protein, sugar, calcium and other substances vital to maintaining proper body function. The kidneys also produce hormones that help regulate the blood pressure in the body, make red blood cells and strengthen bones (Mayo Clinic Health Letter, January 11, 2021, pp.1-2).

Did you know? Poorly controlled blood sugar can harm blood vessels in your body, including the ones in your kidneys, causing kidney function to worsen (Mayo Clinic Health Letter, January 11, 2021, p.2).

Did you know? When a person dies, hearing is the last sense to go, while the first sense to be lost is sight.

Did you know? The speed of blood moving in the body is 2 miles per hour.

Did you know? The top foot speed of a human is 28 mph.

Did you know? The human body consist of 60% water.

Did you know? Every day a healthy body ensure that it does not contract cancer thousands of times every days. To do so the body sends special enzymes scuttling around to inspect DNA strands for faults and fix them before they turn into tumors.

Did you know? The average human body contains approximately four ounces of salt.

Did you know? Only 7% of the population are left-handed.

Did you know? people do not get sick from cold weather, but rather from being indoors a lot more in winter.

Did you know? The speed of a human sneeze is around 100 mph.

Did you know? The speed of hair growth is approximately 0.16 millimeters per hour.

Did you know? there are **6 vitamins** that can be added to your diet to reduce hair loss. These vitamins include D & B vitamins such as B2 (riboflavin), B3 (niacin), B6 and B7 (Biotin). In addition, one should also add to their diet vitamins C, E, Zinc & A. However, keep in mind that vitamin A deficiency can leads to hair loss, but getting too much of it can also cause hair loss (healthscamsnews.com).

Did you know? Hair cells are most active in the morning. Hair does not all grow at the same time. Each hair is on a separate and slightly staggered schedule. In general, hair grows about half a millimeter per day, and the average adult with a full scalp has around 100,000 hairs on their head. So that is a combined 50 meters of hair growth every single day (Woman's World 2021).

Did you know? Rising temperatures increase scalp oil production, making dandruff flakes larger and stickier. For flake-free sculp use 2 crushed aspirin tablets and apply it to your scalp, because it has salicylic acid that stops the growth of yeast that causes the condition. You need to add the aspirin to your shampoo and massage it onto your scalp for 2 minutes before rinsing. Studies show that it will end itching and flaking in about three days, as well as prevent dandruff flare-ups from taking place (*First for women*, June 15, 2020, p.31).

Did you know? People that have more Zinc and Copper in their hair are believed to be more intelligent than the rest of us. These people most often have natural red/orange color hair.

Did you know? Redheads require more anesthesia to be sedated than those with other hair colors (Reader's Digest, June 2021, p.117).

Did you know? Bright people are more likely to find dark jokes funny.

Did you know? The speed at which fingernails grow is 0.004 millimeters. The nails that get the most exposure and are used most frequently grow the fastest. Fingernails grow most quickly on the hand that you write with and on the longer fingers. On average, a nail grows about one-tenth of an inch each month.

Did you know? Fingernails can provide hints to the status of your overall health, through their color, shape and texture (THE DAILY, AARP August 16, 2021).

Did you know? Without a pinky finger, our hands would lose 50% of its strength.

Did you know? If you are right-handed, you will tend to chew food on your right side of your mouth. If you are left-handed, you will tend to chew your food on your left side.

Did you know? The average person's left hand does 56% of the typing.

Did you Know? Blondes typically have more individual hairs on their heads than brunettes. Redheads have the fewest of the three.

Did you know? The average human eyebrow has 550 hairs, and the average human beard has more than 15,000 hairs.

Did you know? Our eyes are always the same size from birth, but our nose and ears never stop growing.

Did you know? The average human beard has 15,000 hairs.

Did you know? The glands in our mouth produce an incredible 1.5 liters of saliva per day. Without saliva, our mouth would dry up and become overrun with bacteria and we would not be able to digest our food. In addition, the average person produces about 25,000 quarts of saliva in a lifetime, that is enough to fill two swimming pools.

Did you know? Fifteen million blood cells are produced and destroyed in the human body every second.

Did you know? Red blood cells take about 60 seconds to complete circulating in the body, delivering oxygen and keeping the body energized. Each cell lives for about 40 days, before being replaced by a younger one, and makes about 60,000 trips around the body.

Did you know? The average human speaks at a rate of up to 150 words per minute. That is a lot of information, which is conveyed in a short amount of time, making spoken conversation one of the most effective ways to communicate (Discover Magazine, January/February 2020, p.73).

Did you know? The brain does not stop working. It is estimated that between 50,000 to 60,000 thoughts pass through it each day on average. That is about 35-48 thoughts every minute of the day.

Did you know? Multitasking hijacks your frontal lobes, which are the brain's higher order thinking center, and in doing so, it reduces creativity, increases errors, lowers your ability to focus on what is most important, and increases problems with sleep, stress, and memory. So says Sandra Bond Chapman, PhD, the founder, and chief director of the Center for Brain Health at the University of Texas at Dallas.

Did you know? In 2011 study it was found that students who went to bed late instead of turning in early did the best on intelligence tests measuring reasoning, math, and languages skills.

Did you know? People who went for 24 hours without sleep, had a cognitive functioning, and responding speed that is worse than if they had a blood alcohol contents of 0.10 percent, which is 0.2 percentage points higher than the legal limit for driving under the influence.

Did you know? People whose minds wander the most tend to score highest on basic IQ tests, according to a study in *Neuropsychologic.*

Did you know? Chronic stress and lack of sleep suppress the immune system's function.

Did you know? A Harvard Medical School study found out that those people who achieved REM sleep, were better able to detect positive emotions in other people, while those who did not were more sensitive to negative emotions. The study concluded that dreams during REM sleep help the brain to process negative emotions safely.

Did you know? A vacation can help a person be more productive in life, and meditation reduces anxiety, depression, and stress. In addition, laughter increases the feel-good hormones Dopamine and Serotonin. This in turn decreases pain and improves resiliency.

Did you know? Lack of social connections carries a risk that is compatible to smoking up to 15 cigarettes per day. In addition, developing meaningful bonds with others is critical for your happiness and health too (Health Magazine, March 2020, p.92).

Did you know? Happy people tend to be healthier than those who are not happy. If you want to be happy, take time to enjoy life's little pleasures. Meik Wiking, CEO of the Happiness Research Institute in Copenhagen said, "The tiny moments are actually the big things in life." In addition, Kristin Neff, PHD, associate psychology professor at the University of Texas at Austin and coauthor of *The Mindful Self -Compassion Workbook* had another piece of advice as to how to be happier in life. She suggests that we should have compassion for ourselves and not be so harsh on us when things do not go smoothly in our lives. She claims that we need to remember that our setbacks or anxiety is normal part of being human. Jodie Eisner, PsyD, a clinical psychologist based in New York City, believes that one needs to accept the things that we cannot change and that we need to acknowledge our current reality without passing judgment, and remind ourselves that things are not good, or bad, they just are (Health Magazine, March 2020, pp.93-95).

Did you know? You can burn an extra 500 calories every day if you stand or walk whenever you can, and just keep your body moving. Try also swaying while you brush your teeth or listening to music.

Did you know? Pounding away on a flat treadmill puts you at higher risk of an overuse injury. It is better to walk or run-on varied terrain because the body will constantly readjust to evenly distribute the stress on joints.

Did you know? When we have a "gut feeling" are we just imagining it? No, we are not. According to research, hunches are the result of our brains' receiving and processing information so fast that our conscious minds do not even realize it yet.

Did you know? If you are feeling overwhelmed and stressed, step outside, or open a window. Researchers say getting more oxygen to the brain is a quick and effective stress reliever. "Taking in a deep breath of fresh air can immediately shift your neuro-chemistry," says Deborah Serani ,PsyD, a psychology professor at Adelphi University and the author of *Living with Depression*. In addition, the American Psychological Association recommends the fresh air approach too (Reader Digest, May 2020, p.22).

Did you know? Looking at blue spaces, like water, tends to make us happier, reduce our stress levels, and make us more sociable. Simply spending 10 minutes by a fountain can act as a mini vacation (Health Magazine, June p.89).

Did you know? According to a 2016 study, employees who have sunlight and natural elements in the workplace, report higher satisfaction with their work and become more efficient and productive workers (Health Magazine, June 2020, p.91).

Did you know? The longest cells in the human body are the motor neurons. They can be up to four and a half feet long and run from the lower spinal cord to the big toe.

Did you know? The average human body has enough fat to produce at least seven bars of soap.

Did you know? Tufts University experts claim that people who consume a lot of refined grains are at greater risk of developing dangerous abdominal fat around the intestines that is linked to many diseases such as heart disease, stroke, Type 2 Diabetes and heart attacks. It is all due to the fact that abdominal fat (belly-white fat) releases excess inflammatory compounds called cytokines into the body and that in turn undermines the immune system and leads to many health problems. The health problems include atherosclerosis, cancer, diabetes, strokes, liver failure, hypertension, sleep apnea and kidney damage (Health & Nutrition Letter, Tufts University, 5 Health Reports from Tufts p.5 & Newsmax Magazine Natural Cures 2021, p.33).

Did you know? Cancers associated with obesity, which are typically diagnosed at higher rates in people over 65, are now on the rise in younger people, according to a study published in *JAMA Network Open*, 2019;2(8): e100261.

Did you know? Breast cancer is more deadly for men than women. Researchers believe that it is due to the fact that men are not checked for it like women are, typically once a year (Reader's Digest, June 2020, p.46).

Did you know? Lung cancer claims more lives than breast, ovarian, colon, and prostate cancer combined. Even if you never smoked or only smoked occasionally or quit smoking, you are still at risk. Why? This is because most of us have been exposed to second-hand smoking during our lifetime. We also probably were exposed to radon, asbestos, emissions from indoor wood-burning stoves or fireplaces, and even to cooking oil, all of which can trigger deadly lung cancers. Even worse is that the symptoms are frequently ignored or mistaken for other problems until it is too late (Ultimate Women's Guide to Beating Disease, 2018, p.35).

Did you know? High blood pressure, high Cholesterol, or even high blood sugar put you at a higher risk for colon cancer (Ultimate Women's Guide Beating Disease, 2018, p.48).

Did you know? A high blood pressure has been associated with cognitive decline, because it can damage small blood vessels in the brain and that will hinder your memory and your thinking ability. In addition, it also increases your risk of a heart attack and a stroke. Just losing as few as 2.2 pounds can lower your blood pressure. In addition, cutting sodium intake by 50% can cut your risk of fatal stroke by about 85% according to the Global Council on Brain Health (https://info.prevagen.com).

Did you know? If you have high blood pressure, just 30 minutes of daily exercise can lower it for the rest of the day. However, it is important that you continue to see your doctor on a regular basis. In addition, you need to continue to monitor your blood pressure daily too (Better Homes & Gardens, March 2021, p.26).

Did you know? Tylenol won't raise your blood pressure the way Advil, Aleve, or Motrin sometimes can (Health Magazine, September 2021, p.27).

Did you know? Exercise is not just for weight loss. The benefits of exercise extend far beyond just losing weight. Walking at a moderate pace for 30 minutes a day gives very substantial heart health benefits to people of all ages.

It also tends to boost brain health and reduce cognitive decline in older people (AARP Bulletin, March 2019, p.18 & May 2021, p.6).

Did you know? Researchers found out that compression pants have the power to bump up our metabolism by about 15% if worn while we are active. It has to do with the fact that they support the circulatory system and speed up oxygen through our bodies, maximizing fat loss (Woman's World, 2021).

Did you know? There are two major kinds of body fat. White fat, the most abundant type, is what you feel when you "pinch an inch" on your mid-section. Brown fat, found mainly in the neck region and it is used by the body for energy. So, it tends not to be stored by the body like the white fat does, according to Scott Kahan, MD, director of the National Center for Weight and Wellness in Washington, DC.

Did you know? Even though people tend to believe that white fat is bad to have, it delivers important health benefits. It cushions and protects our vital organs, and it helps us keep warm. Furthermore, it stores calories for later use, keeping us from starving when food is scarce. However, excess white fat cells stored in the abdomen or around the inner organs such as the liver and gut releases inflammatory chemicals and other molecules that can increase the risk of heart disease, liver disease, diabetes, and health conditions. In contrast, fat that is stored in your arms, legs, or hips does not tend to do much harm.

Did you know? Scientists found out that sometimes white fat can be turned into brown fat when we exercise. One study points to a hormone called Irisin which our muscles produce when we exercise, that helps to convert the white fat to brown fat.

Did you know? Brown fat may also ward off diabetes. According to a study in *Cell Metabolism*, individuals with higher amount of brown fat have smaller fluctuations in blood sugar and thus have a reduced risk of developing diabetes.

Did you know? Infants are born with high levels of brown fats, which helps to regulate their body temperature. However, they will lose some of this brown fat as they age. Unfortunately, an adult human typically has small amount of it.

Did you know why it is so healthy for you to exercise? When you do so, the skeletal muscles, especially the large muscles of the butt and thighs, release immune protective compounds called Myokines during exercise. The Myokines are believed to have positive effects on metabolic disorders, Type 2 Diabetes and obesity.

Did you know? Increasing the amount of physical activity, can extend your lifespan, according to a study published in BMJ 2019;366:14570.

Did you know? Exercise at every age has been shown to improve memory, concentration, and other cognitive functions. It is linked to an increase in circulation, an increase in bringing oxygen and nutrients to the brain, while also helping remove waste. In addition, studies have shown that you can actually increase your body's response to insulin after just a week of regular walking (97 Favorite Foods Every Senior Should Eat, p.36).

Did you know? Adult's aged 65 and older who exercise four times a week, cut their risk of getting dementia in half, compared to those who are not active at all, or are active one day a week. In addition, managing your cardiovascular risk factors seems to reduce also the risk of dementia too. As we age, our joints, ligaments and cartilage wear down, and we rely on muscles to stabilize the ball joints in the hips and shoulders. Therefore, exercise is essential to keep

these joints working pain free (AARP Bulletin, March 2019, p.20 & Cleveland Clinic, Heart Advisor, Vol.21A -DGHHAST, August 2021, p.3).

Did you know? The best exercise is in the pool. It all has to do with the fact that water provides resistance but does not have s high impact on the joints like running does (AARP Bulletin, March 2019, p.20).

Did you know? When men sit with their wallets in their back pockets, it tends to cause them to have lower back pain. This is because the wallets in the back pockets tend to distort their lower lumber portion of their spines. This can eventually weaken and destabilize their spines as well (AARP Bulletin, March 2019, p.20).

Did you know? Worldwide, almost a third of people over age 65, fall each year. Dance activities such as the tango, folk dancing, or swing dancing reduce this risk by about 37%, according to a new study. The reason is due to the fact that dancing improves balance, mobility, and lower body strength (Reader's Digest, March 2021, p.46).

Did you know? Walking 7,000 steps a day can lower eye pressure and glaucoma risk, according to research from UCLA. Those who were the most physically active decreased their risk by up to 73% compared with less active subjects (Health Magazine, June 2020, p.32).

Did you know? Climbing stairs is ideal exercise because it is both aerobic exercise and strength exercise (Nutrition Action Health Letter July/August 2020, p.5).

Did you know? Eyes are the window to your body. The eye doctor may be able to spot symptoms of high blood pressure, cardiovascular disease, diabetes, and even colon polyps before they become dangerous, all by looking at your retina (Health Magazine, June 20, p.32).

Did you know? Studies have linked poor sleep to increased anxiety, and anxiety may disrupt sleep. So, it is a good idea to turn off electronics well before bedtime and keep a regular sleep schedule.

Did you know? Researchers found out that getting a good night's sleep is essential for our health. In fact, sleeping soundly for 7-8 hour helps to lose belly fat, lowers stress and reduce out-of-control cravings.

Did you know? Daily exercise is one of the best remedies for anxiety. Exercise causes the brain to produce pain and stress-relieving chemicals.

Did you know? What is good for your heart tends to be also very good for your brain (Cleveland Clinic, Heart Advisor, Vol. 21A – DGHHAST p.3).

Did you know? When healthy, the liver and the kidneys play a crucial role in supporting the immune system.

Did you know? The human heart creates enough pressure while pumping to squirt blood up to 30 feet.

Did you know? Humans have 60,000 miles of blood vessels, and the hard-working heart pumps about 2,000 gallons of blood through those blood vessels every day.

Did you know? Our liver is remarkably busy over the course of a day. It manufactures cholesterol, vitamin D & blood plasma. It identifies the nutrients that our body needs, and stores some away for future use. It also filters 1.53 quarts (1.43 liters) of blood every minute and produces a quart (0.94 liters) of bile every day to help break down the food we eat. It is like a technologically advanced factory plant running inside of us.

Did you know? Getting regular vaccinations help the immune system battle infections.

Did you know? People sweat a lot from their feet. A pair of feet has 500,000 sweat glands and can produce more than a pint of sweat a day.

Did you know? The droplets from a human sneeze can travel at a speed of 100 miles per hour or more. So, it is good practice to cover your sneeze.

Did you know? Your skin is actually an organ. In fact, it is the largest organ in the body with an average surface area of about 18 square feet equal to about 2 square meters. The average human sheds about 1 million skin cells every single day. That amounts to about 1.5 pounds each year. So, the average person will lose around 105 pounds of skin by age 70.

Did you know? Every square inch of skin on the human body has about 32 million bacteria on it. However, the vast majority of them are harmless.

Did you know? The small intestine is about four times as long as the average height of an adult person. Its length is about 18 to 23 feet.

Did you know? The cells in our stomach-lining produces an alkaline substance every few milliseconds to neutralize stomach acid. If they did not do this, our stomach would digest itself because some of the acids produced are strong enough to dissolve even metals. However, after a few days, despite the body's effort to neutralize stomach acid, the stomach ends up digesting its lining and therefore we end up generating a new stomach lining every three to four days.

Did you know? Poor gut health is more deadly than smoking. America's top cardiologists found that cigarette smokers are often healthier than those with gut issues. That means that the keys to fighting weight gain, fatigue and heart issues are all in our guts.

Did you know? A-pack-a-day smoker will lose approximately 2 teeth every 10 years.

Did you know? Researchers found out that current and former smokers, as well as obese or overweight people, and those who consume alcohol, have a higher risk of developing Rheumatoid Arthritis (RA) than people who have never smoked, drank alcohol, or have a normal body weight (Women's Nutrition Connection, May 2021, Volume 24, Number 5, p.2).

Did you know? Arthritis and other autoimmune issues can have a negative impact on the immune system. However, there is currently no consensus as to what actually causes arthritis. The word "arthritis" comes from the Greek word *arthron* (joint) and *itis* (inflammation). It is a broad category that includes more than 100 different rheumatic diseases and conditions, including Rheumatoid Arthritis, Fibromyalgia, Osteoarthritis, Gout, Lupus, and Lyme Disease. Nearly two-thirds of adults with arthritis are younger than 65. Arthritis is more common among women (26 percent) than men (19 percent) and more prevalent among obese individuals. It is estimated (in 2021) that 27 million adults have osteoarthritis and 1.3 million have Rheumatoid Arthritis in the U.S. (Newsmax, May 2021, pp.92-93).

Did you know? Different forms of arthritis affect people of all ages, and most are not senior citizens. For example, Rheumatoid Arthritis (RA) typically shows up between the ages of 40 and 60, and Juvenile Idiopathic Arthritis begins in children 16 and under. At times, some cases begin in infancy, even Osteoarthritis (OA), which is commonly associated with aging, can begin causing symptoms at an age that is far from old.

Did you know? For 50 years doctors have used Nonsteroidal Anti-inflammatory Drugs (NSAIDs) to treat the symptoms of arthritis, but these drugs actually do not cure the disease. In reality, prolonged use of NSAIDs inhibit cartilage formation and actually can worsen the arthritic conditions. Furthermore, more than 16,500 patients with arthritis die annually from the toxic effects of NSAIDs (Newsmax, May 2021, p.93).

Did you know? People with arthritis are prone to have lower levels of gut microbiota diversity. This can lead to pro-inflammatory gut microbes to dominate the gut biome, which can in turn trigger an inflammatory response throughout the body (Women's Nutrition Connection, May 2021, p.1 & p.6).

Did you know? In order to manage and reduce the symptoms of arthritis, it is recommended that one should stay physically active by walking, swimming and bicycling.

In addition, it is advised to maintain a healthy weight and take supplements that include vitamins A, B6, B12, C as well as take Boswellia, Glucosamine, green tea and Turmeric. Furthermore, it is advised to stay away from foods that boost inflammation in the body such as refined sugar and processed foods. Eat a whole-food diet, with as much organic produce as possible, including plenty of fruits and vegetables along with fatty fish, peas and beans, nuts and olive oil. In addition, one should drink adequate amounts of water because it was found to help patients significantly improve their condition (Newsmax, May 2021 p. 93 & Tufts University, Health & Nutrition Letter, June 2021, p.6).

Did you know? Research suggests that Turmeric may ease arthritis pain. Turmeric works similarly to a prescription COX-2 inhibitor, but without the side effects (Arthritis Foundation, AF-FY21-27SEC-INS-25-T).

Did you know? You should not stick out your tongue if you want to hide your identity. As with fingerprints, everyone has a unique tongue print.

Did you know? Your tongue is the only muscle in your body that is attached at only one end.

Did you know? In order to stay healthy our body needs to have a good quality of sleep every night. Poor quality of sleep is associated with increased stiffness of the arteries in the body as well as increased cholesterol plaque. If you want to have a better night's sleep, avoid afternoon naps, and caffeine within six hours of bedtime, as well as stop using your computer or cellphone before bedtime (Reader's Digest, February 1, 2021, p.65).

Did you know? Snoring can be a sign of sleep apnea, a life-threatening sleep disorder that can harm your body. About 10% of people who snore have sleep apnea. It has to do with people stopping to breathe in during sleep as often as 300 times every night. That can lead to a stroke or heart attack.

Did you know? About 75% of what we think we taste actually comes from our sense of smell. Along with sweet, salty, sour, and bitter, there is a fifth taste called *'umami'*, which describes the savory taste of food. The word *'umami'* is actually a Japanese word that means literally 'deliciousness'. People taste *umami* through taste receptors that typically respond to glutamates, which are widely present in meat broths and fermented products, cheese, and soy sauce to name a few.

Did you know? Our body cells regenerate themselves every single day without any prompting. This means that we end up having an entirely new set of taste buds every ten days, new nails every 6-10 months, new bones every ten years and even a new heart every 20 years.

Did you know? Our nose is not as sensitive as a dog's nose, but it can detect about 50,000 different scents.

Did you know? Humans are born with two fears: falling and loud noises. Every other fear is learned.

Did you know? If the human eye were to be a digital camera, it would have 576 megapixels.

Did you know? We blink approximately 28,800 times every day, with each one blink lasting just a tenth of a second. This is a voluntary reflex the body uses to keep the eyes clean and moist. Keep in mind the fact that our eyes need to be in top shape because about 90% of the information we process is visual.

Did you know? In order to kick the common cold out of your life, you need to keep your hands away from your face, especially from your eyes and nose. In addition, get plenty of rest. When you fall behind on sleep, you are more susceptible to catching a cold. Furthermore, taking 500mg of Ester C, slow-release Vitamin C, twice a day every day without a gap, may reduce your chances of getting a cold altogether. Try it! You've got nothing to lose!

Did you know? Vitamin C may protect the endothelium, the layer of cells that lines blood vessels, which may help reduce risk of heart disease and dementia.

Did you know? We do not lose most of our body heat through the head. Only 10% of our body heat is lost through our head (The Old Farmer's Almanac, Fall & Winter 2020, p.20).

Did you know? Most of our body's energy is expelled via heat. Our body produces the same heat as about 25 regular 60-watt lightbulbs over the course of a single day.

Did you know? We do not catch a cold from cold temperatures. We catch it from the cold virus.

However, cold weather can weaken our immune system, making it easier to catch a cold (The Old Farmer's Almanac, Fall & Winter 2020, p.20).

Did you know? If you are stranded and thirsty, you should not eat snow or ice, because it will lead to internal injuries. If you have no water, try to melt ice in a plastic bag between the layers of your clothes (The Old Farmer's Almanac, Fall & Winter 2020, p.21).

Did you know? When you exercise, even in cold temperatures, you can sweat, and in cold weather you will lose even more water through your breath than you would at warmer temperatures. Dehydration is dangerous in cold weather. It hinders the body's ability to produce heat (The Old Farmer's Almanac, Fall & Winter 2020, p.21).

Did you know why do we shiver? Shivering means that our body is trying to warm up, and that is good. Shivering is happening involuntarily. It is one of the ways that our body automatically responds to heat loss that threatens to lower our core temperature. Shivering is when skeletal muscle contracting, and it can actually triple our body's heat production (The Old Farmer's Almanac, Fall & Winter p.21).

Did you know? Researchers found out that cold weather can affect your heart health. When temperatures drop below 32 degrees Fahrenheit the risk of heart attack in older adults increases by much (*JAMA* Cardiology, Oct.24, 2018.

Nutrients, Foods, Diet & Health

Did you know? Dr. Sam Walters, a practicing physician and a former NASA Nutrition Scientist, recommend that we should try to minimize exposure to **five poisonous foods for our brain**. The **first** is **MSG** – monosodium glutamate, the **second** is **Aspartame**, sold under the label NutraSweet or Equal. Aspartame and MSG are both "excitotoxins" because they "excite" or stimulate the brain cells the wrong way. They are made from sugar molecule and 3 chloride ions. When chloride is combined with carbon, it becomes an unwanted contaminant. This is how actually pesticides and herbicides are created. The **third** is **Sucralose**, sold under the label Splenda. The **fourth** is **Diacetyl**, the buttery flavor in microwave popcorn. Keep in mind that it will not appear on the labels as such but rather as "artificial butter flavor" or "natural flavors." Diacetyl is a brain toxins that can cross the blood-brain barrier (a defense mechanism that prevents harmful substances from entering the brain) and form plaques on the brain, and that in turn will lead to memory decline. If you still would like to eat popcorn you could make your own at home by using the stove or an air popper and add to it your own ingredients. The **fifth** one is **Aluminum**. Aluminum unfortunately can be found everywhere. It is in drinking water, supplements, antacids, antiperspirant, cans of soda, foils, and is also commonly used in cookware. So, one should look for/ aluminum-free deodorants, baking powder, antacid and avoid aluminum cookware to mention a few. (clearstateofmind.com).

Did you know? A poor diet can increase and prolong inflammation in your body, while a good diet can protect your health. Chronic inflammation can lead to heart disease, cancer, diabetes, stroke, Parkinson's and Alsheimer's diseases (Dr. Russell Playlock in Newsmax Magazine, Natural Cures 2021, p.28).

Did you know? A bacon, egg, and cheese breakfast biscuit at a popular fast-food restaurant contains 13 grams of saturated fat - more than half of the recommended total for an entire day (Iris Cantor Women's Health Center, Women's Health Advisor, October 2021 p,7).

Did you know? Diet has a huge impact on disease risk in general. About 30% of all cancers are linked to poor dietary habits, according to Anna Taylor, lead outpatient clinical dietitian at the Cleveland Clinic's Center for Human Nutrition. Diet rich in vitamins and minerals can help the body better prepare itself to fight off anything that may come its was. This is especially important as we get older, since our immune response declines as we age. There are about eight superfoods that will give us a boost such as probiotic foods that include plain Greek yogurt, pickles in salty water (not in vinegar), kombucha, kimchi, kefir and sauerkraut. We also need to eat foods that contain prebiotics such as garlic, whole grains, onions, bananas, asparagus, ginger, blueberries, and other dark berries to mention a few.

Did you know? Researchers found out that eating breakfast has a great positive impact on heart health (Woman's Health, August 2021).

Did you know? All oats are nutritious as long as other ingredients are not added to them. They contain fiber rich whole-grains, and they are rich in beta-glucan, a soluble fiber associated with reducing cholesterol levels and colon cancer risk in humans (Tufts University, Health & Nutrition Letter, October 2021, p.8).

Did you know? Steel-cut oats are preferable to rolled oats for breakfast because they have more intact structure to slow blood sugar rise. What is important to consider is that both rolled, and steel-cut oats are better choice than instant varieties, which boost blood sugar more and also come with undesirable added ingredients like sugar. (Tufts University, Health & Nutrition Letter, October 2021 p. 8).

Did you know? Canola oil is one of the few cooking oils that contains healthy Omega 3 fats. However, corn and soybean oils are the worst, because they are hydrogenated.

Hydrogenated oils have tons of harmful chemicals that cause inflammation (Eating Well, August 2021).

Did you know? The sulfur compounds in garlic tend to help lower cholesterol and blood pressure (EatingWell, August 2021).

Did you know? Avocados tend to stabilize blood sugar and fight metabolic syndromes. They also tend to be a major player in cancer-fighting, because avocados contain phytochemicals that are as powerful as some chemotherapy treatments, and they also help reduce inflammation and DNA damage. Furthermore, they contain Carotenoids and Lutein, the kind of antioxidants that are valuable for healthy eyes. In addition, they also contain Zeaxanthin, Alpha-Carotene and Beta-Carotene as well as significant quantities of Vitamin E. Even though they are calorically dense and high in healthy fats, they actually contribute to great weight lose because they reduce hunger by keeping blood sugar and fat-storing Insulin in check. The healthy fat that avocados contain includes monounsaturated fatty acids and serum lipids. In addition, they contain plenty of Oleic Acid, the same healthy fat that is found in olive oil that lowers bad cholesterol as well as blocks the development of Arteriosclerosis and helps in preventing breast cancer and other cancers. However, it is advised not to eat the pits because they can cause intestinal discomfort or other health issues for some.(http://thenutritionwachdog.com).

Did you know? Avocado pits or seeds have been used medicinally for generations. In South America avocado pits have been used as a treatment of inflammation, Diabetes and Hypertension. The pits and the seeds contain phenolic compounds, which are known to prevent cancer, cardiovascular disease and other degenerative illnesses. (https://thenutritionwatchdog.com

Did you know? A Canadian research found out that eating one avocado daily can help folks shed about 2 pounds in 4 days. It all has to do with the fact that it contains gut-healing soluble fiber that turns into gel in the gut, ensuring slow, and thorough digestion of food (First for women, August 30, 2021, p.27).

Did you know? Researchers found out that high intake of water-rich fruit and veggies like cauliflower, melon, radishes, romaine lettuce, peppers, tomatoes and cucumbers can help people over 50 lose weight successfully. Why? Because these foods tend to be low in calories and yet they will make people feel full and therefore turn off their craving for more food consumption (Woman's World August 2021).

Did you know? Researchers found out that fresh vegetables are not always best. In fact, they concluded that frozen vegetables actually might be healthier. It all has to do with the fact that produce chosen for freezing tends to be at their peak, containing the most vitamins and minerals (EatingWell, August 2021).

Did you know? Eating foods labeled low-fat sometimes means that you are eating as many calories as the full-fat version, because food companies tend to add more carbs and sugar to the food so it will tase good (EatingWell, August 2021).

Did you know? A new discovery by Harvard University researchers and others, found out that Capsaicin in chili peppers helps the human body burn all type of fats. So, taking the right amount of it can give you a lot of health benefits. However, in order to achieve great success with losing fats you would need to eat a lot of chili peppers and they can aggravate your digestive system in a big way. Today one can find a new supplement on the market called Capsimax by MST (Millennium Sports Technologies) that can help you lose fat without aggravating your digestive system.

Did you know? Food labels that say "no nitrites" do not mean that there are really contain no nitrites. It just means that the nitrites used are not synthetic, but rather come from celery or other natural sources. However, keep in mind that nitrites, synthetic or not, are still bad for your health (Consumer Reports, 2021 p.10).

Did you know? Eggs with a "no hormones" claim are not different from eggs that do not have the "no hormones" claim. The reason has to do with the fact that by U.S. law, chickens that produce eggs cannot be given hormones. So, do not waste your money on false claims (Consumer Reports, 2021 p.5).

Did you know? Zinc is an essential element that our body does not make on its own. Zinc is necessary for the activity of over 300 enzymes that aid in metabolism, digestion and nerve function processes. It is also critical for the development and function of immune cells, skin cells health, DNA synthesis, protein production as well as needed for our senses of taste and smell. It also reduces the risk of infections and promote better immune response in older adults. The most absorbable form of Zinc is Zinc citrate or Zinc Gluconate. Zinc Oxide on the other hand, is poorly absorbed. Zinc occurs naturally in foods like shellfish, meat, poultry and dairy, and is also tends to be added to other foods, such as breakfast cereals and wheat flour. The common cause of Zinc toxicity is taking too much Zinc, which can cause both acute and chronic symptoms such as decreased "good" HDL cholesterol levels, headaches, nausea, vomiting, diarrhea and abdominal cramps. It can also cause deficiencies in other nutrients such as Copper and Iron. The recommended daily intake (RDI) of Zinc is 11mg for adult man and 8mg for adult women (http://www.healthline.com/nutrition.zinc#function pp.1-11).

Did you know? Pumpkin seeds are high in zinc and therefore they tend to heal, repair and regenerate tissue quickly (Arthritis Foundation, AF-FY21-27SEC-INS-25-T).

Did you know? Plant-based foods are best for your health when they are unprocessed in their original form, or minimally processed. Ultra-processed foods of both plant and animal origin are linked to the development of chronic diseases, according to Dariush Mozaffarian, MD, DrPH, Dean of the Friedman School and editor in chief of Tufts Health & Nutrition Letter. In addition, be aware that, plant-based products that mimic meat are highly processed and are not proven to be better for your health, even though they are clearly better for the environment (Health & Nutrition Letter, Tufts University, August 2021 p.1).

Did you know? 9 foods that can help you ger rid of an upset stomach include: white rice, oatmeal, chamomile tea, bananas, ginger, plain yogurt, papaya, apple sauce, and chicken broth (1000LifeHacks.com).

Did you know? Marshmallows relieve toothaches, asthma, sore throats and arthritis (1000LifeHacks.com).

Did you know? High Iron levels can stand in the way of weight loss and make you tired. Wine, eggs and beans can reduce the amount of Iron absorbed, making slimming easier. In addition, use a non-iron pan (Woman's World, August 2021).

Did you know? Plant foods that contain lots of prebiotic fiber such as leeks, garlic, greens, bananas, apples and kiwi, to mention a few, tend to trigger reduction in calorie absorption. In addition, they also turn off cravings and activate genes linked to effortless weight control (Woman's World, August 2021).

Did you know? Researchers in the University of Wisconsin suggest seasoning meals with ½ tsp. of a potassium-rich salt like Nu-Salt or Morton Salt Substitute because it can help prevent heat-triggered muscle aches. The reason our muscles tend to ache at times is due to increased perspiration that result in electrolyte and mineral losses through our skin. So, when blood levels of muscle-relaxing potassium dip too low, it can lead to stiffness, cramps and muscle spasm (First for women, August 30, 2021, p.31).

Did you know? About 97% of us lack the nutrients that keeps the gut lining from eroding, leading to brain fog, fatigue and stuck-on fat. Our intestinal lining is only one cell thick and would cover about more than 2,700 square feet of surface area, for an average size person, if stretched out. When it is in good shape it will allow only select nutrients to enter our blood stream. But when the lining is damaged, it develops tiny gaps that let undigested food particles, toxins and waste into the bloodstream, causing major health issues for us. Without soluble fiber to feed the 'good' bacteria, 'bad' bugs will attack the gut wall, creating holes that trigger health problems and weight gain. So, when good bacteria fueled by soluble fiber, the good bacteria crowd the bad one allowing the mucus layer to rebuild and speed weight loss too *(First for women,* August 30, 2021, p.26).

Did you know? Adding 2 Tbs. of fresh ground flaxseeds (that contain insoluble fiber) to your diet will make you feel fuller faster and help to eliminate waste faster from your body. In addition, British scientist found out that the seeds also helped most people to lose weight in a faster pace (*First for women*, August 30, 2021, p.27).

Did you know? Since hair cells are most active in the morning it is a good idea to eat a hair-helping breakfast that incudes egg yolks (Woman's World, 2021).

Did you know? Heal your gut with plant foods that contain lots of prebiotic fiber such as leeks, onions, garlic, greens, bananas, apples and kiwis, to name a few. They tend to trigger the same gastrointestinal changes as gastric bypass surgery, so you will reduce calorie absorption, turn off cravings and activate genes linked to effortless weight control (Woman's World, 2021).

Did you know? Researchers found out that high levels of sodium, as well as refined sugars and flour in your diet may increase your eye disease risk as you age (healthscamsnews.com).

Did you know? As we age, we have to make sure to eat foods that are rich in Lutein, Zeaxanthin, Carotenoids and powerful antioxidants in order to keep our eyes healthy. It is therefore advised, to include in our diet, egg yolks, dark leafy greens like kale, broccoli, peas and spinach as well as sweet corn.

Did you know? In order to keep our eyes healthy, we need to consume different kinds of vitamins such as for example Vitamin C because Vitamin C is a powerful antioxidant. In addition, our eyes also need Vitamin E to keep tissues strong and functional. Sunflower seeds, almonds and pecans are good source of Vitamin E. We also need to consume fruits and vegetables that have purple skins because they contain powerful antioxidants. These are called Anthocyanins and they tend to reduce inflammation in the retina that is so characteristic of many eye diseases. Anthocyanins can be naturally found in fruits like purple grapes, raspberries, cherries, blueberries, black currants goji berries, cranberries and bilberries. They also can be found in vegetables like red cabbage, eggplant and dark olives. In addition, Beta-Carotene can help the body convert Vitamin A. This vitamin is needed to help people see in darkness or dimly lit environments. It also helps to slow the progression of Macular Degeneration. Beta-Carotene can be found naturally in most orange and yellow vegetables like carrots, sweet potatoes, pumpkins and squash to mention a few (healthscamsnews.com).

Did you know? Our brain is 60% fat. Therefore, it is especially important to include good fat in our diet. Mayo Clinic researchers found out that seniors who ate more good fat and fewer carbs actually had a 44% lower risk of ever developing dementia or even Alzheimer's Disease (pro.nhsreports.org).

Did you know? Dr. Richard Gerhauser, M.D. claims that a diet high in good fat and low carb can lead to faster brain processing speed, better learning and stronger memory. Furthermore, the "forbidden" saturated fats like those in red meat, cheese, eggs, whole milk and real butter are all extremely high in Choline. He stressed that Choline is a super nutrient for our brain because it helps carry signals along brain cells. In addition, since our brain is made of 60% fat, fat is the most important food for our brain cells as well as it will help keep our memory intact. "A fat brain is a healthy brain" (healthgrades.com).

Did you know? Dr. Russel Playlock believes that in order to reduce inflammation in our body we need to limit our exposure to mercury, aluminum, cadmium, lead, pesticides, herbicides, and industrial chemicals (Newsmax Magazine, Natural Cures 2021, p.28).

Did you know? Dr. Russel Playlock found out that Vitamin C, Apigenin, Hesperidin, Vinpocetine, Luteolin, Bromelain, Resveratrol, Quercetin and Green Tea can reduce inflammation just as good if not better than Nonsteroidal Anti-Inflammatory Drugs (NSAIDs) such as Ibuprofen, Naproxen and Aspirin (Newsmax Magazine, Natural Cures 2021, p.28).

Did you know? "Yo-Yo" dieting may be bad for your heart. If you want to lose excess weight, the slow and steady way will help you get there in a healthy and safe way (Healthy Aging, February 2019, p.7).

Did you know? Processed food was not always synonymous with junk food. Processing food goes all the way back for thousands of years, when several methods were employed to keep food from spoiling, such as salting and pickling. Keep in mind that the methods of refrigeration and the use of most modern preservatives were not invented yet. The French were the first to invent canning around 1800. They used canning techniques to keep Napoleon's troops supplied with food during their march across Europe. However, today many companies use preservatives, such as nitrites, as well as other chemicals and also add artificial colors, trans-fats, sodium, and sugar to foods, which can be bad for. Therefore, today processed food is considered, for the most part to be junk food. It is cheap, quick, and easy to get and eat, but it is incredibly bad for us. The National Institutes of Health found out that people who tend to eat processed food end up gaining weight faster than people who ate a whole food diet with the same amount of calories. Our bodies simply were not meant to consume highly processed junk food, and it does not matter how good it tastes.

Did you know? Deli meat labeled "no nitrates or nitrites added" actually means that the nitrate and nitrites used to cure the meat come from celery or other natural sources, not synthetic ones, such as sodium nitrate or nitrite. However, the chemical composition of natural and synthetic nitrates is the same, and so are the health effects on us (Consumer Report, June 2021, p.10).

Did you know? Food safety is important to all of us but especially more so to children because they are vulnerable pound for pound. Why? Children drink 2.5 times more water, eat 3-4 times more food, and breathe 2 times more air than adults. Therefore, they absorb a higher concentration of pesticides than adults (earthjustice.org).

Did you know? Chocolate used to be the food provided only to emperors for nearly 2,000 years. The growing process of the cocoa beans, from which chocolate was made, was finally perfected during the late Incan Empire. Most chocolate today is grown over the west coast of Africa. However, small batches of chocolate also come from the jungles of Peru. The difference between the two places of origin is incredible. Peruvian cacao is not only sweet like regular milk chocolate, but it is also one of the healthiest and the highest in antioxidant foods on the planet. It is 12 x healthier than blueberries, 10 x healthier than kale and 37 x healthier than broccoli. The Peruvian chocolate promotes healthy blood sugar, reduces free radicals & fights inflammation, thereby slowing down aging in the body. It also helps people fall asleep faster and stay asleep through the night, and it even helps to prevent brain aging (coffeeinfo@paleopolan.com).

Did you know? Studies suggest that sipping 8 oz. of cocoa a day can cut your risk of depression and fatigue by about 45%. In addition, according to researchers at Penn State University, consuming cocoa may also help ward off (NAFLD) nonalcoholic fatty liver disease. The reason has to do with the fact that cocoa contains compounds that help the body flush away fat instead of storing it in the liver. (Woman's World, 2021 & *First for Women,* August 30, 2021, p.22).

Did you know? The thyroid gland is one of the most important ones in the body. It controls your endocrine system, which includes all of the glands in the body that are responsible for hormone production as well as metabolism. Thus, it affects your weight, energy, heart health, kidneys and other organs. So, in order to keep your thyroid heathy, one needs to eat foods that can help it stay in good shape. First you need to avoid soy products from your diet including edamame, because most are genetically engineered. You also need to eliminate gluten, especially if you have Hashimoto's Disease, because both gluten and soy can have negative effects on normal thyroid function. In order to keep the thyroid gland healthy, it is a good thing to add cooked bamboo shoots, sea vegetables such as spirulina, kelp, wakame, hijiki, or nori sheets, Brazil Nuts and green vegetables for their chlorophyll. Researchers also found out that chlorophyll can decrease and absorb mold toxins like Aflatoxin B, which can cause liver complications and cancer. Chlorophyll also tends to help boost energy level in the body and remove heavy metals, which may negatively affect the thyroid. You also need to add to your diet, cruciferous vegetables, that may help prevent thyroid cancer. Cruciferous vegetables include cabbage, broccoli, Brussel Sprouts, collard greens, kale, turnip greens, watercress, bok choy, arugula, cauliflower, and mustard greens. In addition, these vegetables tend to also reduce the calcium buildup in the aorta, the body's largest blood vessel, leading to reduction in heart attacks and strokes (www.dherbs.com "What You Should Eat to Help Improve Your Thyroid" pp.1-4).

Did you know? In general, when buying foods, choose the ones that are higher in unsaturated fats. Avoid any food with more than zero trans fats. In most cases you do not need to worry about cholesterol intake unless you have diabetes or are at high risk for it. Avoid products that are high in sodium. Try to keep daily sodium to less than 2,300 milligrams daily (Health & Nutrition Letter, Tufts University, 2021, p.3).

Did you know? There are foods that can actually reduce inflammation in your body and your arthritis pain. They include broccoli, olive oil, blueberries, fish, nuts, tart cherry juice, kelp (harvested from clean ocean water), fermented foods, papaya and green tea (Arthritis Foundation, AF-FY21-27SEC-INS-25-T).

Did you know? Sweet potatoes are brimming with both Vitamin C and Beta-Carotene. These two nutrients are effective in reducing the risk of knee and spine Osteoarthritis. In addition, cumin and ginger are two spices that contain anti-inflammatory properties which can also help reduce the risk of getting Osteoarthritis (Arthritis Foundation, AF-FY21-27SEC-INS-25-T).
(Arthritis Foundation, AF-FY21-27SEC-INS-25-T).

Did you know? EGCG, the chief catechin in green tea, not only protects cells from oxidative damage, but also encourages gut health. Catechins in general are natural antioxidants that help prevent cell damage. They reduce the formation of free radicals in the body, as well as protecting cells and molecules from damage. Green tea was found to reduce *Firmicutes* (unfriendly bacteria) and improves levels of *Bacteroidetes* (friendly bacteria). Green tea can also inhibit NLRP3 inflammation and increase Nrl2, a protein that controls inflammation. According to researchers from Japan, it takes as little as two cups of green tea per day to gain benefit from it (Bottom Line's Health Breakthroughs 2021, p.2).

Did you know? Four years can be added to your life by adopting a plant-based diet.

Did you know? Dark leafy greens such as arugula, collard greens, kale, spinach, bok choy, Roman lettuce, mustard greens, Swiss chard, turnip greens and broccoli are some of the healthiest type of foods to consume on a regular basis. They are nutrient rich as well as low in calories and are also linked with reduced risk of cardiovascular disease (Women's Nutrition Connection, May 2021, Volume 24, Number 5 P.4).

Did you know? You need to put leafy greens in plastic bags at the supermarket to separate them from meat and dirty shopping carts. Keep in mind that salad greens can have bacterial contamination which can cause food-borne illness. So, therefore they need to be washed thoroughly under running water prior to eating (Women's Nutrition Connection, May 2021, Volume 24, Number 5 p.4).

Did you know why it is recommended to consume dark leafy greens? This is because they are excellent sources of many minerals, including iron, calcium, potassium and magnesium. They also provide vitamins C, E, K, and many of the B vitamins as well as phytonutrients, including Beta-Carotene, which has antioxidant properties. However, people that have the tendency to get kidney stones should stay away from eating spinach because it has high oxalate content that can cause them to have kidney stones. In addition, people who are on blood-thinning medications such as Warfarin should check with their physicians before adding leafy greens to their diet, because spinach and kale for example are high in Vitamin K that can lead people to form blood clots (Women's Nutrition Connection, May 2021, Volume 24, Number 5 p.4).

Did you know? The worst foods to consume include processed sugar, and those that have gluten and refined carbohydrates, processed food, trans fat, blackened and barbecued as well as the

Nightshade family of plants (tomatoes, eggplants, and potatoes to mention a few).

Did you know? Sugar is bad for your teeth because according to the ADA, plaque bacteria use the sugar to produce acids that attack the enamel of teeth. Also, acidic food can directly erode the enamel of teeth. So, in order to protect your teeth as much as possible you need to stay away from, or at least limit your consumption of sticky and chewy sweets, starchy snacks, most carbonated soft drinks, alcohol, caffeinated coffee and tea, hard candies, and even avoid chewing on ice (Weill Cornell Medicine, Iris Cantor Women's Health Center, Women's Nutrition Connection, June 2021, p.3).

Did you know? Researchers found out that a gluten-free diet is significantly lower in protein, magnesium, potassium, vitamin E, folate, B vitamins and dietary fiber (Tufts University, Health & Nutrition Letter, June 2021, p.5).

Did you know? Cancer cells like to gorge themselves on glucose. They consume 30 times more sugar than regular cells, and they cannot survive without it (Bottom Line's Health Breakthroughs 2021, p.15).

Did you know? There are many names that sugar hides under. Some of the most common names for sugary compounds are sucrose, fructose, dextrose, galactose, agave nectar, honey, maltose, lactose, beet sugar and corn syrup. In addition, refined breads, regular sodas, yogurts, tomato sauce, and even salad dressing may all be high in sugar (Weill Cornell Medicine, Iris Cantor Women's Health Center, Women Nutrition Connection, May 2021, p.8).

Did you know? High-fructose corn syrup can wreak havoc on your health. Consumption of it will increase your chance of getting cardiometabolic diseases which include stroke, heart disease, Type 2 Diabetes, obesity, high blood pressure, high cholesterol and Nonalcoholic Fatty Liver Disease. When fructose and glucose are combined as high -fructose corn syrup, it contributes to LDL ("bad") cholesterol and triglycerides. It is also bad for the gut microbiota because fructose increases the permeability of the gut barrier. It also tends to cause inflammation throughout the body and insulin resistance in the bloodstream (Weill Cornell Medicine, Iris Cantor Women's Health Center, Women Nutrition Connection, January 2021, p.4).

Did you know? A new study from a team of clinical psychologists at the University of Kansas found out that added sugars can trigger metabolic, inflammatory and neurobiological processes tied to depressive illness. The researchers found out that inflammation is the key physiological effect of dietary sugar related to mental health (Reader's Digest, December 2020/January 2021, p.42).

Did you know? According to a study published in The *BMJ* (February 2021) a regular consumption of refined carbohydrates, about 350 grams per day, of foods such as white breads and desserts, can increase the risk of cardiovascular death, as well as heart attack, stroke, heart failure, and increase the glycemic load - how much food will raise a person's blood glucose level after eating. So, it is best to replace refined carbohydrates with whole-grain carbs to lower your mortality risk in the future (Women Connection, May 2021, Volume 24, Number 5 p.8).

Did you know? Breads that are labeled "made with 21 whole grains and seeds" may just be sprinkled in or added as a topping. In order to purchase a healthy bread, you need to actually look for whole grains toward the top of the ingredients list. In addition, look for breads labeled 100 percent whole grain (CRConsumer Reports, June 2021, p.9).

Did you know? Spanish researchers in 2021 reported in the *Journal of American College of Cardiology* that walnuts in particular, are the best option to protect your heart. They credited walnuts for having rich stores of healthy fats and antioxidants which help reduce heart-damaging inflammation (*First for women,* April 26, 2021, p.26).

Did you know? In a study conducted in 2021, people who ate about an ounce (18 halves) of walnuts per day experienced a lower blood pressure response to high-stress situation than people who did not eat the nuts. It all has to do with the fact that walnuts are rich in inflammation-fighting omega-3 fatty acids (Arthritis Foundation, AF-FY21-27SEC-INS-25-T).

Did you know? Another walnut study was conducted in 2021 by Yanping Li, the lead investigator from the Harvard T.H. Chan School of Public Health. He concluded that even eating a few handfuls of walnuts per week may help promote longevity, especially among those whose diet quality is not great to begin with.

Did you know? When we are young our body produces enough proteolytic enzymes that help the body reduce inflammation and remove toxins from the blood. However, as we get older, our body produces less and less of these substances and therefore, we need to supplement them. Proteolytic enzymes can be found in pineapple (Bromelain), Turmeric, Papain, Devil's Claw, Boswellia, Ginger, Rutin and Citrus Bioflavonoid to mention a few.

Did you know? Cumin and Ginger are two spices that have anti-inflammatory properties.

Did you know? Nondairy creamers can be a significant source of heart-damaging trans-fats. Even creamers labeled "0 trans-fats" can have up to half a gram of this poisonous fat per serving. That adds up if you drink several cups daily. Trans-fats increase levels of unhealthy LDL cholesterol and decrease the levels of healthy HDL cholesterol. Take in consideration that real low-fat 1% dairy creamer is healthier than Half-and-Half. Even better, try evaporated skim milk or use almond or soy milk as alternative to the dairy versions (AARP, February/March 2021, p.25).

Did you know? Our body is designed to store fat. It is all due to the fact that when prehistoric humans existed, storing fat helped us to survive. The reason was that food then was not easy to find. Fat allowed for the storage of energy, and back then, energy translated into survival. The problem that we have today is that our body is still stuck in this ancient habit of favoring fat storage. So, even if we exercise constantly, every day, and eat nothing but chicken, vegetables and fruit, the body will still try to find a way to preferentially store it as fat in the different parts of our body.

Did you know? A high-fat, lower-carb diet is associated with faster brain processing, better learning speed and stronger memory. After all, our brain is made up of 60% fat. Red lean meat, cheese, eggs, whole milk and real butter are all extremely high in Choline. Choline is an important compound that helps to synthesize and transport lipids to the brain and the rest of the body, "a fat brain is a healthy brain."

Did you know? Processed meats like bacon, sausages, hot dogs, jerky and cold cuts, are listed as a Group #1 carcinogens that are linked to cancer risk as in the case of smoking or being exposed to asbestos (Health & Nutrition Letter, Tufts University 2021, p.3).

Did you know? High temperature cooking methods like pan frying and grilling, may produce more carcinogens in meat. Therefore, choose lower temperature cooking methods like baking, braising or roasting to reduce the risk of cancer promoting chemicals in your food (Health & Nutrition Letter, Tufts University p.3).

Did you know? Researchers today believe that brain health may start in the gut. They suspect that the gut microbiome, consisting of all of the various bacteria in the gut, affects everything from our mood to our response to stress. Therefore, it is recommended that we should have a diet rich in prebiotics and probiotics to keep the gut healthy and prevent us from having inflammation in our body that can affect our brain function. That in turn may also help us stay away from depression and anxiety (Harvard Health Letter, October 2020, p.8).

Did you know? Researchers today also found out that our lifestyle and habits influence brain health. To protect the brain, we need to first control our blood sugar levels. Sugar in excess can be toxic the brain causing neurons to die and that can lead to cognitive decline. It is recommended to eat real food not just supplements when possible ((based on Dr. Sanjay Gupta knowledge).

Did you know? Better diet and sleep might help protect our brain and may deter Alzheimer's Disease. Scientists found out that there is correlation between poor quality of sleep, diet, and the early accumulation of the plaques associated with Alzheimer's disease, cognitive impairment and dementia. Part of the reason has to do with the level of the hormone Cortisol in your body. A high intake of refined sugars, salt, animal fats, animal proteins and a low intake of fruits and vegetables can disturb the circadian levels of Cortisol in your body leading to poor quality of sleep. It was also discovered that sleep deprivation can cause a decrease of Creatine in the brain, negatively affecting cognition and your mood. In addition, researcher found out that magnesium deficiency is strongly correlated with insomnia and that potassium is important for adequate sleep duration (Health & Nutrition Letter, Tufts University, 2021 pp.30-31).

Did you know? There are some super healthy foods that one needs to add to their diet in order to improve memory, brain health and lower blood pressure. One is **canola oil,** which is a vegetable oil that is the lowest in saturated fat. If that isn't available, **safflower** and **soybean oil** will be good substitute too. Another healthy food is **blueberries** because they contain antioxidants that help reduce inflammation and oxidative stress in your body. Some studies even suggest that blueberries can even improve your memory. Another healthy food is **cranberries** that tend to help ward off urinary-tract infections and might even prevent periodontitis and gingivitis by keeping bacteria from adhering to the teeth and gums. Another is **avocados** because they contain unsaturated fat, which is a healthy fat that tends to support brain health and even reduces blood pressure as well as contain Vitamin A and 15% of our daily need of Vitamin C. Another is **carrots** because they contain 150% of our daily need of Vitamin A in just half a cup as well as other essential vitamins. A**sparagus** is another healthy food because with just 25 calories in eight medium-size asparagus spears we get 25% of our daily Vitamin A and 15% of our daily Vitamin C, plus essential Folic acid. Yet another is **spinach** because it is rich in Vitamins A and K plus Folate and it is also packed with Lutein which is associated with reduced risk of Macular Degeneration, the leading cause of vision loss and blindness in people aged 65 and older. Another is **broccoli** that contains antioxidants such as Vitamin C and flavonoids needed for brain health. Another is **tomatoes** because they were found to have Lycopene in them that may be protective against prostate cancer and pancreatic cancer in men. They are also good choice for Lutein, and a single medium tomato also contains half the daily value of Vitamin C. Another are **seeds and nuts** that contain Omega-3 as well as antioxidants such as walnuts, almonds and cashews. Another healthy food is **oranges**, which are packed with Vitamin C that helps eyesight and healthy brain function, as well as contain a lot of flavonoids, that can aid in maintaining good memory. **Dark chocolate** is another healthy food because it contains flavonoids, a specific type of antioxidants found in **cacao** that are essential for brain health and seems to encourage blood vessels and neuron growth in the areas of the brain that involve in learning and memory. Another is **fatty fish (not fried)**, like salmon, sardines, mackerel and trout, because they are rich in omega-3 fatty acid that is used for building nerve and brain cells. Another is **eggs** because they contain essential B vitamins, such as Folic Acid, Vitamin B6 and Vitamin B12. According to researchers, B vitamins play a role in proper brain function and mood. Another is **tea (with no added milk)** because a freshly brewed tea has phytonutrient antioxidants that tend to reduce heart disease (https://info.prevagen.com & Health & Nutrition Letter, Tuft University, 2021 p.3 & pp.24-27).

Did you know? In general, farm-raised fish should not be eaten because of the high concentration of antibiotics that they are fed, in order to prevent them from getting diseases that are more prevalent due to being in a tightly confined area with other fish. If this is not enough reason not to eat such fish, know also that they are fed with raw sewage daily, in some Asian countries, such as in the case of Vietnam, China and the Philippines. It is therefore better to buy wild-caught fish from North America, Hawaii or New Zealand.

Did you know? Omega-3 fatty acids are crucial for cell health and for supporting many body systems including the immune system. Omega-3 fatty acids can be found in foods such as in salmon, tuna and sardines, as well as in vegetables-based oils, flaxseed and nuts. It is recommended that one should eat about four ounces of fish twice per week (Women's Connection, May 2021, p.6).

Did you know? According to the American Heart Association (AHA) you can increase your life expectancy if you include in your daily routine, brisk walking, or go up and down a flight of stairs a few times, or practice yoga or dance for 10 minutes a day. However, be sure, to first, consult your doctor before beginning a new exercise program (*Renew* by United Healthcare, p.8).

Did you know? A study in 2017 by the Stanford University School of Medicine found out that a low-fat diet rich in fruits, vegetables, and whole grains is more effective in lowering LDL – "bad" cholesterol, than low-fat diets that do not focus on these foods.

Did you know? Lemons contain not only citric acid but also magnesium, bioflavonoids, Vitamin C, pectin, calcium and limonene, all which tend to super charge the immune system so that the body can fight infection. Lemons also help to lower the activity of free radicals and increase the breaking down of body fat, also known as adipose tissue. Therefore, it is a good thing to drink lemonade first thing in the morning in order to help keep the body healthy for the rest of the day (http://thenutritionwatchdog.com).

Did you know? Red wine may help improve blood vessel health and protect against high blood pressure. In addition, a research done in 2020 by the University of Iowa, found out that red wine in particular and cheese (aged old preferred) reduces cognitive decline in people too. Thanks goes to the calcium and B-12 in cheese and resveratrol in wine, all of which improve blood flow to the brain to prevent the cell damage that causes brain fog and memory decline. However, one should drink red wine in moderation (**First *for women,*** April 26, 2021, p.26).

Did you know? Our brain not only contains fat but also water. Therefore, just 2% dehydration has a measurable impact on memory, processing speed and analytical thinking. So, in order to keep the brain and body healthy we need to make sure to drink water and be active and not just sit down a lot. Brisk walking or other exercise tends to boost blood flow to the brain, reduce inflammation and promotes the growth of new brain cells.

Did you know? Drinking water keeps everything working efficiently in your body as well as helps to increase metabolism too. In addition, if you drink a glass of water before you eat, it will curb your appetite, so you will eat less and will not gain too much weight (FC&A, Medical Publishing p.21).

Did you know? Mayo Clinic cardiologists found out that dehydration can lead to strokes and heart attacks. They also discovered that drinking water at a certain time of day maximizes its effectiveness on the body. So, two glasses of water after waking up will help activate the internal organs. One glass of water 30 minutes before a meal will help digestion. One glass of water before taking a bath will help lower blood pressure. Furthermore, drinking one glass of water before going to bed not only avoids stroke or heart attack, but also prevent nighttime leg cramps. Why? Because when the leg muscles do not get enough hydration, they can cause a person to have cramps and a Charlie-Horse.

Did you know? If you stop getting thirsty, you need to drink more water. Why? When a human body is dehydrated, its thirst mechanism shuts off.

Did you know? People over 60 tend to have a lower water reserve. This is part of the natural aging process. They also frequently do not feel like drinking water, because their internal balance mechanism does not work very well. So, because of this they usually stop feeling thirsty and consequently stop drinking fluids and end up dehydrated. Dehydration is severe when it happens because it effects the entire body. It may cause abrupt mental confusion, lack of attention, irritability, a drop in blood pressure, increased heart palpitations, angina (chest pain), coma and even death.

Did you know? Drinking very cold water (not room temperature) can interfere with a number of healthy bodily processes and actually be detrimental to our wellbeing. Cold water will rob us of nutrients, it can also cause us to have sore throat, as well as cause an increase in our chance of having headaches. In addition, cold water may contain dirty water coated with bacteria and fungus. It is also believed that drinking cold water during a meal can promote hardening of oils in the food and lead to fat deposit in the intestine (http://thenutritionwatchdog.com/what-cold-water-does-to pp.1-2).

Did you know? If you want to jump-start your metabolism you need to drink a cup hot water first thing in the morning. Hot water increases body temperature at the rate in which your metabolism burns calories. It is also a wonderful natural treatment for a cold. It can naturally dissolve phlegm and clear your airways and soothes sore throat symptoms as well. Furthermore, as body temperature rises, it activates the process of sweating, which leads to the flushing of toxins from the body through the pores of the skin. In addition, it also helps the kidneys to flush waste material out of the body, along with toxins. (http://thenutritionwatchdog.com/what-warm-water-does-to pp.3-10).

Did you know? If you do not like to drink hot water first thing in the morning you can instead drink warm water with fresh lemon juice. Why to add to your warm water lemon juice? Because lemons contain vitamin C, pectin, calcium, citric acid, magnesium bioflavonoids, and limonene, all of which supercharge our immune system so that our bodies can fight infection. In addition, it will also lower the activity of free radicals and increase the break down of body fat, known as adipose tissue (http://thenutritionwatchdog.com/what-warm-water-does-to pp.9-10).

Did you know? People who take glucosamine supplementation were found to have lower risk of death from cardiovascular disease, cancer, respiratory disease, digestive diseases, or from other cause ((Annals of the Rheumatic Diseases, Life Extension Magazine, November 2020 p.17).

Did you know? Caffeine increases the power of aspirin and other painkillers, which is why it is found in some medicines like migraine medications for example.

Did you know? A pinch of instant espresso powder, or a splash of strong coffee can bring out the chocolate flavor in brownies and cakes.

Did you know? Researchers discovered that men who drank one beer a day lowered their cholesterol levels and increased their blood levels of heart-healthy antioxidants, as well as reduced their levels of fibrinogen, a protein that contributes to blood clots. In addition, they found out that red wine might be even more beneficial because of the Resveratrol, an antioxidant found in the skin of red grapes used to make red wine. However, be aware that too much alcohol can lead to heart failure, liver damage, obesity, and even certain types of cancer. So, whether you like to drink beer or red wine, make sure to drink just one or two drinks a day (Reader's Digest, February 2021, p.64).

Did you know? Kidney stones are actually crystals that are formed in your urine. There are four types of kidney stones: Calcium, Uric Acid, Cystine and Struvite. The most common type of stones in the U.S. is the calcium type. It was found that the biggest factor that contributes to the development of calcium stones is lack of liquid intake. People should drink 12 or more cups of water per day. Water also keeps everything working efficiently in your body and helps to increase metabolism. In addition, it is good to cut back on salt intake, since salt can increase the amount of calcium in the urine. Furthermore, if you are prone to kidney stones, try to limit or eliminate the following foods: berries, spinach, nuts, chocolate, tea and beer (Eat to Beat the Top 27 Health Problems for Seniors by The Editors of FC&A, Medial Publishing Booklet, 2017, p.7).

Did you know? The biggest hidden source of salt in the American diet is bread, which does not taste salty. We eat a lot of it in dinner rolls and pizza crusts (AARP, Bulletin, March 2019, p.18).

Did you know? Soluble dietary fiber that can be found in whole grains as well as in many fruits, vegetables, nuts beans and seeds, tends to delay the absorption of carbohydrates. That in turn, reduce the blood sugar spike after a meal and may help reduce the risk of developing Type 2 Diabetes. It is recommended that you consume 25 to 30 grams of fiber per day (Health & Nutrition Letter, May 2021, p.3).

Did you know? Consuming raw fruits and vegetables daily, unlike canned or cooked varieties, tends to reduce depression, low mood and irritability. It all has to do with the fact that they contain fiber and antioxidants that increase the production of mood-boosting brain chemicals (***First for women***, April 12, 2021, p.26.)

Did you know? Food rich in fiber supports the growth of good bacteria in the gut, which is especially important when you have arthritis. It may also promote weight loss, lower blood sugar levels, reduce the body's cholesterol absorption, reduce the chance of getting colon cancer and other types of cancer as well as fight constipation.

The recommended daily intake of fiber for women is 25 grams and 38 grams for men (Women's Nutrition Connection, May 2021, Volume 24, Number 5, p.1).

Did you know? The best high fiber foods to consume are: pears, strawberries, avocadoes, apples, raspberries, bananas, blueberries, blackberries, carrots, beets, broccoli, artichokes, brussels sprouts, kale, spinach, tomatoes, lentils, kidney beans, split peas, chickpeas, cooked black beans, cooked edamame, cooked lima beans, baked beans, quinoa, oats, popcorn, Marcona almonds (are much healthier than the regular almonds), chia seeds, pistachios, walnuts, sunflower seeds, pumpkin seeds, sweet potatoes, and dark chocolate that has a cocoa content of 70-95 or higher and is not loaded with added sugar.

Did you know? A diet that includes bananas or other foods that are rich in potassium can help offset some of the sodium's harmful effects on blood pressure (AARP Bulletin, May 2021, p.13).

Did you know? People who eat about an ounce (18 halves) of walnuts a day, tend to experience a lower blood pressure response to a high-stress situation, than people who do not eat nuts. The reason has to do with the fact that walnuts are rich in inflammation fighting omega-3 fatty acids (Arthritis Foundation, AF-FY21-27SEC-INS-25-T).

Did you know? Pistachios are one of the most nutritious foods that you can eat. They contain as much protein as an egg and have healthy fats and antioxidants. Compared to other popular nuts, pistachios are one of the richest food sources of potassium, Vitamin

B-6, Beta-Carotene, Lutein and Zeaxanthin (good for eye health), fiber, selenium (good for thyroid health) as well melatonin. If you eat them before bed, they will help you sleep, as they are one of the most melatonin rich foods. In addition, eating them will help you burn fat as well as improve your cholesterol and keep your heart healthy. Furthermore, they will also help balance your blood sugar. The fiber that they contain is considered to be "prebiotic" the kind that feeds your healthy gut bacteria and keeps your gut lining healthy. In the past, pistachios used to come from the Middle East, however today most pistachios come from California (https://thenutritionwatchdog.com & www.healthhouseinfo.com).

Did you know? One pear with skin has 6 grams of fiber. An apple has 4 grams, an orange has 3 grams, a banana has 3 grams, a cup of blueberries has 4 grams, and a cup of raspberries has 8 grams of fiber (Nutrition Action Health Letter, September 2020, p.11).

Did you know? Researchers found out that apples have many beneficial effects on human health including regulating blood sugar, helping improve heart health and also having an antioxidant effect on the body. In addition, apples also keep our body weight healthy, because they contain fiber and phenolic compounds. Furthermore, studies show that both fiber and phenolic compounds in apples also protect us against many diseases. Apples also contain polyphenol that help to prevent heart disease, protect our brain health as well as lower blood pressure. Apples in general are better source of carbohydrates for diabetics because they have a slow effect on blood sugar absorption. Researchers also found out that eating more apples tends to increase the number of healthy bacteria in our gut. They, in particular, increase the Clostridiales and Bacteroides species that tends to influence gut health and general health. If we want to have the best weight loss effect scientists believe that we should consume Granny Smith apples because they have more non-digestive compounds than other types. Researcher also advise to choose organic apples over conventional ones because regular apples are high in pesticides residues and petroleum-based waxes that are used to coat the apples (https://thenutritionwatchdog.com).

Did you know? Peaches and apples can exacerbate symptoms in people with pollen allergies, but it turns out that celery can as well. Both cooked and uncooked celery can cause swelling of the throat, lips and tongue, so if you have a pollen allergy, you should probably steer clear of eating it. In addition, be sure to read the labels on packaged food because celery is often added as an ingredient in soup and salad dressing, as well as to other prepared foods.

Did you know? In 2018 top doctors discovered that mushroom extract contains active breast-cancer fighting and blocking compound. The compound is called Conjugated Linoleic Acid. It tends to suppress the hormones that fuel breast-tumors, so they literally starve to death (Ultimate Women's Guide, Beating Disease 2018, p.48).

Did you know? Dietary intake has a big impact on gut microbiota composition and function. In order to keep the gut microbiota happy and healthy we need to stay away as much as possible from taking too many antibiotics. Why? Antibiotics tend to kill off the beneficial bacteria along with the harmful ones. Eating probiotic food and probiotic supplements while on antibiotics may help support beneficial gut microbe populations. Also, eat food rich in fiber. Fiber is prebiotic that may encourage healthy microbes to multiply in the gut. Gut microbes turn fiber into SCFAs, which may have anti-inflammatory and other helpful roles. Therefore, it is advised to eat fruits, vegetables, nuts, beans and whole grains daily. In addition, add probiotics to your diet such as yogurt as well as fermented food like fresh sauerkraut, kimchi, hard cheese and kombucha tea (Health & Nutrition Letter, Tufts University, December 2018, p.4).

Did you know? Whole grain are seeds of certain plants, and they are associated with many health benefits, including lower risk of cardiovascular disease, Type 2 Diabetes, cancer and digestive issues like constipation to mention a few. For a grain to be considered whole, it must have all three parts - the bran, the germ, and the endosperm. The bran is the outer skin of the seed that is fiber rich and a source of a number of vitamins and minerals. The germ, the embryo of the seed, contains healthy fats, some protein and more vitamins and minerals. The carbohydrate rich endosperm is the largest part of the seed (Health & Nutrition Letter, Tufts University, May 2021, pp.4-5).

Did you know? In order to prevent muscle shrinkage due to age or inactivity it is recommended that you include beans in your diet. Why? Beans are packed with protein, fiber and antioxidants, and are practically fat free. However, not all beans are alike. The best beans that contain the most antioxidants are red beans, small red kidney beans and pinto beans (Arthritis Foundation, AF-FY21-27SEC-INS-25-T).

Did you know? NASA scientists discovered an ingredient that can be found in chili peppers that can help block arthritis pain. It is called Capsaicin, the natural ingredient that gives chili peppers their eye-watering strength. Today you can find it in a product called PainBloc 24. The formula has been clinically shown to provide long lasting relief of arthritis pain by helping block joint pain at the source of the pain signal and it is recommended by the American College of Rheumatology (Reader's Digest, October 2020, p.38).

Did you know? Oregano has been used all the way back in ancient Grecian times as a highly effective medicinal herb. The Greeks used it for wounds, insect bites, snakebites, and for digestive and respiratory infections. Oregano essential oil has been proven to kill bacteria, viruses, fungal infections, ringworms, and parasites, including Giardia, an amoebic infection. It was also proven to be effective against even antibiotic-resistant pathogens.

In addition, it was found to be highly effective against food poisoning, stomach flu, Candida infections, eczema, sinus infections, nail fungus, acne, insect bites, warts and more. Oregano tends to help alleviate osteoarthritis and other inflammatory conditions such as Rheumatoid Arthritis. It is because it contains natural compounds that have many of the same effects as the powerful anti-inflammatory COX-2 inhibitor drug, Celecoxib (Celebrex). Oregano actually also protects the heart by helping to prevent blood clots and irregular heart rhythms. When taken internally it is best to purchase and take it as a prepared capsule. However, oregano is strong and can be irritating, so you need to dilute it in a carrier oil when you plan to use it on your skin (thenutritionwatchdog.com & Bottom Line's Ageless Health, Ageless Beauty, 2020, p.7).

Did you know? A study in 2017 by the U.S. Department of Agriculture founded that cranberries contain more antioxidants than almost any other fruit. They offer protection against a variety of diseases and can even help ward off some of the effects of aging. Cranberries contain tannins that help stop bacteria from adhering to the digestive tract. So, by eating cranberries one will be able to avoid UTIs - urinary tract infections and keep the urinary tract healthy. It is advised to take 500mg of cranberry extract a day or more and drink a lot of water. However, you should not drink cranberry juice instead, because it has a lot of sugar, and the sugar in the juice will make you gain weight (Eat to Beat the Top 27 Health Problems for Seniors by Editors of FC&A, Medical Publishing booklet 2017, p. 2 & Nutrition Action Health Letter, November 2020, p.9).

Did you know? Olives are loaded with monounsaturated fats, which slow sugar absorption in the intestines. The effect is so powerful that eating just 5 or 6 olives can cut the risk of hunger-causing blood-sugar dips in half for four hours (*First for women*, 12/21/2020, p.31).

Did you know? Eating fat has nothing to do with getting fat. The actual cause of obesity has to do with excess consumption of sugar and starchy carbohydrates. This in turn leads to high levels of blood sugar, excessive release of insulin, deposition of deep fat in the abdominal area, and chronic inflammation (Newsmax Magazine, Natural Cures 2021, p.34).

Did you know? There are 5 foods that you should try to avoid. Of the five, chips, French fries and fried seafoods usually contain trans-fat that can lead to increasing the risk of high cholesterol levels in your body. The other two are doughnuts and regular soda. Both have a lot of sugar. Sugar is linked to obesity, tooth decay, and heart disease ((Eat to Beat the Top 27 Health Problems for Seniors by Editors of FC&A, Medical Publishing booklet 2017, p.3).

Did you know? Not all breads are alike or healthy for you.

Whole wheat or other whole grains or enriched or wheat or unbleached wheat flour are all not very healthy breads to eat. In order to have a good and healthy loaf of bread it should contain 100% whole grain or100% whole wheat, as well as at list 3 grams of fiber and 2 grams of fat or less per serving. In addition, the bread that will trigger fast weight loss for you and make you actually feel full faster is pumpernickel bread (Woman's World, 2021 & Eat to Beat the Top 27 Health Problems for Seniors by Editors of FC&A, Medical Publishing booklet 2017, pp.2-3, Woman's World, 2021, p.5 & Nutrition Action, October 2021, p.13).

Did you know? If you ran out of gum or mints and you still want to have fresh breath, use a slice of cucumber and press it to the roof of your mouth with your tongue for about 30 seconds. The phytochemicals in the cucumber will kill the bacteria in your mouth that causes the bad breath.

Did you know? Some medications can affect nutrient absorption levels. Proton Pump Inhibitors (PPIs) that help to reduce the amount of acid that is pumped into your stomach tend to reduce the absorption of B12 and calcium levels since both need acid to be absorbed in the GI tract. This medication will also lower the magnesium levels in your body. Furthermore, Statin drugs that lower our LDL (bad) cholesterol tend to reduce the amount of CoQ10 enzymes in the body. This enzyme has an important task in our body. It converts food into energy, keep cells healthy, protects DNA with antioxidants and supports heart and blood vessel health. Another kind of medications are diuretic drugs that help our body eliminate excess fluid through the kidneys and may cause a person to eliminate too many electrolytes and reduce magnesium, potassium and calcium levels. Another example is the diabetic drug Metformin, it can cause a person to be low on folic acid and Vitamin B12. Other offenders that will reduce nutrient absorption are anticonvulsant medications and corticosteroids which can cause low levels of Vitamin D and calcium. Certain Parkinson's Disease medications can also cause the body to be depleted of Vitamin B6 and B12 (Women's Nutrition Connection, Well Cornell Medicine, October 2020, p.1 & p.6).

Did you know? Researchers at the Medical University of Vienna, Austria in 2020 found out that acid reflux drugs may trigger allergies. These drugs are known as PPIs, Proton Pump Inhibitors. These drugs tend to reduce stomach acid. Other acid-reducing medications called H2 Blockers also will increase the allergy risk but to a lesser degree.

Did you know? Cholesterol-lowering statins can cause severe myopathy (muscle pain or weakness) in about one out of 10,000 people per year (Nutrition Action Health Letter, May 2021, p.7).

Did you know? Acid reflux occurs when stomach acid backs up into the esophagus due to a weakened valve. Some foods tend to cause or can aggravate acid-reflux too. They include fried and fatty foods, highly spiced foods, coffee, alcohol, tomatoes, carbonated beverages, and citrus fruits. In addition, it can take place when eating large meals, eating too quickly, or eating too close to bedtime.

Did you know? Chewing sugar-free gum, excluding mint-flavor, tend to reduce acid in the esophagus by increasing saliva production as well as increase swallowing more often.

Did you know? If you want to reduce the occurrence of acid reflux, also known as GERD - Gastroesophageal Reflux Disease, the most important thing you should try to achieve and maintain first is a healthy weight. In addition, you should also try to avoid smoking, drinking alcohol, eating fatty or fried foods, tomato sauce, chocolate, mint, garlic, onions and caffeine. Try to eat a healthy diet, one that is rich in whole grains, fruits, and vegetables and low on red meat and added sugar. Furthermore, it is also a good idea to avoid lying down after a meal for at least three hours when possible. You should also keep your head elevated in bed and try to sleep on your left side. Sleeping on your right side can trigger the lower esophageal sphincter to relax and let stomach acid travel to your mouth. In addition, do not sleep on your back because it will let acid escape from your stomach to your mouth (Mayo Clinic Health Letter, January 2021, p.8 & Consumer Report On Health, May 2021, p.8).

Did you know? CBD, a chemical compounds, found in marijuana and hemp was used medically in Asia as far back as 1800 BC. In addition, many American medical journals from the 1700s cited that hemp seeds and roots can be used as treatments for incontinence and skin inflammation, and that it is not addictive.

Did you know? Some small studies from the year 2021 found out that CBD can relieve symptoms of Multiple Sclerosis, Rheumatoid Arthritis, high blood pressure, anxiety, insomnia and even reduce seizures. Animal studies show that it has promise for helping with nerve pain, diabetes, depression and more. It has no known serious risks, but it can cause fatigue, weight loss, and diarrhea. Before you plan to start taking CBD, please consult with your doctor, because it could interact with some medications (Healthy Aging, Icahn School of Medicine Mount Sinai, October 2020, p.4).

Did you know? Spices are loaded with antioxidants and anti-inflammatory compounds that have health benefits. Among the most potent are ginger, turmeric, cayenne, garlic, rosemary, sage, and cinnamon.

Did you know? China is the largest producer of garlic in the world, and they use people's poop or even chickens' poop to fertilize their fields. U.S. is the second in line to produce garlic.

Did you know why the people in India suffers five times less from Alzheimer's Disease than people in the United States? It all has to do with the food they eat on a regular basis. The Indian traditional dishes include spiced curry, and curry is high in the spice turmeric. The most active ingredient in turmeric is *Curcumin*, which tends to boost mental energy, memory, increase focus and help you learn faster because *Curcumin* actually dissolves the amyloid plaques that are the hallmark of Alzheimer's disease (National Scientific Special Brain Health Edition, Winter 2021, p.18 & Real Cause Real Cure, Bottom Line Books, pp.146-147).

Did you Know? Customizing the Mediterranean diet known also as MIND to more severely restrict red meat and increase the consumption of greens can help reduce Nonalcoholic Fatty Liver Disease (NAFLD) and promote the loss of intrahepatic fat, which is fat that originates in the liver (Women's Nutrition Connection, May 2021, Volume 24, Number 5, p.3).

Did you know? The MIND diet recommends getting five or more serving of nuts each week and eating beans four or more times a week, poultry and berries at least twice a week, and fish at least twice a week too. Researchers reported that those that adhere to this diet reduce their risk of having cognitive impairment, including Alzheimer's Disease as well as Parkinson's Disease or other type of dementia (Women's Nutrition Connection, May 2021 Volume 24, Number 5 p.3 & Tufts University, Health & Nutrition Letter, June 2021, p.3).

Did you know? Researchers in 2021 from the University of British Columbia found out that combining the best of both the DASH (Dietary Approaches to Stop Hypertension) diet and the Mediterranean - style diet, known as MIND, that emphasizes unsaturated fats found in plant foods especially the monounsaturated fats found in olive oil, contribute to greater brain benefits, such as protecting memory and thinking ability to a greater extent. People who followed these combined diets most closely were about 53% less likely to develop Alzheimer's Disease than those who did not. The research also found out that even small changes tend to reduce the risk for Alzheimer (Health & Nutrition Letter, Tufts University p.1, Women's Nutrition Connection, May 2021 Volume 24, Number 5 pp.2-3, Newsmax, May 2021, p.90).

Did you know? The Nordic diet tends to encourage weight loss and it lowers blood pressure. Its emphasis is on whole grains such as rye, barley and oats, as well as legumes like beans and peas, berries and other fruits and vegetables, especially cabbage and root vegetables like potatoes and carrots. This diet also includes fatty fish such as salmon, mackerel and herring (Women's Nutrition Connection, May 2021, Volume 24, Number 5 p.2)

Did you know? If you want to really succeed in losing weight you should adhere to time-restricted eating for five days per week and stay with it for good. Eat only during an eight-hour period every day and you can choose the time most convenient to you and your schedule. During the remaining 16 hours in the day, you can drink water, diet drinks, coffee or tea with no milk or sugar (Women's Nutrition Connections, May 2021, Volume 24, Number 5 p.2).

Did you know? Most people are unaware that when they skip a meal or go for a long time without eating, their body shifts to a survival mode and craves food, which may cause them to overeat beyond fullness at the next meal. Then the body will shift gears and start storing the extra food as fat. So, if you want to lose weight, the correct way is to eat low-fat high-carbs meals a few times a day, not just once a day (Better Homes & Gardens, March 2021, p.114).

Did you know? To stop overeating, it is advised to eat complex carbs such as whole grains, high-fiber fruits, and veggies. The reason behind this is that they are digested more slowly than simple carbs, so they prevent blood sugar dips. In addition, it is also recommended to eat protein or healthy fat because it tends to slow the rate carbs break down, helping the blood sugar and your energy to remain steady (Better Homes & Gardens, March 2021, p.114)

Did you know? Coffee contains many thousands of compounds that affect human health. These include Caffeine, Chlorogenic Acid, Melanonids and Pentacyclic Diterpenes, Kahweol and Cafestol to mention a few (http://thenutritionwatchdog.com).

Did you know? Researchers found out that drinking three caffeinated beverages in a day such as coffee, tea or soda, can increase the migraine risk for some people.

In addition, even though caffeine is a headache trigger, some of the very medications that supposedly treat headaches contain caffeine (Reader's Digest, October 2020, p.35 & healthscamsexposed.com).

Did you know? Coffee may bring health benefits to people who drink it, but not all cups of coffee are created equal. Unfiltered brews of coffee like French Press or Turkish coffee as well as Expresso have a lot of a compound called cafestol that can raise the "bad" LDL cholesterol levels in your body. However, drip-filtered coffee, instant coffee and percolator coffee have negligible amount of the compound (Harvard Women's Health Watch, November 2020, p.3).

Did you know? What you add to your coffee can affect your health too. So, if you add sugary syrup, heavy cream, or regular sugar to your coffee, you will turn your coffee into a high-calorie beverage that may lead to excess weight gain and a higher risk of diabetes (Harvard Women's Health Watch, November 2020, p.3).

Did you know? Studies consistently in 2021, show that people who drink black coffee live longer than people who do not. In addition, it may also keep your coronary arteries clear, and it may lower your risk of cognitive decline. The current conservative recommendation is to drink only 3 cups of coffee per day (Reader's digest, February 1, 2021, p.66 & Newsmax, May 2021, p.83)

Did you know? Another study from 2021 has found that one cup of coffee per day can reduce your risk of developing alcohol related Cirrhosis of the liver by about 22%. Furthermore, two cups per day can reduce it by up to 43%, three cups can reduce it by 57%, and four cups a day can reduce it the most by 65% (http://thenutritionwatchdog.com).

Did you know? Researchers in 2020, at the Kyushu University in Japan, found out that drinking plenty of green tea and coffee are both inked to lower risk of dying from any cause among people with Type-2 Diabetes. The reason is due to the fact that these beverages contain various bioactive ingredients needed to keep the body strong.

Did you know? Coffee will not actually clean out your arteries, but it could help protect against cardiovascular disease. Researchers found out that people who drank 3-5 cups of coffee a day were about 41% less likely to suffer from coronary artery Calcium deposits than non-coffee drinkers. In addition, it was founded that coffee intake may lower the risk of Type-2 Diabetes Furthermore, people that drank more than five cups of coffee a day actually saw greater risk for arterial plagues than moderate drinkers (Health & Nutrition Letter June/July 2020 p.3 & Health & Nutrition Letter, Tufts University p.3).

Did you know? Resent research conducted in 2021 has founded out that drinking your daily coffee may help protect your liver from alcohol-related cirrhosis. Remember that a little bit of alcohol may actually be healthy but overdoing it on the other hand is extremely dangerous to your health and can cause liver cirrhosis, and liver scarring that can lead to liver failure (https://thenutritionwatchdog.com).

Did you know? Researchers also founded out that coffee might actually be beneficial for your heart too and will reduce your risk of having Type 2 Diabetes and Alzheimer's Disease, as well as reducing your chance of getting liver cancer and certain types of other cancers. Coffee contains biologically active phytochemicals that include chlorogenic acid, lignans, trigonelline and melanoidins. They all help to feed the healthy organisms in the gut and improves the way the body processes sugar and fat. Coffee also helps reduce oxidative stress by neutralizing harmful substances, called free radicals, that can damage body cells. In addition, coffee contains some important nutrients and Vitamin B3 (niacin). Furthermore, caffeine in coffee stimulates the central nervous system (CNS) which controls both emotions and attention span. Research also found out that those who had caffeine tend to feel less sad and they performed better when solving problems. That is because caffeine causes the CNS to block out brain chemicals that make us feel distracted and that cause symptoms of depression, like headaches and stress (Harvard Women's Health Watch, November 2020, p.3, **First** for Women, July 27, 2020, p.20, Newsmax, May 2021, p.83).

Did you know? Coffee drinking keeps you alert during the day, but it also gives you many health benefits. Coffee is rich in several different types of antioxidants which help fight off disease-causing free radicals. For example, coffee contains the antioxidant Melanoidin that has antibacterial and anti-inflammatory properties. It also contains Trigonelline, which may help prevent the development of dental cavities. It also has a fat-burning potential by boosting the metabolic rate by as much as 10% in obese people and 29% in lean individuals. In addition, it also contains several healthy nutrients such as B12, B5, Manganese, Potassium RDI, Magnesium and Vitamin B3. The caffeine in coffee may even be good, according to Harvard Medical School, for your brain health and can have a longer-term effect on your thinking skills (www.prevagen.com/brain-health-tips/top-4-health).

Did you know? According to Harvard Health Letter from 2021, coffee drinking is associated with a lower risk of depression among women, a lower risk of fatal prostate cancer among men, and a lower risk of stroke among both men and women. It also was found to protect against Alzheimer's Disease and a lower risk for some cancers like Estrogen-Negative Breast Cancer. In addition, coffee may also help boost your metabolism and brain power, as well as potentially lower Type-2 Diabetes risk. In addition, it will also help protect your liver from alcohol related Cirrhosis, and liver scaring, which can lead to liver failure. Researchers suspect that the reason why coffee is so good for your health is due to the fact that it contains many antioxidants which have significant anti-inflammatory properties (http://thenutritionwatchdog.com).

Did you know? According to a German study, both caffeinated and decaffeinated coffee exacerbate gastroesophageal reflux. Which indicate that the caffeine by itself does not cause the problem, but rather the ingredients in the coffee.

Did you know? The best, high- quality coffee tends to be acidic, and even more so with cheap coffee. Acid can be hard on sensitive stomach. So, adding a small pinch of baking soda to your cup of coffee can improve the tase of the coffee as well as neutralize its acidity to avoid stomach upset.

Did you know? Edible mushrooms are loaded with nutrients and are beneficial to add to our diet. They contain fiber, copper, phosphorus, potassium, selenium, zinc, riboflavin, niacin, thiamin, folate, and Vitamin D. Furthermore, when mushrooms are exposed to UV light, they tend to contain double the amount of Vitamin D. In addition, eating mushrooms will not have impact on our calorie's intake, sodium or fat levels in our bodies (Women's Nutrition Connection, May 2021, Volume 24, Number 5 p.3).

Did you know? Thousands of years ago, humans produced Vitamin C in their bodies. However, now it is no longer the case. However, unlike humans, most animals still produce their own Vitamin C even today.

Did you know? Researchers discovered lately, after carefully studying the old records from the 1918 Flu pandemic, that the reason why so many millions of people died at that time was due to the lack of Vitamin C in their bodies.

Did you know? During the Age of Exploration, about 2 million sailors died because they suffered from scurvy that resulted from lack of consuming Vitamin C.

Did you know? Vitamin C, also known as ascorbic acid, is necessary for the development, growth, and repair of all body tissues. It is also involved in the proper functioning of the immune system, the formation of collagen, wound healing, the maintenance of cartilage and bones, and iron absorption, to name a few.

Did you know? Eating more Vitamin C rich foods such as tomatoes, oranges and strawberries, can have youthful effects on skin, like reducing wrinkles and age-related skin dryness in middle-aged women. Its antioxidant properties also help to protect against the ultraviolet rays of the Sun and help to keep the skin firmer via collagen synthesis (EatingWell Magazine).

Did you know? One cup of mango supplies roughly two-thirds of a day's recommended intake of Vitamin C, 10% of a day's Vitamin A, a decent dose of blood-pressure-lowering potassium, and three grams of fiber (www.NutritionAction.com).

Did you know? A ten-year study at the University of California, Los Angeles of 11,000 people, found out that people who took 300-500 mg of Vitamin C or more, had an increased life span up to six years for men and one year for women. In addition, death rates were significantly lower among those with higher Vitamin C levels in their blood. People with the highest Vitamin C levels, had half the risk of dying from different causes of disease alone. The chances of dying from cardiovascular disease were reduced by 71% in men and 59% in women (Ultimate Health Special Report, Number 3 p.3).

Did you know? Women over 65 face double the stroke risk. However, in 2017 researchers found out that higher amount of Vitamin C intake – at least 133 milligrams per day- reduces the risk of stroke by 30 percent. In addition, smokers who supplemented their diet with Vitamin C cut their risk of stroke by 70 percent (Eat to Beat the Top 27 Health Problems for Seniors, by The Editors of FC&A, Medical Publishing booklet, 2017, pp.11-12).

Did you know? Not all C vitamins on the market are alike. The regular ones absorb quickly in your body and do not give you coverage for the entire day since they are water soluble and get flushed out from your body rapidly. However, today you can find Ester-C 24 Hour Immune Support 500mg (or more) that is stomach friendly (vegetarian coated tablets) and will last longer than the regular Vitamin C in your body. Alternatively, you can get Vitamin C in drops called Nano C, if it is difficult for you to swallow pills in general.

Did you know? Vitamin B-12 plays an essential role in nerve function. A shortfall of B-12 is associated with depression, dementia and decreased cognitive function, as well as anemia. Unless you are a vegan you will be able to get enough of it by eating beef, chicken, egg, and dairy products. However, as we age our ability to absorb B-12 is reduced by changes in our digestive systems, as our stomachs naturally begin to produce less stomach acid. Keep in mind that antacids such as proton-pump inhibitors (PPIs) like Prevacid will reduce stomach acid as well as reduce the absorption of diabetic medications. Furthermore, celiac disease will also effect the absorption of Vitamin B-12. In addition, researchers found out that people that produce low levels of stomach acid due to atrophic gastritis (thinning of the stomach lining due to inflammation) tend to also exhibit B-12 deficiency (AARP Bulletin June 2021, p.32 & Nutrition Action Healthletter, September 2021 p.7).

Did you know? B-12 supplement, or fortified foods can be easily absorbed by the body without stomach acid, unlike the naturally occurring B-12 (Nutrition Action Healthletter, September 2021 p.7).

Did you know? Dr. Bredesen and his team of researchers in 2020 found out that dementia is not related to genetics. They claim that it can be reversed if diagnosed early, and if one should include in their diets B vitamins especially Vitamin B12. This vitamin is water -soluble vitamin that is also involved in red blood cell production, brain health, and DNA synthesis. However, not all Vitamins B12 are alike. The natural form of Vitamin B12 – Methyl cobalamin, rather than Cyanocobalamin, the synthetic one, tends to be very affective in helping to reduce brain shrinkage and problems with thinking, boost mood for less blues, and improve the mental energy and quick recall of memory. (National Scientific, Special Brain Health, Winter 2021, p.12).

Did you know? Collagen actually makes up 75% of our skin and 70% to 80% of our ligaments, tendons and joints.

During our late 20's, the body's natural ability to produce collagen begins to wane by 1-2% each passing year. When we hit middle age, our body will have less than half the amount of collagen that our body needs. So, it is important to take collagen supplements on a regular basis. However, not all collagen supplements are alike. The good ones have 5 types of collagen and is naturally hydrolyzed - the kind that our body can easily and rapidly digest. Bio Trust Ageless Multi-Collagen seems to be a good kind to add to our diet.

Did you know? Collagen helps maintain the integrity of our connective tissues such as our joints, muscles and cartilage, which is the rubber-like tissue that protects our joints. With age our body's collagen level decreases, and the risk of developing degenerative joint disorders increases. So, it is a good idea to take collagen supplements to reduce overall joint pain. Collagen also is responsible for strengthening muscles, enhancing skin complexion, reducing wrinkles, improving hair health, slow follicle thinning, promote heart and artery health as well as heal wounds.

Did you know? Many seniors fail to get enough collagen on a daily basis, the specific protein bones are made of and it is hurting their bones. The reason has to do with the fact that they tend to eat less protein. Less of a protein intake also decreases calcium absorption and affects bone formation and breakdown.

Did you know? There are 6 superfoods that you need to eat after you turn 50 years old that will help you stay healthy. **1. Berries** - because they are high in fiber, Vitamin C, anti-inflammatory and antioxidant. **2. Dark-green leafy vegetables** - because they supply a significant amount of folate, a B vitamin that promotes heart health and helps prevent certain birth defects. In addition, Folate is also necessary for DNA duplication and repair which protects against the development of cancer.**3. Seafood** - fish such as salmon, cod, tuna and trout are lean source of protein and a good source of Vitamin B12 that help to maintain or regain muscle. **4. Nuts and seeds** - have protein and fiber and are important sources of healthy fats. **5. Cottage Cheese** - is a great source of whey protein, which helps stimulate muscle protein synthesis and it's also high in calcium and Vitamin D. **6. Beans and legumes** - beans help to reduce cholesterol because they are loaded with fiber and protein, and they are also a low-calorie food as well as rich in iron, potassium and magnesium.

Did you know? Seaweed tends to detoxify some of the pesticides, chemicals, heavy metals and pathogens that we have been exposed to during our lives. The seaweed that is easy to find in the Asian section of many grocery stores or on Amazon is called 'dulse' (https://www.aarp.org/health/healthy-living/info-2021).

Did you know? B vitamins such as folate, B6 and B12 – Methylcobalamin, are essential to protect the health of the brain. These vitamins help keep the levels of homocysteine, an amino acid, in a healthy range in the brain. Otherwise, the brain will start shrinking. Higher levels of homocysteine in the blood are associated with greater risk for age-related cognitive decline, such as impaired thinking and memory, as well as Alzheimer's Disease. In addition, Vitamin B12 maintains the protective cover that surrounds the nerves, so nerve impulses keep moving fast, ensuring effective nerve-impulse transmission (Environmental Nutrition, March 2016 p.6 & National Scientific, Special Brain Health Edition, winter 2021, p.17).

Did you know? Folate is important in order to maintain good health and it is especially important for pregnant women. Folate decreases the risk of an unborn baby to develop serious birth defects called NTDs - neural tube defects. It was also found to lower homocysteine levels, which, in turn, improves arterial flow in people that have cardiovascular disease. Folate can be found in fortified cereals, instant oatmeal, avocado, romaine lettuce, peanuts, raw spinach, orange juice, navy beans and green peas, to mention a few (Eat to Beat the Top 27 Health Problems for Seniors, by The Editors of FC&A, Medical Publishing 2017, pp.5-6).

Did you know? Healthy hair needs the sulfurous amino acid cysteine for strength and shape. Low cysteine levels make hair thin, brittle and weak (New Health Revelations p.3).

Did you know? Selenium is a powerful antioxidant that is one of the most essential minerals for our health. It contributes to the health of the thyroid, testosterone level, heart, and immune system.

Did you know? The thyroid gland contains the largest amount of selenium. Selenium and iodine work together to protect and maintain the proper function of the thyroid gland. The thyroid produces hormones which govern, among many other things, our metabolism, including the level of fat-burning in the body.

Did you know? A study published in September 2020 analyzed the relationship between thyroid conditions such as hypothyroidism, Hashimoto's, hyperthyroidism and how they relate to COVID-19. It was found that people with these thyroid conditions have a higher risk of having severe COVID-19 infections (info@paleoplan.com).

Did you Know? It was found that over 78% of Americans are deficient in both sulfur and selenium in their diet. The reason is due to the fact that the farmers in the U.S. are using chemical fertilizers that remove sulfur and selenium from the soil. Without these elements the body is unable to get rid of toxins, acid residues, chemicals, fungi, bacteria and carcinogens. So, without a constant supply of trace minerals, we are, in effect, dying each day through cellular degeneration (New Health Revelations p.4).

Did You know? Selenium was found to promote killer T-cells, which are part of our immune system, which engulfs harmful substances that enter our body. The prestigious journal, *Microbial Ecology in Health* reports that "selenium is critical to the health of living organism and that the world's population doesn't get enough of it." Selenium also helps slow down the appearance of aging. It is essential to eliminating toxins from the body and keeping health problems at bay. It was found that people with the highest selenium in their blood scored 10 years younger on tests of cognitive function. Selenium also helps support glutathione's efforts to keep the immune system strong. Glutathione carefully scours the body for hidden toxins, bacteria, fungi, chemicals, carcinogens and acid residues, and remove them. It does it by helping the system recycle and produce more glutathione. Glutathione is 5,000 times more powerful than any other antioxidant in your body. Since it works at the cellular level and restore lasting energy. No wonder Dr. M. OZ believes that "Glutathione is the Superhero of Antioxidants". Furthermore, Dr. Troy Lund indicated that glutathione is highly concentrated in the epithelial lining of the lungs. So, it helps protect us from inhaling free radicals. The epithelial is a thin lining found in our respiratory tract that moistens and protects our airways and it highly effective in keeping out pathogens, bacteria, infections and other foreign particles from our lungs (New Health Revelations, pp. 3-11).

Did you know? Researchers in 2021 found out that the role of sulfur in the human body is much more profound than previously taught. They realized that it makes cell walls more permeable and that it is also helping to supply oxygen for building healthy new cells which the body does on a daily basis. So, sulfur is actually nature's perfect anti-aging and health rejuvenating superfood (New Health Revelations, p.5).

Did you know? Sulfur and selenium can only be found today where there is volcanic activity, and because Iceland has the world's longest chain of volcanoes that cross the entire country, their soil is extremely rich with these minerals. Therefore, many Icelanders are much healthier than the population of the U.S. and other countries around the world (New Health Revelations, p.4).

Did you know? Today one can find an incredibly good supplement called SELENEXGSH that can eliminate the deficiency in our body of selenium and sulfur as well as nourish our hair follicles, by helping to deliver oxygen and nutrients to the hair cells, so hair can grow thicker, and strong again. It also raises the glutathione level in the eyes to help safeguard our vision and our entire health (New Health Revelations, p.7 & p.9).

Did you know? Proper levels of potassium and magnesium are among the most important elements to keep our body healthy. Potassium helps keep our cells, tissues, and organs' electrical system working properly. Magnesium helps protect against heart attack risks, strengthens muscles and tissues, as well as lowers blood pressure (Reader's Digest, February 1, 2021, p.68).

Did you know? Magnesium is involved in over 600 reactions in the body including in the metabolism of food, the synthesis of fatty acids and proteins, protein formation, the transmission of nerve impulses, muscle movements, and gene maintenance. It needs to be consumed about 100 milligrams a day. Researchers found out that 50% of the people in the United States and Europe do not get the recommended amount of magnesium in their diet. It is also important to note that magnesium levels in soil in general are lower than they use to be. Furthermore, the use of chemicals such as fluoride and chlorine in water make magnesium less available. In addition, the daily use of sugar and caffeine also deplete magnesium supplies within the body. Magnesium deficiency can lead to a range of chronic health issues. It can cause calcium deficiency, poor heart health, weakness, anxiety and high blood pressure, Type 2 Diabetes, fatigue, respiratory issues, poor memory and confusion. Good sources of magnesium include bananas, spinach, dark chocolate, cocoa powder and cacao, almonds, coffee, and seeds like pumpkin, sunflower, flax, sesame, chia, hemp and flax seeds. Keep in mind that calcium from milk and refined sugar can interfere with magnesium absorption, so drink your coffee black and use honey instead of regular sugar.

Did you know? If you are having bleary eyesight after you spent some time browsing the web or reading a book, eat a dark chocolate bar made of 72% cocoa or higher. The polyphenols in the sweet treat deliver nutrients and oxygen to the retina, enhancing the eye's ability to have clearer vision within a short time (*First for Women*, July 27, 2020, p.4).

Did you know? Today phones, TV's, computers and LED bulbs emit massive amounts of blue light that our eyes and nervous systems are not designed to handle. These in turn disrupt our circadian rhythm, and in most cases, can make falling asleep and getting up early difficult. It has to do with the fact that, blue light interferes with the sleep hormone melatonin. Research also indicates that just six hours of artificial blue light causes a drop in energy-generating mitochondria in cells. It is advised to set your devices on night-mode to reduce blue light. Furthermore, Dr. Breus advises to wear amber-tinted glasses that filter out blue light 2 hours before bed, a method that actually can increase sleep by about 52%. In addition, Dr. Gundry recommends walking outside between the hours of 10am and 3pm, when the red-light wavelengths in sunlight are strongest, in order to reset the circadian clock and stimulate the mitochondria to make energy. If you have no time to go outside you can invest in a device that emits red light like Joovv; at Joovv.com (*First for women*, April 5, 2021, p.35 & Consumer Reports *On Health*, May 2021, p.12).

Did you know? Most people do not realize that more than 75% of the sodium that they ingest comes from restaurants, prepackaged, and processed foods (Environment Nutrition, March 2016, p.6).

Did you know? Eating a cantaloupe has the power to help offset the negative effects of sodium in your body. It is because it contains a lot of potassium - the heart-protective mineral that can help ease tension in the blood vessel walls, thereby lowering your blood pressure, reducing the risk of a stroke, and keeping your heart healthy and strong (Consumer Reports On Health, and The Answers to Good Health 2021, p.1).

Did you know? Over consumption of sugar can cause a harmful condition known as "metabolic slowdown." The warning signs include belly flab, brain fog, slower metabolism, tiredness, constipation and difficulty in concentration. This symptoms manifest themselves slowly over time (buzz@am.conservativebuzz.com).

Did you Know? Sugary beverages increase insulin resistance, which raises the risk for cardiovascular disease. Furthermore, fructose consumption, like drinking fruit juices, can stimulate weight gain around the waist, which in turn can also lead to cardiovascular disease. Therefore, one should limit, or completely eliminate the consumption of beverages that have sugar, whether it is soft drinks or fruit juices (The Week, June 14, 2019, volume 19 issue 928 p.17).

Did you know? According to Dr. Amy Lee, high-fructose corn syrup is very addictive and will make you eat more than you should. In addition, it will more likely turn into fat than real sugar, which is a real risk factor for diabetes.

Did you know? Simple sugars can be harmful because they are rapidly broken down into glucose and absorbed by the body. Glucose promotes inflammation in the body. This in turn is linked to Macular Degeneration, cancer and heart disease (Macular Degeneration Research, a BrightFocus Foundation Program brightfocus.org/cure AMD).

Did you know? In order to control your blood sugar naturally it is advised that you add barley to your diet (Ultimate Women's Guide to Beating Disease 2018, p.129).

Did you know? New research in *Clinical Nutrition* found out an easy way to slash diabetes risk by eating 200 grams of sardines (about two cans in olive oil) weekly. The fish's *taurine*, omega -3s, calcium and vitamin D, all help to increase the "good" HDL cholesterol, improve the glucose breakdown, lowering triglycerides and also reducing blood pressure in the body- all of which reduce diabetes risk (*First for women*, August 30, 2021, p.22).

Did you know? Most people are unaware that excess blood sugar can upset the balance between HDL "good' cholesterol and LDL "bad" cholesterol. When glucose is in high level in your blood, it tends to latch on to the "bad" LDL cholesterol. This in turn makes the LDL "bad" cholesterol remain in your bloodstream for a long period of time. So, it is important to keep your sugar level in your blood in a good range (Health & Wellness, Blood Sugar News, Winter 2021, p.8).

Did you know? Eating two to three kiwi fruits a day can help reduce harmful blood triglyceride levels. The fruit also can help raise your HDL "good" cholesterol levels. In addition, it is rich in vitamins C and E as well as the minerals potassium, magnesium, copper and phosphorous (Reader's Digest, February 1, 2021, p.67).

Did you know? Doctor Julian Whitaker found out that there are three powerful ingredients such as **Berberine**, **Cinnamon** and **Chromium** that can help improve your blood sugar and lipid levels. However, the secret is to take a combination of all the three ingredients in the right dosages and forms. So, he came up with a supplement called **Berberine GlucoGold** that can help keep your blood sugar and lipids in check in a more natural way (Health & Wellness, Blood Sugar News, Winter 2021, p.3).

Did you know? High blood sugar occurs when your body does not make enough insulin or does not use it effectively. So, in order to lower your blood sugar levels naturally, you may want to do exercise regularly, maintain a moderate weight, reduce your carb intake, increase your fiber intake (especially the soluble fiber), drink plenty of water, reduce portion sizes, and choose foods with a low glycemic index (yogurt, barely, oats, beans, lentil and non-starchy vegetables to mention a few). In addition, you also need to manage your tress levels, monitor your blood sugar levels often, get enough good quality sleep, eat foods rich in chromium (meats, whole grain, fruits, vegetables and nuts) as well as those rich in magnesium (dark leafy greens, squash and pumpkin seeds, tuna, whole grains, dark chocolate and bananas). Furthermore, you should include cinnamon in your diet as well as Berberine and Fenugreek seeds (www.healthline.com/nutrition pp.1-14).

Did you know? Age and a family history of diabetes can affect your chances of developing the disease. However, a small number of bad daily habits can significantly increase the risk. So, you need to avoid skipping breakfast, avoid sitting more than 30 minutes at a time, avoid drinking more than one or two glasses of wine per day, avoid chronic sleep deprivation, smoking and eating highly processed foods every day (www.aarp.org/health).

Did you know? Sitting too long can cause a release of a hunger-promoting hormone. To make a difference, it is a good idea to stand up for five minutes every hour. In addition, a recent study found out that sitting all day long in an office also puts you at a greater risk of having heart disease. Furthermore, men who drive for 10 hours a week have an 82% higher risk of death from CVD (cardiovascular diseases). So, it is better to have a job in which either you are on your feet often or you work at a standing desk if one is available for you. Also, do not forget to get at least 150 minutes of real exercise (not strenuous) into your week (AARP, February/March 2021, p.25 & p.28 and Woman's World 2021).

Did you know? Type-2 diabetes is fast becoming a real epidemic in the world. This has been due to the global expansion of sugary foods, sugary soft drinks and the reliance of people on processed foods that are cheaper and easier to prepare than most healthy foods and that are heavily advertised by major food corporations (nutritionwatchdog.com).

Did you know? Type-2 diabetes has the potential of being completely reversed if one would follow a series of lifestyle changes that dramatically reduce or eliminate sugar and starches from their diet (nutritionwatchdog.com).

Did you know? Berberine is a powerful plant extract that has been used in China for more than 2500 years to treat Type-2 diabetes. Not only does it reduce Hemoglobin A1C levels, but it also improves the Triglyceride, LDL (bad) cholesterol and blood pressure of an individual taking it on a daily basis. Berberine also helps people lose weight by reducing the size of fat cells and inhibiting their storage capacity. However, Berberine tends to enhance the production of brown fat cells, a type of fat cells that burns energy instead. Brown fat is the kind of fat that the body burns right away. Berberine has been also found to enhance memory and cognitive function in people (nutritionwatchdog.com).

Did you know? In addition to its great benefits for Diabetes, Berberine is helpful for other health issues as well including high cholesterol, hypertension (high blood pressure), anti-aging, gastrointestinal infections, heart disease, immune challenges, joint problems and low bone density (nutritonwatchdog.com).

Did you know? Honey affects your body in about the same ways as corn syrup, even though it contains trace amounts of phytochemicals from its floral sources and from the beehive. Honey gets broken down in the body into glucose and fructose in proportions that are similar to sugar and high-fructose corn syrup (Health & Nutrition Letter, Tufts University p.2).

Did you know? In order to heal your arteries, reduce inflammation, and boost your insulin sensitivity, naturally, you need to add cinnamon to your diet. A mere ¼ teaspoon of cinnamon reduces fasting blood sugar levels by about 29%, lowers triglycerides by 30% and lowers LDL (bad) cholesterol by 27% (Ultimate Women's Guide to Beating Disease, 2018, p.129).

Did you know? Nuts, such as almonds and walnuts, can help fight cardiovascular disease. You can add nuts to your diet without worrying much about gaining weight. In fact, some people even lost weight when tree nuts were added to their diets. It all has to do with the fact that eating nuts will make you feel full fast. In addition, the body uses a lot of energy to digest it. Keep in mind that some children and people can be very allergic to nuts and not know it (Tuft University Health & Nutrition Letter, December 2020, p.4).

Did you know? All nuts are good for you, but research shows that walnuts in particular may help regulate food cravings (Better Homes & Gardens, March 2021, p.116)

Did you know? Resveratrol is a polyphenol, an antioxidant, and a disease fighter that helps protect the heart and circulation. It can also lower cholesterol and blood sugar levels and helps prevent clots that can lead to heart attack and stroke. It can be found in the skin of red grapes and in dark grape juice. Other foods that have small amount of resveratrol include peanuts, peanut butter, pistachios, cocoa, dark chocolate, and berries such as blueberries and cranberries. Resveratrol is best consumed from food because supplements seem to have low bioavailability and low absorption (Women's Nutrition Connection, Weill Cornell Medicine, October 2020, p.8).

Did you know? Peanut butter has a lot of protein, fiber and heart-healthy monounsaturated fats. However, keep in mind that a tablespoon has nearly 100 calories, and that many peanut butters have added sugar (AARP, February/March 2021, p.25).

Did you know? America's obesity epidemic is being fueled by ultra-processed foods loaded with synthetic flavors, preservatives, added sugars and salt. In addition, people tend to eat more of the ultra-processed foods than the unprocessed foods (The Week, June 14, 2019, volume 19 issue 928 p.17).

Did you know? Not all carbs are alike. Some are healthy, and some are not. There are two types of carbohydrates, simple carbohydrates, that absorb fast in your body and make you gain weight, and complex carbohydrates that actually can make you lose weight. Simple carbohydrates include anything that contains sugar and white refined wheat products as well as potatoes. Complex carbohydrates include vegetables and fruits. Fruits are sources of healthy carbs, since they provide fiber and plenty of nutrients, and their sweet taste comes from natural sugars rather than added sugars. In addition, there are other healthy carbs including whole grains, legumes such as lentils, beans (navy, kidney, pinto, black, cannellini, lima) and peas, as well as low-fat or fat-free plain milk and yogurt (Women's Health Advisor by Well Cornell Medicine, Volume 20, p.1).

Did you know? Iceland, a small island country, is ranked one of the healthiest in the world. For decades, scientists and doctors could not figure out the cause for it. Many speculated that maybe it was due to the high consumption of fish. However, today modern medical research has found out that it is not the case. They discovered that it was the volcanic Icelandic soil that contained Sulfur and Selenium, which played a major role. These nutrients tend to deep-feed and rejuvenate body's cells. Sulfur in particular, increases the permeability of cells to allow for optimal oxygen transport into cells and to carry sickness causing waste out of the cells in your body. In addition, Selenium fights illness by elevating Glutathione, which promotes the production of Killer T-cells that engulf harmful substances that enter our body. However, today Sulfur and Selenium have been almost entirely stripped out of our diet because farmers around the world uses chemical fertilizers that remove it from the soil.

Did you know? Being on a high-protein diet for an extended period of time can cause harm to our health. Excess amounts of protein in our diet tend to be stored as fat, and over time it can lead to weight gain. In addition, it can also be harmful to the kidneys as well as increase the risk of heart disease. Furthermore, it can also contribute to temporary headaches, irritability, nausea, bad breath and sleeping problems.

Did you know? Beef is actually significantly more nutritionally healthy for us (and environmentally healthy and sustainable too) than any type of chicken or pork. It all has to do with the fact that chicken and pork, unlike beef, have excessive amount of Omega-6 fatty acid in their food. That in turn enters our food supply and too much of Omega-6 in our diet cause degenerative diseases like heart disease, diabetes, cancer and Alzheimer's Disease (Mike Geary' Nutrition Watchdog Ezine Newsletter).

Did you know? Cows that are fed grains instead of grass have higher concentration of Omega-6 fats in their body and when their meat is consumed by humans it causes inflammation in our bodies. Therefore, it is much healthier to eat meat from cows that are fed grass (Newsmax Magazine, Natural Cures 2021, p.41).

Did you know? Milk of grass-fed cows tend to have higher levels of heart-healthy Omega-3 fatty acids and antioxidants carotenoids (Consumer Reports, August 2021, p.18).

Did you know? If you like to grill meat, it should be marinated first in order to reduce the production of carcinogenic compounds called Heterocyclic Amines (HCAs) that form under high heat.

Did you know that not all soy protein is alike?

Avoid highly processed soybean oil and isolated soy protein, which can be found in protein powders and energy bars. Instead, consume whole soybeans, edamame, tofu, tempeh, soymilk, and miso. In addition, in order to reduce heart disease risk, the Food and Drug Administration recommends people to consume 25 grams of soy milk or tofu per day (Women's Nutrition Connection, Weill Cornell Medicine, October 2020, p.6).

Did you know? Researchers found out that when women do not get enough Calcium, they gain weight. It is due to the fact that when Calcium is in short supply, the body releases large amount of Calcitriol, a hormone that helps retain Calcium and also signals the body to make more fat and decrease fat burning. Therefore, the researchers recommend that women eat three low-fat dairy servings a day (FC&A, Medical Publishing p.21).

Did you Know? Excess amount of Calcium in your arteries, on the other hand, can lead to heart attack and stroke. So, by eating at least 45 grams of cruciferous vegetables daily, like Brussels sprouts, cauliflower or cabbage that are rich in Vitamin K, may prevent

Calcium deposits in your arteries (Better Homes & Gardens, January 2021, p.97).

Did you know? An ice cream scoop can be used for more than just ice cream. You can use it to measure meatballs into even portions, divide cookie dough onto baking sheets, and spoon cupcake batter into muffin cups.

Did you Know? If you want to prevent blueberries or chocolate chips from sinking to the bottom of muffin or cake batter, you need to slightly coat them first with flour.

Did you know? Flour has heat absorbent properties and also has strong antioxidant properties. Thus, it helps if you got burnt to apply it within 15 minutes of receiving the burn and apply it for ten or more minutes. So, keep a bag of flour in your fridge in case of accidental burn in the kitchen.

Did you know? Do not waste money on eggs that are labeled as raised with "no hormones". By law in the US, chickens that produce eggs cannot be given hormones. So, eggs with a "no hormones" claim are no different from eggs that do not have "no hormone" claim. In addition, eggs are safe to eat up to five weeks after the "sell by" date. If you want to know when those eggs were packed, just look at the number under the "sell by" date. The three-digit number in the middle of the numbers printed on the case, let say for example 060 = 60 – 59 (31 days in January + 28 days in February) = eggs that were packed on March 1st (Health & Nutrition Letter, Tufts University, 2021, p.1 & CRConsumer Report June 2021, p.5).

Did you know? Eggs contain every vitamin except Vitamin C, and they are one of the most nutritious foods you can eat. The yolks actually contain almost all of the good nutrients that your body needs. Eggs deliver Lecithin to help the body break down and utilize cholesterol. They are also rich in Choline, a nutrient that prevents fat accumulation in the body. If you add a little milk or cheese to your scrambled eggs, you get complete protein, like as if you were eating a piece of steak (www.healthhouseinfo.com).

Did you know? Eggs are loaded with appetite - controlling protein, vitamins, minerals, powerful antioxidants, healthy cholesterol, and saturated fat (healthy fat). Eating eggs will also help you control the hormones in your body and blood sugar levels too. In addition, researchers found out that eating eggs for breakfast instead of carb-based food leads to less food cravings during the day.

Did you know? Hair cells are most active in the morning, and eating eggs, especially the yolks at that time, will help your hair grow faster and fuller in most cases (Woman's World, 2021, p.5).

Did you know? Eating eggs occasionally in moderation will not probably raise you risk of health issues such as heart attack, stroke, or heart failure. However, consuming a lot of eggs can increase the risk of heart failure in people.

Did you know? Oatmeal (quick, old -fashioned, or steel-cut) makes a great whole-grain breakfast. Each half-cup (dry) of plain, rolled oats has 4 grams of fiber- roughly half of it is the soluble kind that helps lower cholesterol (www.NutritionAction.com.)

Did you know? Spanish researchers found out that drinking 12 oz. of eggnog three times weekly could cut the risk of colds by about 33%. It is all due to the fact that the Choline in eggs and the amino acids in milk, energize the white blood cells in the body to boost the production of germ-fighting antibodies (*First for women,* 12/21/2020, p.33).

Did you know? UCLA researchers found out that pomegranates tend to boost mental concentration. Why? This is because they are packed with a compounds that increase the levels of the brain chemical Serotonin, which helps a person feel calmer and more clearheaded in just about 72 hours *(First for women,* 12/21/2020, p.55).

Did you know? Not all salts are alike. Sea salt does not contain much Iodine, while iodized salt has Iodine added to it. Iodine is an element that we need in order to produce certain hormones. Low levels of Iodine can contribute to Hypothyroidism, which is an underactive thyroid, which can cause a person to develop a goiter, which is the enlargement of the Thyroid Gland. Most Americans get enough Iodine from dietary sources such as eggs, enriched grains, dairy products, and seafood. However, vegetarians and vegans do not have enough Iodine in their food, so it is essential for them to add iodized salt to their diet (Healthy Aging, Icahn School of Medicine at Mount Sinai, October 2020 p.8 & Health, May 2020, p.14).

Did you know? Eating less salt helps support healthy immune function. Researchers found out that some of the immune cells in the blood known as Granulocytes were less effective against bacteria when levels of glucocorticoids increase as result of consuming an extra six grams of salt per day. Why? This is because glucocorticoids tend to inhibit the function of Granulocytes that primarily attack bacteria. So, when Granulocyte function is impaired, infections tend to be more severe (*Science Translational Medicine,* Life Extension Magazine, November 2020, p.18).

Did you know? A vegan diet is not the same as a vegetarian diet. A vegan diet excludes all animal-based or animal-derived ingredients. This means no meat, poultry, seafood, eggs, dairy, honey, or certain marshmallows and gummy candies that contain gelatin. You also cannot use cosmetics that have been tested on animals either, or wear clothing made from wool, fur, or leather. A vegetarian diet on the other hand, means that the majority of the food comes from plants, but one tends to still include some fish every now and then. (Health, May 2021, p.14).

Did you know? Wines contain Histamine and tannins found in grape skins. Some people produce less of the enzyme that breaks down Histamine, therefore when those people have a glass of red wine, their Histamine level may go up and cause their blood vessels to dilate. Dilated blood vessels in the brain can cause headaches. Increased levels of tannins are another possible reason that can lead to headaches in people because it tends to raise the levels of the neuro-transmitter Serotonin. Keep in mind that there are variety of wines and not all contain the same amount of Histamine and tannins. So, one needs to experiment with a variety of wines to see which one will work best in the future. Keep in mind that alcohol-related dehydration can also cause headaches. So, it is advised to drink a glass of water after finishing to drink a glass of wine (Health, January/February p.52).

Did you know? It was discovered that headache caused by summer heat can be cured by consuming watermelon juice. Just one glass a day works wonders usually, (www.healthhouseinfo.com).

Did you know? Histamine is a compound made by the body and also is found in many foods too. Its role is to cause an immediate inflammatory response. It actually serves as a red flag in our immune system, telling the body about potential attackers, and it can help fight infections or heal injuries. It is also part of the body's sleep/wake cycle. However, if our body does not break down Histamine properly, it builds up in our bloodstream. The result is suffering from fatigue, body aches, allergy-like symptoms and more. By the way, 80% of sufferers tend to be female and over the age of 40. It was found that a top cause of overload is actually a genetic deficiency in DAO, an enzyme that breaks down Histamine (*First for women,* April 26, 2021, p.37).

Did you know? If you have problem with Histamine-rich foods, you should avoid eating them after lunch because the Histamine in them will keep you up at night. These Histamine-rich foods include aged cheeses, fermented foods, and vinegar, nuts, processed meats, chocolate, avocados and spinach. You also should avoid alcohol, and black and green tea because they block DAO, an enzyme that breaks down Histamine. Doctors today recommend taking DAO supplement (Histazyme, Amazon.com) 15 minutes before meals and to cook meals with olive oil, as well as eat wild-caught salmon several times a week, because the fatty acids in those foods boost DAO levels in the body (*First for women*, April 26, 2021, p.37).

Did you know? Quercetin, a nutrient found in foods like apples, fennel and onions tends to lower Histamine levels in the body by 96% to boost energy. Turkish researchers in 2021, are testing it to prevent and treat COVID-19 infections. In addition, Dr. Fred Pescatore, an integrative physician, recommends taking 500 mg of Quercetin twice a day to combat COVID -19 (*First for women*, April 26, 2021, p.37).

Did you know? Potato starch, which is made by heating and cooling potatoes, acts as fertilizer for beneficial gut bacteria, and according to researchers from Yale University it may speed the recovery from COVID-19. It all has to do with the fact that potato starch tends to break down microorganisms in the gut into *Butyrate*, a fatty acid that has been shown to lower the risk of viral respiratory infection. To get the benefits from the potato starch you should purchase Bob's Red Mill Gluten-Free Unmodified Potato Starch (in supermarkets) and add 1tsp. to your food (soup) every day over six days until you get to 2 Tbs. daily. Keep in mind that adding too much starch to your diet all at once, or too fast can cause you to have digestive discomfort (*First for women*, April 26, 2021, p.38).

Did you know? Drinking alcohol does not kill brain cells, as commonly believed. However, it significantly diminishes the production of new cells. A 30-year study from the United Kingdom found that drinking even only two to three drinks per day does long-term damage to the brainpower of an individual. In addition, it was recently found that people who sometimes drank enough alcohol to the point of losing consciousness were roughly twice as likely to eventually develop dementia. Therefore, you should be careful not to drink too much all at once (Reader's Digest, March 2021, p.44).

Did you know? Caffeine and alcohol will not help you stay warm, since they actually hinder the body's ability to produce heat. They can also cause the core temperature of your body to drop. Instead, it is better to drink warm water or consume a sugary beverage. Sugar will give you the fuel your body needs to produce energy in order to warm your body (The Old Farmer's Almanac, 2020, p.20).

Did you know? Some foods can trigger headaches beside caffeine in individuals such as aged cheeses like mozzarella, brie, cheddar, Swiss and Bleu Cheese especially if you take Monoamine Oxidase Inhibitor (MAOI) medications. In addition, citrus fruits can also cause headache flairs. Also, some types of beans such as fava beans, Italian beans, and lima beans contain Tyramine, which can increase the risk of contributing to headaches in people too (Healthscameexposed.com).

Did you know? Some dairy foods have little or no Lactose, such as cheddar and Swiss cheeses. The bacteria used to make yogurt 'digests' the Lactose in the milk. Also, research suggests that many Lactose intolerant people can, in most cases, handle up to 15 grams of Lactose – which is about a cup of 1% milk at a time, especially with a meal (Consumer Reports On Health, May 2021, p.9).

Did you know? Drinking enough water keeps our body functioning optimally. Researchers found out that people who drank at least six glasses of water a day were less tired, and they were happier and more optimistic than otherwise. The reason is due to the fact that drinking water increases the flow of blood and oxygen to the brain as well as improves concentration, memory, energy, mood and emotional balance (*First for women*, April 26, p.42).

Did you know? Green tea was found to be more beneficial than black tea. They also found out that regular tea drinkers (2 to 3 cups per day) may help lower cholesterol, manage blood sugar, promote weight loss, protect against several forms of cancer, boost immunity, and reduce inflammation. Keep in mind that if you want to maximize the health benefits of tea, you need to drink it without milk.

The protein in milk decreases the concentration of many of the tea's beneficial phytocompounds (The Old Farmer's Almanac Boys Town, 2020, p.12 & www.healthhouseinfo.com).

Did you know? New study found out that 4 or more cups of green tea and 2 or more cups of coffee per day may help protect your liver and keep it healthy.

Did you know? Green tea is very healthy to drink, but white tea is even healthier for your heart, because it contains flavonoids that may help keep blood vessels open and it will also break down fat in your body (Consumer Reports On Health, 2021, pp.1-2.

Did you know? Researchers in Loma Linda University in California found a link between drinking 2 cups of milk daily to an 80% increase of breast cancer risk, and those who drink ¼ cup daily increased their risk by about 30%.

Why? This is because most cows' milk contains hormones and having excess hormones can promote the growth and spread of cancer cells, especially hormone-sensitive illnesses like breast cancer. In addition, they believe that replacing cows' milk with nondairy alternatives, when possible, can reduce the risk by about 62% (*First for Women*, July7, 2020, p.20).

Did you know? Sugar is vital to your brain health, which is the biggest guzzler of sweets in your body. The brain uses up to 400 calories worth of glucose each day (Dr. Drew Ramsey article in https://healthscamsexposed.com/2017/09/ why-sugar-should-be-a-vital-part-of-your-everyday-diet/).

Did you know? There are many different forms that sugar can be found. Fructose, which is found in many processed and artificial foods as well as in soft drinks, is not good for your body because it has no real nutritional value. However, glucose and more complex carbohydrates found in fruit, maple syrup, honey and other natural food are considered healthier to consume because they are naturally occurring sugars and not artificially created (Dr. Drew Ramsey https://healthscamexposed.com/2017/09/ why-sugar-should -be-a-vital-part-of-your-everyday-diet/).

Did you know? If you do not include in your meals every day small quantities of healthy carbohydrates, your body will convert stored fat to energy. This is how people on "ketogenic" or "paleo" diets lose weight. However, if you want to stay healthy and still lose weight you need to **practice moderation** when it comes to eating – especially with regards to intake of sugar and carbohydrates Do not completely avoid consuming them for a long period of time, because it is not very healthy practice for your body (Dr. Drew Ramsey https://healthscamexposed.com/2017/09 Why-sugar-should-be-vital-part-of-your-everyday-diet/).

Did you know? Eating a whole piece of fruit is much better for us than drinking juice. It all has to do with the fact that juice can cause a spike in blood sugar and a resultant spike of insulin, and that in turn signals to body to enter a mode of fat creation and storage. On the other hand, fruits naturally contain fiber and complex sugars that tend to slow the metabolism of the sugars from the fruit (Dr. Drew Ramsey https://healthscamexposed.com/2017/09 why-sugar-should-be-a-vital-part-of-your-everyday-diet/)

Did you know? Glycemic Index (GI) tells us how quickly foods containing carbohydrates affect your blood sugar level when eaten by themselves. GI scores are rated as: low: 55 or below, moderate; 56-69 and high: 70 and above. The lower the GI score, the more slowly the rise in blood sugar when eating sugar and carbohydrates. Most whole fruits have in general a low to moderate GI. Many fruits are also packed with essential vitamins like A and C as well as fiber.

Did you know? To calculate the GL ourselves we can use this formula: GL= the G (glucose), multiplied by the grams of carbohydrates, divided by 100.

Did you know? We need carbohydrates because they provide energy to our cells in the body. However, in order for our bodies to use carbs for energy, we need insulin. When our bodies do not produce enough insulin or we are unable to use it, we end up having Type-1 Diabetes. When our bodies do not produce enough insulin, we end up having Type-2 Diabetes.

Did you know? Many fruits have a low GI score such as: cherries (GI of 20), grapefruits (GI of 25), prunes (GI 29), pears (GI 38), apples (GI of 39), oranges(GI of 40), plums (GI 40), strawberries (GI of 41), peaches GI of 45) and grapes (GI of 53), to mention a few (reviewed by Dr. Titu Budania – MBBS, MD).

Did you know? Researchers found out that eating a fresh grapefruit before a meal does in fact make a person lose weight, as well as improve insulin sensitivity. Thereby, it helps a person to control the insulin and blood sugar levels too. On the other hand, consuming grapefruit can interfere with people's medications and vitamins intake.

Did you know? Lemons & limes are not the same even though they have a lot in common. They are actually totally different citrus fruits. Lemons, formally known as Citrus limon, grow on a small evergreen tree that is actually native to Asia and are typically grown in moderate climates. On the other hand, limes, formally known as Citrus aurantifolia, are thought to be hybridized fruit and actually come in several varieties form various parts of the world and grow better in tropical and subtropical regions. In addition, limes are harvested before they ripen, while lemons are picked when ripe, yellow and mature. They both contain a good amount of Vitamin C, or Ascorbic Acid, which helps to strengthen the immune system so the body can fight colds, flu, and other pathogens. Vitamin C is also a powerful antioxidant, which helps prevent damage to the DNA in our cells, and also protects and helps insure we have healthy cell production and reduces the chance of us having cancer. Furthermore, Vitamin C also helps to enhance iron absorption form foods, it is also valuable for the heart, by helping us fight heart disease, lower blood pressure and decreases the amount Calcium in the urine. That in turn helps to prevent the formation of kidney stones. In addition, drinking lemon or lime water can help with weight loss. The sour flavor actually helps you feel slightly more satiated. (https://thennutritionwatchdog.com/lemons-vs-limes-which-is-healthier/? pp.1-11).

Did you know? Dried fruit can boost your fiber and nutrient intake and supply your body with large amounts of antioxidants. However, on the other hand, they also tend to be high in sugar and calories and can cause problems when eaten in excess. Dried fruits in most cases contain up to 3.5 times the fiber, vitamins and minerals of fresh fruit. However, Vitamin C content is significantly reduced when the fruit is dried. In addition, dried fruit generally contains a lot of fiber and is a great source of Phenolic and Polyphenol antioxidants. These antioxidants are associated with numerous health benefits such as improved blood flow, better digestive health, decreased oxidative damage and reduced risk of many diseases. Be aware that sulfites are added to some dried fruit to preserve color, which may cause adverse effects if you have sensitivity to them. You also need to keep in mind that died fruits that are improperly stored and handled may end up containing fungi and toxins. Avoid dried fruit with added sugar known as "candied fruit" as they may increase your risk of obesity, heart disease and even cancer (healthline.com).

Did you know? Baking soda can help lower Uric Acid levels and relieve Gout symptoms according to GoutDiet.org, as well as help people who suffer from acid reflux or GERD, and those that suffer from ulcers.

Did you know? Going overboard with ingesting baking soda can cause undesired side effects, because it is extremely high in Sodium, so it will raise your blood pressure and too much Sodium is linked to kidney and health issues in healthy people.

Did you know? Baking soda, also known as Sodium Bicarbonate, is actually a chemical salt that occurs naturally as a mineral Nahcolite. This mineral was discovered in 1928 when it was found in a lava tunnel at Mount Vesuvius, Italy.

Did you know? Most of the U.S. baking soda comes from Green River, Wyoming, and it is mined from Trona ore. Trona deposits were molded over four million years ago after the evaporation of great salt lakes in Wyoming. Trona also comes from Kenya, Egypt, Venezuela and the deserts of Central Asia.

Did you know? According to a meta-analysis published in *Molecules*, researchers found out that green tea may be an immune booster, helping fight both cold and influenza viruses. However, one has to have the habit of drinking it regularly every day.

Did you know? If you want to lose weight or keep from overeating and stay in shape and not feel hungry after eating your meals, you need to drink 8 oz. of water before each meal. Why? Water will fill you up and make you feel full (**First** *for women,* April 26, 2021, p.30).

Did you know? Drinking water after eating reduces the acid in your mouth by 61%. In addition, drinking a glass of water before you eat may help digestion and curb your appetite.

Did you know? Our body works overtime to digest our food and the process starts before food even hits the mouth. When we smell food, our mouths automatically produce more saliva to prepare the digestive system to work. In an average healthy body, it takes about 6-8 hours for food to pass through the stomach, and two days to complete the digestion process. The average person will eat about over 50 tons of food in a lifetime.

Did you know? Skim milk tends to be the most hydrating drink you can get. Its sugar, protein, and fat slow the emptying of fluid from the stomach, and its Sodium acts as a sponge, keeping water in the body. Oral rehydration solutions, such as Pedialyte, are effective in keeping water in the body as well. Just drinking plain water will not do a good job to hydrate the body (Reader's Digest, June 2020 p.48).

Did you know why dark chocolate is healthier than milk chocolate? Dark chocolate is considered healthier because it contains more cocoa that is rich in phytonutrients - plant compounds that have antioxidant, ant-inflammatory, and anti-carcinogenic effects associated with many health benefits. Some nutrition experts advise choosing chocolate with a minimum of 70% cocoa. On the other hand, milk chocolate tends to have more added sugar than dark chocolate and a smaller percentage of cocoa (Women's Health Advisor, Weill Cornell Medicine, October 2020, p.7 Volume 20).

Did you know? Dark chocolate, of at least 75 percent cocoa is very heart-healthy to consume. It is rich in healthful flavonoids, particularly flavanols that can help according to the AHA lower the risk of heart disease. In addition, they can also lower the risk of insulin resistance, high blood pressure in adults, and high cholesterol. Furthermore, they also help fight the DNA damage that causes aging symptoms like wrinkles, graying hair as well as boost cognitive function by improving cerebral blood flow, thanks in part to its high flavanol content. Recent research has also found out that the antioxidants in dark chocolate have a strong ability to fight the DNA damage that could lead to cancer development, as well as reduces certain inflammation enzymes that could encourage cancer growth. Moreover, research shows that dark chocolate may actually help you keep cravings in check, which can help you keep the pounds off. Recent studies have also found out that even the smell of dark chocolate tends to reduce appetite and improve satiety. (Reader's Digest February 1, 2021, p.67 & https://blog. paleohacks.com/health-benefits-of-dark-chocolate/).

Did you know? Eating chocolate while studying helps the brain retain new information easily. It is all due to the fact that chocolate is super high in Magnesium, and Magnesium is needed for over 300 metabolic functions, including helping to grow new neurons so messaging is more accurate, and helping to strengthen connections between brain cells that lead to memory formation Magnesium also improves learning ability and decision making as well as helps to retrieves short memories from the prefrontal cortex area of the brain. It also detoxifies tissues from heavy metals, pesticides/ herbicide chemicals, and environmental poisons and toxins (National Scientific, Special Brain Health Edition, Winter 2021, p.14 & p.17 & www.healthhouseinfo.com).

Did you know how Nutella came about? After WWII, chocolate was in short supply in Italy. So, Pietro Ferrero came up with an idea of how to stretch the little chocolate supply by using a new recipe. His new recipe included a little cocoa, sugar, and hazelnuts. Today we call it Nutella.

Did you know? The National Health and Nutritional Examination Survey found out that 68 percent of the population of the US is deficient in Magnesium. People over the age of 50 who tend to experience more mental decline, including lack of physical energy, headaches and irritability, tend to be deficient in Magnesium (National Scientific, Special Brain Health Edition, Winter 2021, p.14 & p.17).

Did you know? Magnesium was reported by the American Academy of Neurology and the American Headache Society as "effective" for preventing migraines. It is also well known that people who suffer from migraine headaches have lower levels of Magnesium in their blood and tissues (National Scientific, Special Brain Health Edition, Winter 2021, p.14).

Did you know? Magnesium is shown to benefit blood sugar levels. Magnesium deficiency has been linked to a higher risk of developing Diabetes. Studies have linked individuals with higher Magnesium intake with up to about 47% lower risk for developing Type-2 Diabetes. Magnesium rich foods includes pumpkins and squash seeds, tuna, dark chocolate, bananas, avocados, beans and whole grains.

Did you know? Researchers found out that in order for our body to absorb Magnesium better from the food we eat we also need to combine it with food that contains Chromium. When we eat these foods regularly it will prevent us from having deficiencies and reduce our risk of having blood sugar problems.

Did you know? Adding one tablespoon of unsweetened cocoa as well as 2 grams of fiber to your smoothie will help your body drop excess pounds.

Did you know? There are five inexpensive foods that can defend your eyes against cataracts and Macular Degeneration such as: strawberries, green tea, sweet potatoes, salmon and kale.

Did You Know? Scientist found out that one can rev up brown fat by being exposed to cold temperatures of 66 degrees Fahrenheit or lower. In addition, they also found out that you can boost your brown fat production by eating foods that Ursolic Acid, a substance that is found in high concentrations in apple peels, cranberries, blueberries, plums, and prunes. You can get rid of the white fat cells by using cooling treatments called CoolSculpting. It literally freezes fat cells to death and the body will remove the damaged cells over several months. On the other hand, 104 degrees Fahrenheit for sustained amount of time can cause the white fat cells to die. This is the mechanism used in popular laser and radio-frequency lipolysis weight-loss treatments. Nevertheless, one should always aim to have healthy diet and exercise so the white fat cell will not be reproduced.

Did you know? Eating foods rich in vitamins and minerals promotes higher white blood cells production and lowers inflammation. You should have diet that is anti-inflammatory. It should include a few carbohydrates with each meal but should be limited in quantity, such as one slice of bread per day. Avoid diet foods and beverages with Aspartame, as it is carcinogenic, damages the brain, and worsens atherosclerosis. Also avoid soy products, as they are high in Manganese, Fluoride, Aluminum, and Glutamate, which can make Diabetes worse (Newsmax Magazine, Natural Cures 2021, p.47).

Did you know? Vitamins and minerals do wonders to our health. However, the flip side is that certain deficiencies can wreak havoc. So, it is important to make sure that we are at least not deficient in Vitamin B12, Vitamin D, Magnesium and Potassium, to mention a few.

Did you Know? Potassium is a mineral that plays numerous roles in the body and one of those roles is that it

activate specific enzymes that assist in protecting lung tissue from invading viruses and it also lowers blood pressure as well as helps your heartbeat stay regular. However, too much of it can cause irregular heartbeat, confusion, temporal paralysis, incredibly low blood pressure, weakness, and coma. Overdose of potassium from natural sources is nearly impossible. However, it is possible to consume too much of it via potassium salts which can lead to nausea, vomiting, and even cardiac arrest (Health & Nutrition Letter, Tufts University p.2 & myfooddata.com).

Did you know? Vitamin C may reduce your risk of stroke, especially if you smoke, and oranges are one of the best sources of Vitamin C. Strawberries, brussels sprouts, broccoli and red bell peppers are also excellent sources of it (Reader's Digest, February 1, 2021, p.66).

Did you know? Broccoli is loaded with Vitamin C, Carotenoids, Potassium and folate too (www.NutritionAction.com).

Did you know? Researchers found out that people who consumed brightly colored antioxidant pigment called Carotenoids from vegetables and fruits, as well as consume Vitamin C from fruits were 25% to 50% less likely to get Diabetes (Harvard Health Letter, October 2020, p.8).

Did you know? Research on vitamins in 2021 found out that taking a **high-quality** of multivitamins every day can reduce all manner of health problems and risks of death by as much as 70% (https://www.healthscamsnews.com & the study published by the Journal of Breast Cancer Research and Treatment.

Did you know? The American Journal of Clinical Nutrition indicated that vegetarians can be at risk of cardiovascular problems despite the fact that their diets have been heart healthy. It was found that vegans - who do not eat animal products – and even lacto-ovo vegetarians – who do eat eggs and dairy – were often deficient in levels of Vitamin B12. Lack of Vitamin B12 can affect your heart and cause anemia and nerve problems. So, it is a good idea to supplement your diet with multivitamins and eat foods that is fortified with Vitamin B12. (www.healthhoseinfo.com).

Did you know? Calcium is crucial to heart, bone, dental, nerve and blood health. Men and women 50 years or older need between 1,000 to about 1,200 milligrams of Calcium per day. The best way to get the amount of Calcium one need is from food, such as dairy products, leafy greens, Calcium fortified orange juice, canned sardines and salmon, tofu, and almonds to mention a few. However, consuming too much Calcium can lead to Hypercalcemia when there is above-normal level of Calcium in the blood. That in turn can cause nausea, vomiting, confusion and other neurological symptoms, as well as can lead to a higher risk for kidney disease and aggressive prostate cancer (Harvard Health Letter, January 2021, p.5).

Did you know? The immune system tends to weaken with age. The best way to protect yourself from infections is to follow a healthy lifestyle. Reduce or eliminate completely processed food from your diet. Eat fruits, vegetables, whole grains, low-fat dairy, and lean proteins, especially fish that contain anti-inflammatory Omega-3 fatty acid. Also limit or avoid red meat, and minimize your intake of sugar-sweetened beverages, and desserts. It is also important to keep being active and walk regularly, avoid smoking, and get adequate sleep. Make sure that you are up with your vaccinations and have an annual physical checkup visit with your primary doctor. In addition, get in the habit of washing your hands frequently and thoroughly, using soap and hot water (Women's Health Advisor, Weill Cornell Medicine, October 2020 p.7 Volume 20 & **First** *for women* June 7, 2021, p.28).

Did you know? Immune-boosting foods protect us in several ways. They provide us with antioxidants, reduce inflammation, stimulate the immune system to do its job and help to fight infection and inflammation. These foods include onions (by the way if you toss onions in the freezer for 15 minutes before you cut them you won't tear up), mushrooms, spinach, tomatoes, plain yogurt that contain five probiotics and garlic. Garlic has been used for centuries to support a healthy cardiovascular system and it tends to also help maintain cholesterol and blood pressure levels already withing the normal range. Allicin is the powerful active component in garlic most responsible for garlic's heart healthy benefits. Garlic also helps support your natural immune defense and support a healthy immune system (The Ultimate Women's Guide 2021 & Garlic.com).

Did you know? Nearly 50 percent of the US population was found to have Vitamin D deficiency at one point or another. Vitamin D, a fat-soluble vitamin, plays a critical role in the body. One of its many important functions is to regulate our immune response which keeps inflammation at bay. This may be why low levels of Vitamin D have been linked to severe COVID-19 symptoms. In addition, without enough Vitamin D circulating in the bloodstream, the body will not be able to absorb all the Calcium it needs for bone growth and strength. It also protects your cells and DNA, insures that the nervous system will properly work, regulates the circulation system, balances blood sugar, and energizes the muscles too. Vitamin D is unique because it is not found in fresh fruits and vegetables, like most other essential vitamins. The body obtains it through sun exposure and by consuming some certain foods such as eggs yolk, cheese, soy milk, fortified cereals, beef liver and fatty fish. Fatty fish not only provide the body with Vitamin D but also with Omega-3 fatty acids. Herring contains the most Vitamin D, but others including salmon, catfish, sardines, mackerel, and bluefish are also high in this important vitamin (healththoroughfare.com & Health, January/February 2021, p.42).

Did you know? People with arthritis were found to have low levels of Vitamin D in their body (Women's Nutrition Connection, May 2021, p.6).

Did you know? Not all D vitamins are the same. Vitamin D-3 seems to be best absorbed in the body. In addition, it tends to cut breast cancer risk in half (Ultimate Women's Guide to Beating Disease, 2018, p.61).

Did you know? We can produce Vitamin D in adequate amount while being exposed to sunlight for about 20 minutes each day. However, not all people in the world can be exposed to sunlight every day. It depends on the region and climate where they reside and their daily schedule. It is also difficult to get enough Vitamin D from the food we eat (such as fish or fortified milk). In addition, if we consume Vitamin D or stay in the sunlight once in a while it will not help us be protected from illnesses. Therefore, we need to supplement our diet with about 1,000 IU of Vitamin D3 per day for some insurance (healththoroughfare.com & Harvard Health Letter, Harvard Medical School, January 2021, p.1).

Did you know? The recommended form of Vitamin D is Vitamin D3, known as Cholecalciferol, because it absorbed better in the body than Vitamin D-2. Vitamin D-3 is the natural form of Vitamin D that our body makes from sunlight. Supplements are made from the fat of lamb's wool. Vitamin D in general helps the body to absorb Calcium and Phosphorus needed to keep bones strong. In addition, it also helps support a healthy brain, heart, teeth and lungs. Furthermore, it keeps the immune system strong and can regulate insulin levels. Moreover, it keeps our energy levels up and enhances our mood, too (Healththoroghfare.com).

Did you know? Low levels of Vitamin D in the body can lead to Rickets in children and Osteomalacia in adults as well as Osteoporosis in older people. In addition, it was discovered that people with low Vitamin D levels are more likely to develop severe COVID-19 illness. That includes all the bad things that one can think of such as

suffering hyper-inflammation in the cytokine storm, getting on ventilators and even dying (healththroughfare.com).

Did you know? The scientist from the University of Oxford found out that B vitamins slow brain deterioration caused by disease or injury by 700% (*First for women,* June 15, 2020, p.37).

Did you know? Cucumbers contain 96% water and most of the vitamins that we need every day. One cucumber has the following Vitamins: B1, B2, B3, B5, B6, and Vitamin C. It also has Calcium, Folic Acid, Iron, Magnesium, Phosphorus, Potassium and Zinc. In addition, cucumbers have been used for centuries by European trappers, traders, and explorers for quick meals to thwart off starvation (www.healthhouseinfo.com).

Did you know? Vitamin A is needed in the body for overall health, especially when it comes to vision, immunity, internal organs and reproductive health. It also helps support our lungs heart and kidneys (https://blog.paleohacks.com/why-you-need-vitamin-a/).

Did you know? There are two forms of Vitamin A active and inactive. The active one is known as Retinol, and it is found in animal products. The inactive one is found in plant-based foods. In order to get enough Vitamin A from plant-based foods the body needs to convert a massive amount of Beta-Carotene to Retinoids, a difficult process for the body to do. By the way not all people are able to convert Beta-Carotene into Retinoids. Those who suffer from suboptimal thyroid function, or Diabetes, as well as infants, and children are unable to properly convert the inactive Vitamin A to Retinoids (https://blog.paleohacks.com/ why-you-need-vitamin-a/).

Did you know? The top sources of Vitamin A that contain active form are organ meats such as beef liver, wild-caught salmon, and egg yolks to mention a few. If you plan to supplement your diet artificially with Vitamin A pills you need to be careful, because getting too much of it can cause toxicity and Osteoporosis. It is better to just take multivitamins that includes vitamin A, D as well as others (https://blog.paleohacks.com/why-you-need-vitamin-a/).

Did you know? Scientists found out that nursing home residents who had low blood levels of Zinc were at a significantly higher risk of pneumonia. It has to do with the fact that Zinc helps to boost our immune system as we age. Zinc helps to improve the function of T-cells- a special type of white blood cell that targets and destroys invading bacteria and viruses. Zinc supplementation not only increase the number of T-cells, but it also improves their effectiveness, too. In order to add more Zinc to your diet you should consume shellfish, oysters, crab, pork, turkey, beef, cocoa, cashews, peanuts, chickpeas, mushrooms, and pumpkin seeds. In addition, it was found that intelligent people tend to have more Zinc and Copper in their hair (Health & Nutrition Letter, Tufts University, June/July 2020, p.4 & healthscamsnews.com).

Did you know? The high Zinc content in pumpkin seeds promote healing and helps repair and regenerate tissue faster (Arthritis Foundation, AF-FY21-27SEC-INS-25-T).

Did you know? Cashews and strawberries are the only fruits whose seeds grow on the outside.

Did you know? The banana cannot reproduce itself. It can be propagated only by the hand of humans.

Did you know? Pineapple is not a single fruit. It is made up of a group of berries that have fused together. It is rich in Vitamin C. It also may enhance your weight loss, as well as improve your digestion. Furthermore, it will also keep your bones healthy, and it is packed with disease-fighting antioxidants.

Did you know? Melatonin, known as the sleep hormone, can also help combat viruses and it was found to decrease the entry of viruses into cells. In addition, it prevents cell damage and stop cellular processes that aid in tumor growth. According to researchers, this hormone has anti-inflammatory and immunity-enhancing benefits, plus it increases the activity of antioxidant enzymes that protect cells and tissues against damage and disease. In order to increase Melatonin in the body beside having adequate hours of sleep is to eat pineapple and tart cherries daily as well as take 1-3 mg. of Melatonin 30 minutes before bedtime (*First for women*, June 15, 2020, p.34, April 5, 2021, p. 35 & June 7, 2021, p.33).

Did you know? A leaky gut is often the result of a lack of dietary fiber. This in turn causes inflammation and a dysregulated immune system.

Did you know? There are 7 superfoods that will greatly benefit your immune system including yogurt, garlic, blueberries, kiwi, mushrooms, salmon, beans and tea (black or green) (http://www.aarp.org/health/healty-living/info-2021/superfoods).

Did you know? Non-Alcoholic Fatty Liver Disease (NAFLD) is a very common form of liver disease in the U.S. among people who are obese or overweight. Excess fat tends to accumulate in the liver, often in response to diets high in starches and sugar. People with NAFLD are at high risk of developing liver inflammation that can lead to Cirrhosis, advanced scarring, and liver failure. Recently researchers found out that obese people who have this problem can improve their liver health without even weight loss by fast walking or light jogging during the week (Health & Nutrition Letter, August 2021, p.2).

Did you know? In order to protect yourself against fatty liver buildup and improve your liver function, it is a good idea to walk at least 30 minutes a day. It all has to do with the fact that when the muscles are moving, they quickly burn blood fats for fuel, before the fats can soak into your liver. and cause trouble. In addition, it is a good thing to consume cruciferous vegetables such as broccoli, cauliflower, kale and Brussels' sprouts because they contain phytochemicals that keep inflammation in check as well as *indole* that helps break down liver fat, so the liver can function optimally. It is a also a good thing to add fruits and vegetables to your diet that are rich in BCAAs, including avocado, coconut, dandelion greens, mushrooms, okra, papayas and squash. If one does not like to consume these vegetables and fruit, one can instead take a natural supplement called Hepagard. It includes the following ingredients: Milk Thistle, N-Acetyl Cysteine, Dandelion root, Artichoke leaf and Choline Bitartrate. In addition, one can have another option of just taking 500 mg. of *silymarin* twice a day, once with breakfast and once with dinner. *Silymarin* increase the body's levels of liver detox enzymes by about 43%. The supplement that contains the recommended dose of silymarin is called Life extension Advance milk Thistle - LifeExtension.com (*First for women* June 7, 2021, pp.28-29 & Women's World 10/11/2021, p.17).

Did you know? Studies show that eating more fruit like the delicious papaya, which boast over 300% RDA of Vitamin C, leads to fewer wrinkles, with less thinning and dryness of the skin.

Did you know? Eating 3 tablespoons of mix nuts helps reverse Metabolic-Syndrome factors like excess weight.

Did you know? Food rich in fiber support the growth of good bacteria in the gut, which is especially important when you have arthritis. Keep in mind that people with arthritis tend to have lower levels of gut microbiota diversity. A condition that can lead to pro-inflammatory gut microbes to dominate, and that will trigger a cascade of positive inflammatory effects throughout the body (Women's Nutrition Connection, May 2021 Volume 24, Number 5 p.6).

Did you know? Nuts are actually the seeds of plants. Most are the seeds of trees. Peanuts, however, are the seeds of legume. Nuts contain healthy unsaturated fats, protein, fiber and other nutrients. For example, peanuts and pecans contain lots of B vitamins, almonds are rich in Calcium and Vitamin E, walnuts have lots of Folate, Vitamin E, and Alpha-Linoleic Acid (ALA, an Omega-3 fatty acid).In addition, all nuts contain Magnesium (Harvard Health Letter, September 2019, p.3).

Did you know? Scientists found out that people who ate about an ounce (18 halves) of walnuts a day experienced a lower blood-pressure response to high-stress situation than people who did not eat the nuts. In addition, walnuts are rich in inflammation-fighting Omega-3 fatty acids (Arthritis Foundation, AF-FY21-27SEC-INS-25-T).

Did you know? Beans are packed with protein, fiber and antioxidants, and are fat free. Therefore, when eaten they can prevent muscle shrinkage and help keep muscles stronger and the joints moving freely. The best beans to consume are red beans, small red kidney beans and pinto beans (Arthritis Foundation).

Did you know? Tart cherries mimic the effects of NSAIDs, like Advil, without the side effects (Arthritis Foundation, AF-FY21-27SEC-INS-25-T),

Did you know? Epidemiological research found out that eating whole-grain food, including whole-grain versions of pasta, can reduce risk of various conditions, including heart disease, Diabetes, and several types of cancer. Some even suggest that it may help in weight loss and control, since fiber increases satiety (Wellness Letter, University of California, Berkeley, October 2020, p. 4 & *First for women*, April 26, 2021, p.42).

Did you know? According to a new study from Australia, people who had the highest intake of fiber from foods such as beans, nuts, whole grains and vegetables had about 80% greater chance of living a much longer and healthier life than those who do not consume or add fiber to their diet (Health & Nutrition Letter, Jun/July 2020, p.40).

Did you know? High-fiber foods, like green beans, chickpeas or strawberries, can help prevent weight gain and may even promote weight loss, without the need to go on a diet. Researchers found out that by increasing the intake of fiber by 8 grams per 1,000 calories it will result in loss of about 4/1/2 pounds. It was also found out that the Polyphenols in strawberries, may keep your skin looking younger (EatingWell magazine).

Did you know? According to research distaste for veggies might be genetic. They found out that 25% of people carry a gene that makes cruciferous vegetables (broccoli, cabbage, brussels sprouts, and others) taste bitter. So, instead these people can try sweet veggies such as carrots and beets (Reader's Digest, Sept. 2020, p.54).

Did you know? Cooking at home more frequently will help you consume less calories than if you were to take out food or eat in a restaurant, as well as save you money per year.

Did you know? The easy way to enhance corn's natural sweetness is to add a little sugar to the water (4tsp. per gallon of water) when boiling. The *sucrose* will not make the corn too sweet, but it will prevent the kernels' natural sugars from escaping during the boiling process (*First for women,* June 15, 2020, p.77).

Did you know? Eating foods labeled low-fat sometimes means you are actually eating as many calories as the full-fat version, as well as getting more carbs and sugar.

Did you know? Oils that are high in "healthy" unsaturated fats- like avocado, canola, olive and safflower – are linked to a lower risk of heart disease and stroke (Consumer Reports, June 2021, p.8).

Did you know? Canola oil is one of the few cooking oils that has healthy Omega-3 fats.

Did you know? It is believed today, after extensive research, that coconut oil actually is not healthy alternative to vegetable oil because it raises LDL ("bad") cholesterol, which in turn increases the risk of heart disease. However, coconut oil is still better than animal oils such as butter, and lard (Health After 50, University of California, Berkeley, September 2020 p.7 & Wellness Letter, University of California, Berkeley October 2020, p.1).

Did you know? Researchers discovered a rice-cooking method that reduces calories by 10% and potentially up to 50% for healthier varieties. Just add a teaspoon of coconut oil to the cooking water, then put the cooked rice in the refrigerator for 12 hours. It all has to do with the fact that the coconut oil's fat transforms digestible starch into resistant starch, which we cannot digest, so we process fewer calories. Cooling promotes the conversion (Reader's Digest December 2020/January 2021, p.39).

Did you know? Scientists discovered that olive oil may lower the risk of malignant breast cancer in women by 68% (Health & Nutrition Letter, June/July 2020, p.2).

Did you know? Frozen vegetables actually are healthier than nonfrozen. Why? This is due to the practice of farmers freezing the vegetables immediately after harvesting, so, they will retain most of their vitamins and minerals.

Did you know? Many of the healthiest breads in a grocery store are kept in the freezer section. These breads, like for example whole-grains sprouted bread, are made without adding preservatives to them, so they can therefore be likely to spoil quickly (AARP Bulletin, October 2020, p.22).

Did you know? A study in 2019 found out that those who ate more vegetables and fruits ended up boosting their scores on thinking and memory tests (Reader Digest, Sept. 2020, p.63).

Did you know? Researchers found out that the left hippocampus was heftier in healthy eaters than in unhealthy ones, regardless of age, sex, weight, exercise habits, or general health. In addition, it was found that eating the right foods, like eating fresh fruits and vegetables, salads, and grilled fish, while skipping the wrong stuff, could help protect against cognitive decline and Dementia (Reader's Digest, Sept. 2020, pp.64-65).

Did you know? Eating fatty fish like wild- caught Salmon or Tuna, which are rich in Omega-3 fatty acid, can boost your skin's defenses against UV damage. Researchers also found out that eating about 5 ounces of Omega-3 rich fish each week can decrease the development of precancerous skin lesions by about 30% as well as reduce the risk of heart attacks and strokes (EatingWell Magazine & www.NutritionAction.com).

Did you know? Most heart attacks occur in the daytime, generally between 6AM and 12 Noon. So, if you are told by your cardiologist to take a baby Aspirin once a day, it is best to take it at night. Why? Aspirin has a 24-hour "half-life"; therefore, if most heart attacks happen in the wee hours of the morning, the Aspirin would be strongest in your system at that time.

Did you know? Exercise, in general, tends to reduce the risk of death after a heart attack. Exercising after a heart attack does not have to be strenuous, and it can just be moderately difficult (Healthy Aging, Icahn School of Medicine at Mount Sinai, May 2021, p.3).

Did you know? Aspirin can last in your medicine cabinet for many years. Remember, when it begins to smell like vinegar, it will be no longer good, and should be disposed of.

Did you know? Red watermelon is a good source of Vitamin C. In addition, it has Lycopene, an antioxidant that may help protect you against heart disease and some types of cancer. Researchers also found out that eating foods that contain water, such as watermelon (92% water), cucumber (95% water), salad greens (90% water), or strawberries (91% water), can help us feel satisfied while eating fewer calories, when compared to just drinking water (EatingWell Magazine).

Did you know? What is good for the heart is good for the brain. Besides healthy eating and staying active, you need to avoid tobacco, minimize alcohol consumption, get adequate sleep and manage stress. By following these suggestions, they will help keep the blood vessels in your brain clear and flexible, which may stave off some form of Dementia (Tufts University, Health & Nutrition Letter, June 2021, p.3).

Did you know? Eating mixed berries like blueberries, strawberries or raspberries will help keep our hearts healthy. A study that was done on women showed that when they ate four or more servings of blueberries per week, they were able to reduce the risk of heart attacks by 34%. Why? Blueberries for example contain health-promoting plant compounds such as Anthocyanins and Ellagic Acid that are especially helpful for blood vessels. The also contain phytochemicals that contribute to the prevention and treatment of cardiovascular disease, cancer and Diabetes (EatingWell Magazine

& AARP Bulletin, March 2019 p.18 & Tufts University, Health & Nutrition Letter, June 2021, p.1).

Did you know? If you do not like to eat berries, you can substitute it with fruits and vegetables with similar colors that have similar phytochemicals, such as purple potatoes, sweet potatoes, red cabbage, spinach and kale (Tufts University, Health & Nutrition Letter, June 2021, p.1).

Did you know? While there is no cure for Dementia, healthy eating may play a role in preserving cognitive health as we age. It was also found that older adults who followed the Mediterranean-DASH Diet, which is rich in vegetables, fruits, whole grains, fish and extra -virgin olive oil -retained more brain cells than older adults who did not follow the diet. This diet is linked to a slower rate of cognitive decline – equivalent to about 7.5 years of younger age. It has to do with the fact that it reduces brain inflammation as well as prevent the buildup of plaque and neurofibrillary tangles, which are suspected to contribute to the symptoms of Alzheimer's Disease. In addition, the DHA and EPA Omega -3 fatty acids found in fish can protect the brain and contribute to improved memory function in older adults. People, who followed the diet most closely, were about 53% less likely to develop Alzheimer's Disease than those who did not. The researchers found out that even a small change reduced the risk for Alzheimer's (Tufts University, Health & Nutrition Letter, June/July 2020, p.1 & June 2021 p.3).

Did you know? Humans can survive entirely on a diet of potatoes and butter, which provide all the necessary nutrients the human body needs.

Did you know? You can lose weight and fat by eating Macadamia Nuts. Why? These nuts contain Magnesium and Palmitoleic Acid that activate fat-burning enzymes inside your body's digestive track.

Did you know? Canadian scientists found out that snacking on purple or red grapes daily can double your fat loss on any diet. The grapes contain Resveratrol, Cyanidin and Vitamin C. These are powerful nutrients that calm the adrenal glands, so they produce 33% less fat-storing hormones.

Did you know? The Sulfur compounds in garlic may help lower cholesterol and blood pressure.

Did you know? Researcher found out that onions tend to control blood sugar similar to drugs (Supermarket Super Remedies by Jerry Baker, p.310).

Did you know? Researchers from Vanderbilt University found out that dieting women who drank just half a cup of water before meals, lost just as much weight and fat as those who drank grapefruit juice or ate grapefruit.

Did you know? If you want to lose weight, the easy way, you should follow Dr. Oz's advice. First you should eat your first meal at 10AM and finish dinner by 6PM. Second, in order to lose fat from the middle section of your body you need to eat omega3-rich walnuts or salmon. Third, adding Thai hot sauce called *sriracha* to your food tends to help burn fat because it boasts 20 different fat-burning chemicals in the body. Third, drinking green tea tend to also speed metabolism in the body (Women's World 10/11/2021, p.23).

Did you know? Scientists found out that Vitamins B-12 plays a vital role in maintaining a speedy metabolism, and by taking adequate levels of Vitamin D, one can increase fat burning in the body by 40%.

Did you know? Just one cup a day of hot cocoa can boosts your good cholesterol (Supermarket Super Remedies by Jerry Baker, p.129).

Did you know? Beer reduces the risk of developing kidney stones by 40%.

Did you know? Nicotine and liquor are worse than caffeine for sleep. Drinking alcohol or using Nicotine before bedtime reduces sleep efficiency and sleep duration (Reader's Digest, Sept. 2020, p.57).

Did you know? Caffeine increases the power of Aspirin and other painkillers, which is why it is found in some medicines.

Did you know? The number of calories burned while eating celery surpasses the number of calories contained in celery.

Did you know? About 90 percent of Type-2 Diabetes cases could be prevented if people were to maintain a healthy weight. Even minimal weight loss can slash Diabetes risk in half. Just losing 5 pounds over two years can lower the risk by up to 47%. In addition, one should stay away from smoking, be physically active, eat a diet that is high in fruits and vegetables. It is also important to also eat more good fats rather than bad fats, eat few simple carbs, eat things high in whole grains, and consume fewer sugar-sweetened beverages as well as avoid refined sugars (Nutrition Action Health Letter 2020 p.3 & Healthy Aging, Icahn School of Medicine at Mount Sinai, May 2021, p.3 & *First for women* June 7, 2021, p.32).

Did you know? People do not need to lose a lot of weight to make a difference in their Diabetes risk. High-risk adults who lost just 5% to 7% of their starting body weight - that is about 8 to 11 pounds for 160-pound person for example -- lowered their risk of Diabetes by 58% (Harvard Women's Health Watch, November 2020, p.6).

Did you know? If you eat at least 20 grams of protein first thing every morning, it will boost your metabolism by 25% for the rest of the day, as well as aid in reducing your appetite so you will consume less calories before lunch (***First*** *for women*, April 5, 2021, p.28).

Did you know? The primary cause of Varicose Veins is a buildup of the clotting protein called Fibrin. Fibrins tend to clog blood flow and causes veins to bulge and stretch. So, one needs to eat food that has Bromelain, which is an enzyme that breaks down Fibrin, and flushes it out of the bloodstream. Bromelain can be found in pineapples for example.

Did you know? Spinach that is frozen immediately after harvesting, NOT fresh spinach, tends to have higher concentrations than fresh of Folate, the mineral linked to a lower risk for hypertension (Arthritis Foundation, AF-Fy21-27sec-ins-25-T).

Did you know? According to a new study from Australia, people who had the highest intake of fiber from foods such as whole grains, fruits, vegetables, nuts or beans had an almost 80% greater chance of living a long and healthy life. They are also less likely to suffer from Diabetes, Depression, Hypotension, Dementia or other disabilities (Health & Nutrition Letter 2020, p.4).

Did you know? Fiber is especially important to add to your diet because it can help flush out toxins from your body. In addition, it can also help with gut health and inflammation, which can result in autoimmune diseases later down the road. It can also help you lose weight because ingesting fiber will make you feel full, and therefore you will eat less food and reduce calories intake.

Did you know? Raspberries and blackberries are low in calories but high in fiber. They have 8 grams of fiber per cup as well as vitamins, minerals and antioxidants. They may protect you from Diabetes, Cancer, Obesity, Arthritis, and other health conditions. So, if you need to pack in more fiber and nutrients into your diet, both of these fruits are great natural options.

Did you know? Scientist, after decades of studies on people all over the world, have discovered that the people who eat no fried fish, but consume vegetables like cabbage, broccoli, cauliflower and Brussels sprouts, berries and nuts especially walnuts, tend to live the longest, and stay in the best of health.

Did you know? If you want to avoid cancer, the first thing you should do is to avoid smoking. Secondly, avoid eating red meat as much as possible. A little is fine, but the more you eat, the higher your risk of getting one of these cancers will be.

Did you know? For women, red meat consumption is TWICE as significant as smoking when it comes to cancer risk.

Did you know? Any meat that has been tweaked to enhance its flavor or improve its preservation by salting, curing, fermentation or smoking, is considered processed, (such as bacon, and cold cuts). These foods are classified as carcinogenic and can increase the risk of cancer in humans (Health & Nutrition Letter, June/July 2020 p.3).

Did you know? If you want to decrease your risk of cancer, try to eliminate processed meats from your diet, such as beef, pork, lamb, sausage, bacon, deli meats, and hot dogs. You should also avoid sugar sweetened beverages and refined grain products. In addition, you will also need to avoid alcohol consumption, because all forms of alcoholic beverage - wine, beer, liquor – contains ethanol, which is a cancer-causing substance. Furthermore, one needs to keep walking and exercising at a moderate level, every day of the week. Being overweight or obese is a known risk factor for cancer too. Losing just a few pounds can lower the cancer risk greatly (Health After 50, University of California, Berkeley, September 2020, p.8).

Did you know? Food rich in flavonoids include apples, berries, black and green tea, broccoli, citrus fruits, grapes, kale, legumes, onions, peppers and red wine, all of which can help decrease cell damage and protect cell membranes from inflammation in our bodies (Women's Nutrition Connection, May 2021, p.6).

Did you know? Humans are the only beings that enjoy spicy foods. In addition, scientists discovered that people who eat spicy food every day have a 14% chances of living longer compared to people who do not.

Did you know? Diet rich in red meat is linked to many health problems, such as heart disease, Type-2 Diabetes, and Colorectal Cancer. In addition, a Harvard-led study published on June 12, 2019, by BMJ, found that boosting the intake of red meat increases the risk for early death (Harvard Health Letter, September 2019, p.8).

Did you know? A study published online on June 10, 2019, by *Circulation* claims that by having three healthy lifestyle changes, it could be possible to increase the lifespans of almost 100 million people around the world. So first, one needs to reduce high blood pressure with medication, secondly, one needs to have less sodium in their diet, and lastly, one needs to reduce the intake of trans-fats (Health & Nutrition Letter, Tufts University, 5 Health Reports from Tufts p.4).

Did you know? There are foods that can clean your arteries. Take oranges, for instance. They are full of Vitamin C, but in addition they have Pectin, a soluble fiber that blocks the absorption of cholesterol, similar to a statin drug. In addition, oranges also contain Folate that helps clear the bloodstream of harmful compounds that can lead to a heart attack. Furthermore, pears are healthy to eat because they also contain a lot of dietary fiber in the form of Pectin.

Did you know? During World War II, the U.S. Department of Agriculture asked Florida orange growers to ramp up production in order to get Vitamin C to the troops. No long after, a Florida based company started selling a new product called Minute Maid orange juice.

Did you know? You can lose some weight and fat by eating Macadamia Nuts. Why? These nuts contain Magnesium and Palmitoleic Acid that activates fat-burning enzymes inside your body's abdominal fat cells.

Did you know? Eating fennel stimulates the production of bile, and that in turn helps to speed up the breakdown of fat in the body, especially the lumpy, bumpy, fat and Cellulite. This is because eating bitter foods regularly, like fennel, can increase metabolism by up to 53% (*First for women*, June 15, 2020, p.27).

Did you know? Adding Turmeric to you diet, which acts as a potent anti-inflammatory, can help the liver break up fatty deposits in the body, so it is advised to get 1 tsp of Turmeric a day. Turmeric has been shown to whittle down waistline fat by 30% (*First for women*, June 15, 2020, p.27).

Did you know? Researchers found out that the spiced curry has powerful effects on heart health. Just consuming half a teaspoon of this spice daily tend to reduce cholesterol and Triglycerides in the body and raise the levels of good HDL cholesterol (Reader's Digest February 1, 2021, p.66).

Did you know? Nutrients in Apricots such as Beta-Cryptoxanthin and Magnesium may prevent Osteoarthritis and ease the pain associated with this condition (Arthritis Foundation, AF-FY21-27SEC-INS-25-T)

Did you know? Scientists also found out that grapefruit contains unique phytonutrients that burn fat and help intensify liver metabolism (*First for women*, June 15, 2020, p.27).

Did you know? Scientists from Georgetown University found out that eating mushrooms can kick-start fat burning in the body within 48 hours of ingestion and can help shed up to 5 extra pounds of belly fat per month (*First for women*, June 15, 2020, p.27).

Did you know? Many of us are deficient in Lecithin (good fat) because some of the foods highest in Lecithin, such as egg yolks, butter, red meat, organ meats (like liver), seafood, and poultry, are high in cholesterol, and we were told to stay away from foods that are high in cholesterol (bad fat.) Lecithin is naturally occurring fat (good fat) that works to break down harmful fats that stiffen cell membranes and slow fat burning. Lecithin also keeps cell membranes pliable and healthy, as well as keeps the metabolism fired up. In addition, it also helps break down fat stored throughout the body including fat from thighs, hips and belly. In addition, it also reduces fatigue and menopausal symptoms as well as improves our immunity. Furthermore, it was found to rapidly reduce body mass without any side effects (*First for women*, April 5, 2021, p.27).

Did you know? It was found that sunflower seeds help the liver banish stubborn fat. The seeds have remarkably high levels of natural Lecithin, which is one of the compounds the gallbladder uses to dissolve and break down fat (*First for women*, June 15, 2020, p.27).

Did you know? It is advised to eat hard-boiled or poached eggs, since higher heat cooking methods, like frying, can reduce the Lecithin content of eggs. In addition, it is also recommended to steam or sauté green vegetables, because gently cooking greens makes their Lecithin more bioavailable, so one can get more bang for their bite (*First, for women*, April 5, 2021).

Did you know? Canadian scientists found out that snacking on purple or red grapes daily can double your fat loss on any diet. The grapes contain resveratrol, cyanidin and vitamin C. These are powerful nutrients that calm the adrenal glands, so they produce 33% less fat-storing hormones.

Did you know? Whole grapes, especially the purple color kind, have over1,600 natural plant compounds including antioxidants and other polyphenols that benefit our health. UCLA researchers found out that consumption of grapes on a daily basis may be very beneficial to the health of our brains (Health Magazine, September 2021, p.61).

Did you know? There are **5** main foods that can cause bone deterioration. They are*: **First**,* soft drinks (even diet soda) tend to lower bone mineral density in older women, which increases the risk for Osteoporosis. This is due to the fact that sodas are packed with Phosphoric Acid which causes increase in the body's acidity level. As result, the body pulls Calcium out of the bones in order to bring the acidity levels back to normal. **Second,** table salt causes loss of Calcium and that in turns weakens bone. **Third,** excess in Caffeine drinking from coffee or soda leads to cause the leaching of Calcium from bones. **Fourth,** hydrogenated oils that are man-made do not contain Vitamin K, which is an essential vitamin for strong bones. **Fifth,** 100% wheat bran contains high levels of Phytates which can prevent the body from absorbing Calcium. So, it is recommended to switch from 100% wheat bran to sprouted grain products instead, since they contain fewer Phytates (Health & Nutrition Letter, Tufts University, 5 Health Reports from Tufts, pp.3-7).

Did you know? People who drank diet soda daily had 36% greater risk of developing a metabolic syndrome and 67% had a greater risk of developing Diabetes. Both of these types of conditions significantly raise the odds of having a stroke or heart attack.

Did you know? You can keep your bones strong by eating dried plums, pumpkins seeds, and cheddar cheese. The pumpkin seeds are loaded with Magnesium. Magnesium helps protect bones from getting brittle and susceptible to injury. Cheddar cheese is not only loaded with Calcium, but also with Linoleic Acid CLA (Conjugated Linoleic Acid) that is a bone builder. Research proves that this acid strengthens bone density in places such as the forearm and hips, where injuries tend to occur most often.

Did you know? People that can benefit the most from animal-based diet are those that have autoimmune conditions, gut/digestion issues, diabetes and obesity (Nutrition Watchdog Ezine 2021).

Did you know? The scientific name for bananas is *musa sapientum,* which means "fruit of the wise men."

Did you know? Although bananas are often pictured as growing on trees, the banana "tree" is actually an herb. The banana is the fruit of this herb.

Did you know? Bananas are naturally radioactive. It is due to the fact that they contain relatively high amounts of Potassium-40, which is one of the radioactive isotopes of Potassium that is found in nature.

Did you know? The banana is a happy fruit. Bananas have Potassium which can help prevent Calcium loss, ulcers, high blood pressure, and even certain kinds of cancer. In addition, it can also help relieve irritable emotions, anger, or depression. The Vitamin B6 in bananas will help to increase your focus and mental acuity. Scientists have found out that eating bananas for breakfast, as a snack, or at lunch, can boost your concentration and keep you more alert during the day.

Did you know? Bananas are "low glycemic" foods because they release energy slowly in the body, preventing your Insulin-levels from spiking.

Did you know? Bananas that are barely ripe (that are a bit green) contain resistant starch, a type of fiber that delays, or "resist," being digested until after it passes through the small intestine. Eating a meal rich in resistant starch is proven to speed fat burning in the body (First for women, August 30, 2021, p.27).

Did you know? The Banana Split is claimed to be invented in both Latrobe, Pennsylvania, and Wilmington, Ohio, in 1907.

Did you know? Holding a banana peel over a bruise for 10 to 30 minutes will remove its color (1000LifeHacks.com).

Did you know? The average person eats about 33 pounds of bananas each year. That is approximately 100 individual bananas per person.

Did you know? Too much Potassium taken as a supplement can cause irregular heartbeat and other side effects such as: confusion, temporal paralysis, low blood pressure and coma.

Did you know? Leafy greens (oxalates), nightshades, grains (gluten) and beans (very high in lectin) are the most toxic plant food for humans (Nutrition Watchdog Ezine 2021).

Did you know? Nightshade is a group of plants that are a part of the *Solanaceae* family. Many nightshade plants are common, and we eat them probably every day. The four most popular nightshade plants that we tend to eat often in large quantities include tomatoes, potatoes, peppers and eggplants. However, they are known to cause inflammation because of a compound that they have called "solanine" which can irritate the digestive tract, and even cause breakdown in red blood cells. They also can cause worsening of Arthritis in many people, as well as exacerbate irritable bowel syndrome, heartburn, acid reflux and other GI issues. In addition, they contain seeds that can be harmful to those who are prone to Diverticulitis (an inflammatory disease of the large intestine). So, if you have Arthritis, sever digestive disorders, or an autoimmune disease it is best to avoid nightshades most or all of the time.

Did you know? Nightshades not only include tomatoes, potatoes, sweet peppers and eggplants. They also include okra, all type of peppers - hot or sweet, sorrel, gooseberries, tobacco, paprika, cayenne peppers and chili powder.

Did you know? Some foods that have been associated with increased risk for Type-2 Diabetes and heart disease are the kind that accelerate inflammation in the body. These foods include refined carbohydrates, French fries and other fried foods, soda and other sweetened beverages, red meat (hot dogs and sausages) as well as margarine, shortening and lard (The Food-Health Connection, Harvard Medical School, pp.2-4).

Did you know? Inflammation in the body can cause joint pain for older individuals. Therefore, the Geriatric Society of the U.S. recommends Acetaminophen like Tylenol, as a first line treatment for chronic pain in seniors because it has fewer side effects than anti-inflammatory drugs like NSAIDs like Ibuprofen (Motrin or Advil). However, statistics from the national database suggest that Acetaminophen overdoses send more than 50,000 people to the U.S. emergency departments every year. It is due to the fact that too much Acetaminophen harms the liver and for some people the cut-off of daily dose is too much, or they took other medications that contained Acetaminophen and they did not realize it (Healthy Aging, Icahn School of Medicine at Mount Sinai, February 2019, p.6).

Did you know? There are foods that will help to combat inflammation such as: olive oil, green leafy vegetables including kale collard greens, spinach, Romaine lettuce, Bok Choy, mustard greens, Swiss chard, turnip greens and even broccoli, nuts like almonds and walnuts, fatty fish like salmon, mackerel, sardines and tuna. Iin addition, fruits such as oranges blueberries, cherries and strawberries are also effective at fighting inflammation (The Food-Health Connection, Harvard medical School p.4 & Women's Nutrition Connection, May 2021, p.4 & Arthritis Foundation, AF-FY21-27SEC-INS-25-T)

Did you know? Mushrooms help combat inflammation and oxidation in the body (Reader's Digest, February 1, 2021, p.66).

Did you know? High-fructose corn syrup is linked to Diabetes and other health problems and so is honey. Even though, honey is healthier than sugar it affects the body in about the same way as sugar. Honey breaks down in the body into Glucose and Fructose in proportions that are similar to sugar and high fructose corn syrup (Health & Nutrition Letter, June/July 2020, p.2 & Women's Nutrition Connection, May 2021, p.5).

Did you know? Honey is still healthier than sugar because it is packed with antioxidants that will reduce oxidative stress. It also contains vitamins, amino acids and minerals such as Phosphorus, Calcium, Potassium and Magnesium. In addition, it also has anti-inflammatory, antiviral, antibacterial and antifungal properties.

However, honey's nutritional values vary based on the nectar source. In general, the darker the honey, the greater its nutritional value. Honey can also help you sleep better. Researchers found out that honey is nature's best sleeping pill because it increases the activity of *Serotonin* – which is a calming neurotransmitter. It also curtails the release of *Orexin*, a substance that can prevent you from falling asleep and keep you from staying asleep. In addition, honey can quell coughing, heal wounds and burns when applied topically, help hangovers, and may help even with itch relief of insect bites (Health, January/February 2021, p.10 & Big Book of Household Tips, BottomLineBooks p.167).

Did you know that children under the age of 12 months should not be given honey to eat? Because children 12 months or younger have underdeveloped immune systems that leave them vulnerable to Botulism. Botulism is a serious form of food poisoning. Dirt and dust containing Botulism bacteria spores can creep into honey and can lead to serious health issues for young children (The Old Farmer's Almanac, Fall & Winter 2020, p.18).

Did you know? New research (2020 - 2021) reveals that artificial sweeteners can spike our blood sugar to dangerously high levels. So, instead of using artificial sweeteners, it is a good idea to use alternatives that can boost our health such as: Stevia, Monk fruit or Manuka Honey. By the way, 1 tsp. of Manuka Honey was found to be enough to neutralize 85% of illness-causing bacteria and halt their spread entirely, according to research in *Microbiology*. The reason has to do with the fact that it contains a compound called *Methylglyoxal* that stops germs from anchoring into cells and causing infection. It is important to keep in mind that the UMF- Unique Manuka Factor - should be at least 10. The higher the UMF, the more *Methylglyoxal* it contains. A good kind to try is Steens Raw Manuka Honey UMF 10+, available at grocery stores and SteensHoney.com (*First for women*, April 5, 2021, p.36).

Did you know? The amount of antioxidants in a plant depends on its color. The deeper the color the more antioxidants it contains. Antioxidants in general tend to boost brain function, improve memory and prevent oxidative damage in the brain. It also improves vision and promotes skin health.

Did you know? Sweet potatoes are not members of the Nightshade family.

Did you know? Sweet potatoes are very nutritious. They are loaded with carotenoids and are a good source of Vitamin K and fiber (www.NutritionAction.com).

Did you know? Sweet potatoes belong to the Morning Glory family and are not related to either yams or white potatoes. They generally come from either Central or South America. They contain a lot of nutrients including massive amount of Beta-Carotene, the nutrient that our bodies turn into Vitamin A. They also contain about 35% - 40% of the necessary Vitamin C that we need for a day. These two nutrients are linked to a reduced risk of knee and spine Osteoarthritis. Sweet potatoes also contain Manganese, Vitamin B6, Potassium, Copper, Niacin, Thiamine and Magnesium. They also help to stabilize blood sugar, and help the body become more sensitive to Insulin. This is due partly to the fact that sweet potatoes are high on fiber content and antioxidants which help to slow the absorption of sugar in the body.

Did you know? Sweet potatoes, yams, and regular white potatoes are actually all from different plant families and are not related to one another. They contain however, a lot of nutrients such as Beta-Carotene that turns in our body to Vitamin A. They also contain Vitamin C, Manganese and Vitamin B6.

Did you know? Yams are a tuber vegetable. They are actually part of the Lily family. Yams originated in Africa and Asia and there are about 600 different varieties of them. However, they are not as nutrient dense or full of antioxidants as sweet potatoes. Yams are higher in calories, carbohydrates and fiber as well as contain a good amount of Vitamin C, B6, Potassium and Manganese. The Potassium and Manganese in yams are vital elements that are good for bones, nerve health, heart function and metabolism.

Did you know? Potatoes alone supply every vital nutrient except for calcium, vitamin A, and vitamin D. They are the are one of the top five most important food crops on planet Earth (littlepotatoes.com).

Did you know? White potatoes come from the *Solanaceae* family, which is related to tomatoes, peppers and eggplant and is considered part of the "nightshade" group of vegetables. There are literally thousands of different types of potatoes.

Did you know? The first potato chips were prepared by Chef George Crum in 1853.

Did you know? Since opening 60+ years ago, Waffle House restaurants have served about 150 waffles every minute.

Did you know? Almonds can prevent joint pain. They are loaded with a substance called Alpha-Tocopherol, which is a form of Vitamin E. The body uses Alpha- Tocopherol to fight inflammation which is a big factor in fighting Arthritis and joint pain. It was also found that Vitamin E may reduce the risk of developing Alzheimer's Disease and other forms of Dementia.

Did You know? Vitamin E is a well-known antioxidant that can protect your body from free radicals that can harm your cells, tissues and organs. However, Vitamin E supplements are not as good for the body as getting it from food. For example, a handful of sunflower seeds will meet your daily requirement for heart-healthy Vitamin E and in addition, will provide you also with healthy fats and fiber that will protect your heart (Consumer Reports On Health, 2021, p.11).

Did you know? Pecans are technically fruits rather than nuts. Also, Pecans are high in protein. One ounce of Pecans contains three grams of protein. They also contain healthy fats, such as Oleic Acid, which is a monounsaturated fat that can help to reduce the risk of developing breast cancer (Life Extension magazine, July 2020, p.89).

Did you know? The all-American brownie was created at Chicago's fancy Palmer House Hotel. It happened when in 1893, the organizers of the World's Columbian Exposition, that took place there asked Bertha Palmer, a Chicago socialite, and the wife of the owner of the Palmer House Hotel, to provide a dessert for the event. She requested that the chef at the hotel make a "ladies' dessert" that would fit into a boxed lunch. Today we call them Brownies.

Did you know? During the late 1920s, Mississippians used to beat the heat by sinking their feet into the mud of the Mississippi River. Somehow, that became the inspiration for the Mississippi Mud Pie, whose dense chocolate resembles the river's muddy banks.

Did you know? In 1912, Cleveland-based candy maker Clarence Crane came up with a sweet that could stand up to the heat. He borrowed a machine use by pharmacists to make pills and came up with a new candy with a hole in the middle of them and called it the Life Saver.

Did you know? According to Harvard Medical School, too much sugar may accelerate the aging of cells. In addition, one sugary soda per day was associated with a decline in test scores.

Did you know? Peanut oil is used for cooking in submarines because it does not smoke unless it is heated above 450F.

Did you know? Olive oil is known for its many health benefits, including an ability to help protect you against cardiovascular disease and mild cognitive impairment (Life Extension July 2020, p.20).

Did you know? Olive oil is not the only healthy oil. Avocado oil is also a healthy oil that provides heart-protecting benefits and has a buttery flavor (Consumer Reports On Health, June 2021, p.1).

General Little-Known Facts

Did you know? 400 million years ago, there were 22 hours in a day and more than 400 days in a year (Weird World 1.pdf).

Did you know? Rainbows can appear at night, they are called "Moonbows" (Weird World 1.pdf).

Did you know? The first people to use superstition were the Neanderthals 50,000 years ago, in Western Asia. The first superstitious belief was of survival in an afterlife. That caused the people who believed it to bury their dead with supplies for their afterlife journey. Superstition lead to religion and one group's superstition became the religion of another.

Did you know? There are only about 4 mammals in all the animal kingdom on this planet who do not make their own Vitamin C. They are Humans, monkeys, Guinea pigs and fruit bats. The reason as to why they cannot make Vitamin C is due to the fact that they do not have the enzyme that converts Glucose in the blood to Vitamin C. Most other animals make their own Vitamin C, such as: horses, goats, pigs, dogs, cats, ferrets, squirrels, to mention a few (Ultimate Health Special Report, Number 3 p.2).

Did you know? The Western United States has more oil in the ground than all the other proven reserves on Earth. Here are the official estimates: 8 times as much as Saudi Arabia, 18 times as much oil as Iraq, 21 times as much oil as Kuwait, 22 times as much oil as Iran, 500 times as much oil as Yemen. However, the reason why we do not extract it is because the environmentalists and others have blocked all efforts to help America become independent of foreign oil (http://www.usgs/newsroom/article.asp?ID=1911).

Did you know? Three of our Founder Fathers, Thomas Jefferson, John Adams and James Monroe were United States Presidents who all were ended up dying on July 4th but in different years.

Did you know? In Arlington National Cemetery the guard takes 21 steps during his walk across the Tom of The Unknown. The reason is based on the 21-gun salute which is the highest honor given to any military or foreign dignity. The origin of the number 21 in the Gun Salute came from the fact that the USA declared its independence on July 4, 1776. So, if you add up the numbers 1+7+7+6, you end up getting the number 21.

Did you know? The founder of FedEx saved his company from bankruptcy by going to Vegas, gambling it's last $500 on blackjack and winning $27,000 – enough to keep FedEx going for another week while it secured additional funds.

Did you know? Every year, more than 300 million tons of plastic are produced worldwide, and around half of the produced materials are designed for single-use purposes. Therefore, recently the researchers at the Ben-Gurion University in Israel are looking into a biodegradation method with bacteria, a more environmentally friendly way to recycle and break plastics down (www.aabgu.org).

Did you know? A dust storm can be 1 mile high and 100 miles wide (AZ Weather Authorities: Monsoon 2021).

Did you know? Most dust particles in our houses are made from dead skin.

Did you know? A tiny amount of lead dust is enough to poison a child and put his family at risk, especially when renovating and removing an old paint. Make sure that you hire an EPA-certified lead-safe renovator to do the job (Solutions by EDF-Environmental Defense Fund Vol.52, No.2 /Spring 2021, p.13).

Did you know? Too much smoke in the atmosphere tends to reduce the amount of rainfall, and less rising warm air can cause less rainstorms (AZ Weather Authorities: Monsoon 2021).

Did you know? As little as 6 inches of rushing water can move a parked car (AZ Weather Authorities: Monsoon 2021).

Did you know? An active monsoon day can produce 100,000 lightning flashes across Arizona, and the average monsoon storm can last between 30 to 60 minutes (AZ Weather Authorities: Monsoon 2021).

Did you know? The first product to have a bar code was Wrigley's gum.

Did you know? Pearls dissolve in vinegar.

Did you know? In order to clean an oven window, you need to use a dishwasher powder tablet (the hard type, not the gel pack kind) dip it in warm water and then use it like a pumice stone to buff the oven window clean. The detergents and the abrasive texture of the tablet will lift off baked-on grease and leave no residue (Women's World, 10/11/21, p.40).

Did you know? Traces of peanuts can be found in dynamite.

Did you know? When you peel a banana from the bottom, you won't have to pick the little "string things" off of it (1000LifeHacks.com).

Did you know? The King of Hearts is the only King without a moustache in a standard dec of cards.

Did you know? Venus is the only planet that rotates clockwise.

Did you know? Baking soda catalyzes Superglue. A light sprinkle will cause even a large amount to set in seconds (1000LifeHacks.com).

Did you know? When filling your car with gas, hold the trigger halfway. By doing so you will get more gas and less air in the gas tank (1000LifeHacks.com).

Did you know? Israel became a cyber superpower in 2021. It is all due to the fact that its enemies keep on cyber attacking it with no mercy. Therefore, the enemy indirectly forced it to develop the greatest protection against these attacks. Today many countries are purchasing the most advanced and sophisticated cyber security systems in the world, from Israel.

Did you know? If you plan to buy a hybrid car, keep in mind that the battery does not last forever, and that after a few years you will need to replace it. Replacement will cost you about 10,000 dollars.

Did you know? The dirtiest item in most restaurants is the menu. In addition, if you order wine by the glass, it is often poured from a bottle that was opened days ago. Furthermore, seafood stews and soups tend to be made from fish that is too old to serve any other way (BottomLine Personal Volume 41 Number 9 page #4).

Did you know? Two hundred Navajo Code-Talkers, who participated in WWII, and helped the USA win the war, also helped to save many lives. They were able to help for example, a company of marines that landed in Iwo Jima and was pinned down by enemy forces. The reason has to do with the fact that the request for help was sent in the Navajo language, and it was translated to English in 20 seconds. If the message for help were to be sent in the English code it would have taken 30 minutes to translate, and by then probably most of the marines would have lost their lives.

Did you know? Almost 90% of forests fires are caused by human negligence, according to the National Interagency Fire Center (Defenders Magazine, Summer 2021, p.17).

Did you know? Japan made all the metals for the 2021 Tokyo Olympics out of discarded smartphones and laptops.

Did you know? Adding a small amount of 7up in a flower vase will preserve them for a much longer time (1000LifeHacks.com).

Did you know? Half of all medical bills tend to contain errors or are hard to read and understand. So, do not pay it right away. Instead, call and check with *Consumer Report.* They will advise you how to quickly deal with the confusing medical bills that you received (CR Consumer Report, June 2021, p.9).

Did you know? In 1964, on the floor of the U.S. Senate, Democrats held the longest filibuster in our Nation's history, 60 days, in an attempt to prevent the passing of one thing -- it was the Civil Rights Act.

Did you know? The real reason why every hotel today in the U.S. offers free ice has to do with Kemmons Wilson, the founder of Holiday Inn. Wilson introduced ice machines and free ice to his customers after staying at competing hotels that charged high prices for ice. Yes, people had to pay for every cube in those days. As the Holiday Inn franchises spread, the free ice trend spread across the country. Nowadays, hotel guests use ice machines for everything from serving cocktails to filling up their coolers.

Did you know? The odds of a Friday falling on the 13th of a month occurs once every 212.35 days (Reader's Digest, June 2020, p.43).

Did you know? The odd of finding a four-leaf clover is one in 10,000 (Reader's Digest, June 2020, p.43).

Did you know? The ZZ plant is native to East Africa and is considered to be one of the most resilient houseplants out there. It only needs watering once a month and can be placed in any type of light other than direct sunlight (Health, January/February 2021, p.10).

Did you know? The line that separates day and night sides on Earth is called the Terminator.

Did you know? The Atlantic Ocean and the Pacific Ocean do not mix. It all has to do with a huge difference in salinity between the clear water of the Pacific Ocean, that comes from melting glaciers, is cool and low in salt, while the water from the Atlantic Ocean has a high salt concentration. Therefore, the two oceans have different densities, which make them almost impossible to mix. It also should be noted that during stormy conditions, mostly in winter, and in summer in the northern hemisphere, there can be as much as 6-foot difference between the two oceans. In addition, if you fly above the Straights of Juan del Fuego, at the tip of South America (South of Argentina and Chili) where the Atlantic Ocean and Pacific Ocean meet without mixing, you will be surprised to see that the Pacific Ocean water is blue in color while the Atlantic Ocean water tends to be on the grayish side.

Did you know? The Great Conjunction is when Earth, Jupiter and Saturn all line up. It happens every 19.85 years. In 2020 it happed on December 17. By the way, while it takes one year for Earth to go around the Sun, it takes Jupiter 11.86 years, and it takes Saturn 29.4 years.

Did you know? The Earth gets 100 tons heavier every day due to falling space dust.

Did you know? The cosmos contains approximately 50 billion galaxies.

Did you know? If you could fly across our galaxy from one side to the other at light speed, it would take you 100,000 years to make the trip.

Did you know? If you attempted to count the stars in a galaxy at a rate of one per second, it would take you about 3,000 years to finish.

Did you know? It is estimated that there are more stars in the Universe than there are grains of sand on earth, but there are more atoms in one grain of sand than there are stars in the Universe.

Did you know? About 25 million children in the U.S. today (2021) cannot read proficiently, about 65% of 4th grade students do not read at a proficient level, and 2 out of 3 children living in poverty have no books to call their own (*Reading* Is Fundamental, RIF.org).

Did you know? Astronauts from Texas who were in space on Election Day 2020 could still cast their vote. Secure ballots were sent to space by Mission Control in Houston. After the astronauts made their choices, they beamed their ballots back to Earth, with their out-of-state address listed as "low-earth-orbit" (Reader's Digest, November 2020, p.26).

Did you know? When NASA started sending astronauts into space, they quickly discovered that ball-point pens would not work in zero gravity. To combat this problem NASA scientists spent a decade and $165 million to develop a pen that writes in zero gravity, upside down, on almost any surface and at temperature ranging from below freezing to over 300 C. These pens are commonly known as the Fisher Space Pen. On the other hand, the Russians did not spend that kind of money and instead their astronauts used pencils in space.

Did you know? Astronomers in 2020 found out that our solar system is wetter than they thought. In 2020 they revealed that the icy dwarf planet Ceres as well as Pluto, Europa, Enceladus and the icy moons orbiting Jupiter and Saturn all have active underground oceans. What it means is that where there is water there can be life. These findings according to the astronomer Alan Stern are "one of the most profound discoveries in planetary science in the Space Age."These findings fueled the hunt for life beyond Earth (Discover Magazine, January/Fabruary2021, p.58).

Did you know? There are 5 small countries in the world as of 2021 that have no airports. These include, Vatican City, San Marino, Monaco, Liechtenstein and Andora (https://www.rd.co/article/ countries-with-no-airports/?).

Did you know? In a study printed in *Scientific Report* researchers found out a quick trick of how to learn new words in a faster way. They discovered that infusing the room with favorite scented incense stick increased the ability to learn new words by about 30% (*First for women,* June 15, 2020, p.42).

Did you know? A "jiffy" is an actual unit of time for 1/100th of a second.

Did you know? Rolex watch company is run by a non-profitable charity trust. The company donates 90% of the profits to it because the founder was an orphan.

Did you know? The first Haley Davidson motorcycle that was built in 1903 used a tomato can for carburetor.

Did you know? In many countries around the world voting is compulsory. Australians for example who do not cast ballots face fines that more than double after first offense. In Belgium, a person who fails to vote for the current election time loses the right to vote for the next ten years. Voting is also mandatory in Ecuador, but only for those who are literate. Here in the USA voting is not mandatory so people take it for granted. Therefore, we have low voter turnout, and our democracy is not well served (Reader's Digest, November 2020, p.25).

Did you know? Rubber bands last longer when refrigerated.

Did you know? Up to and including the year 2020, the citizens of the country Gambia were casting their votes by dropping marbles into a metal drums that had pictures of the candidates. Each drum had a bell inside that rang after a marble was dropped. This also eliminated voter fraud because if the bell rang more than once people that were in charge of it would know that someone tried to cheat the system. This system of voting was so tedious that it was therefore changed. Today, in the year 2021, Gambians will only be able to vote on paper ballots (Reader's Digest, November 2020, p.25).

Did you know? The town of Monowi, Nebraska has a population of 1. The name of that person is Elsie Eiler, who is the mayor of the town and she granted herself a liquor license and pays taxes to herself.

Did you know? In 2007, Scotland spent six months of research and $162,972 to create a new slogan that would boost its tourism. It ended up with "welcome to Scotland".

Did you know? Iceland has no army, and it is also recognized as the world's most peaceful country.

Did you know? The University of Alaska spans four time zones.

Did you know? The state with the highest percentage of people who walk to work is Alaska.

Did you know why the honor guard folds the United State flag 13 times? You probably think that it is to symbolize the original 13 colonies, however this is NOT the case. The 1st fold of the flag is a symbol of life. The 2nd fold is a symbol of the belief in eternal life. The 3rd fold is made to honor and remember the veterans who gave a portion of their lives for the defense of the country, to attain peace throughout the world. The 4th fold represents turning to His divine guidance. The 5th fold is a tribute to the country, right or wrong. The 6th fold is for where people's hearts lie, pledging allegiance to the flag and country. The 7th fold is a tribute to the Armed Forces who are protecting the country and the flag against all enemies, whether they are within or outside the country. The 8th fold is a tribute to the one who enters into the valley of the shadow of death. The 9th fold is a tribute to womanhood and Mothers. The tenth fold is a tribute to the fathers. The 11th fold represents the lower portion of the seal of King David and king Solomon, and glorifies in the Hebrews eyes, The God of Abraham, Isaac and Jacob. The 12th fold represents an emblem of eternity and glorifies, in the Christians eyes, God the Father, Son and the Holy Spirit. The 13th fold, or when the flag completely folded, when the stars are uppermost, it reminds us of our Nations motto, 'In God We Trust.' When the flag is completely folded and tucked in, it looks like a cocked hat, which remind us of the soldiers who serve under George Washington, and the Sailors and Marines who served Captain John Paul Jones.

Did you know? There are 58,267 names now, in the year 2020, listed on the Vietnam Wall, including those added in 2010. In addition, there are three sets of fathers and sons, as well as thirty-one brothers' names on the wall. On the first day of the war 997 soldiers were killed, and on the last day 1,448 killed. In addition, thirty-one sets of parents lost two of their sons too. The largest age group that died were 18 years old, 12 soldiers on the Wall were 17 years old, 5 soldiers on the Wall were 16-year-old, and one soldier PFC Dan Bullock was only 15 years old when he died.

Did you know? The most casualties for a single day in the Vietnam War was on January 31, 1968, when 245 soldiers died. Furthermore, the most casualty deaths for a single month took place on May 1968, when 2,415 casualties were incurred.

Did you know? All 50 states are listed across the top of the Lincoln Memorial on the back of the $5 bill.

Did you know? A dime has 118 ridges around the edge.

Did you know? There are 293 ways to make change for a dollar.

Did you know? The $20 bill is the most commonly counterfeited banknote in the United States (Reader's Digest, June 2021, p.117).

Did you know what events inspired Samuel Morse to come up with the Morse Code? It was due to the fact that while he was out of town his wife had fallen ill and by the time, he got the letter about her situation she was already dead and buried.

Did you know? The Army is the second-biggest employer in the United States after Walmart. It has nearly half a million active-duty troops and another 200,000 in reserve (Reader's Digest, September 2020, p.34).

Did you know? Prior to 1933, members of the 45th Infantry Division wore a Native American symbol of good luck, the swastika, as a nod to the many Native Americans who served in that division. However, after the Nazis adopted this symbol, the members of this division adopted another Native American symbol: a thunderbird (Reader's Digest, September 2020, p.35).

Did you know? Green berets were not part of the Special Forces uniform until 1961, after President John F. Kennedy visited Fort Bragg in North Carolina. On his visit he noticed an officer wearing one and thought that it was a good idea for the unit to adopt it, and so he made it official for the unit to wear it (Reader's Digest September 2020, p.35).

Did you know? The U.S. Postal Service still uses mules to reach communities at the bottom of the Grand Canyon.

Did you know? The USA contains 26 different climate types within its borders. One of the Earth rarest ecosystems exist in southern Florida in the Everglades. It includes about 8,000 square miles. It contains 360 species of birds, 75 different reptiles, 50 types of mammals and other animals, as well as 9,000 humans that live in elevated houses. The most dangerous species in the everglades is the Burmese Python. They were released in the 20th Century by someone who wanted to get rid of their python pets. They can get as long as 20 feet and their population increased by about half a million (Bill O'Reilly.com).

Did you know that the U.S. is the home of the 3 B's? Baseball, football and basketball. Baseball was played for the first time in 1839. Football was developed in around 1874, and basketball was invented in 1891.

Did you know? Ohio is the mother of 7 US presidents, because they were all born there, and they are: Ulysses S. Grant, Rutherford B. Hayes, James A. Garfield, Benjamin Harrison, William Howard Taft, William McKinley and Warren G. Harding.

Did you know? The first radio commercial in the U.S. was broadcast on New York station, WEAF. This took place on August 28, 1922, and was for American estate agent, Queensboro Realty. It was not until 1973 that the UK had its first radio commercial. It ran on Britain's first independent radio station LBC and promoted Birds Eye frozen food.

Did you know? AT&T brought advertising to radio in 1922 when their NYC radio station sold time for "toll broadcasting." The 15-minutes ad was for apartments in Queens.

Did you know? More people live in New York City than in 40 of the 50 states.

Did you know? The Empire State building in New York City has its own zip code.

Did you know? There is enough water in Lake Superior to Cover all of North and South America in one Foot of liquid.

Did you know? Oregon's Crater Lake is deep enough to cover about six Statues of Liberty on top of each other.

Did you know? It would take you more than about 400 years to spend a night in all of Las Vegas's hotel rooms.

Did you know? There is enough concrete in the Hoover Dam to build a two-lane highway from San Francisco to New York City.

Did you know? The only states in the U.S.A. that do not observe daylight savings time are Arizona and Hawaii.

Did you know? The state of Kansas produces enough wheat each year to feed everyone in the world for about two weeks.

Did you know? The Library of Congress contains about 838 miles of bookshelves. That is equivalent to a drive from Houston to Chicago.

Did you know? The entire Denver International Airport is twice the size of the island of Manhattan.

Did you know? The total length of Idaho's rivers could stretch across the United States about 40 times.

Did you know? The Amargosa River flows largely underground for more than 100 miles in the Mojave Desert. Along its course – which begins in southern Nevada and hooks down into California's Death Valley – a network of perennial springs is the only major and consistent source of water in what is the hottest and driest place in North America (Nature Conservancy Magazine, Summer 2021 p.19).

Did you know? A highway in Lancaster, California plays the "William Tell Overture" as you drive over it, thanks to some well-placed grooves in the rood.

Did you know? It you stand on the Earth equator line your body will weigh 3% less.

Did you know? The entire world's population could fit inside Los Angeles.

Did you know? Every day, 2,000 acres of agricultural land in the US are paved over, fragmented, or converted to uses that jeopardize farming (American Farmland Trust).

Did you know? The percentage of Africa that is wilderness is 28% and the percentage of North America that is wilderness is 38%.

Did you know? The Arctic Refuge is America's last largest remaining wild frontier. Even though development has pushed deeper into our world's wild places, the Refuge has remained untouched so far. The Refuge is one of only two U.S. wildlife refuges where polar bears live onshore (The Wilderness Society of the U.S.).

Did you know? The Arctic Refuge is a place with deep generational connection to Native peoples in Alaska. The Gwich'in and the Inupiat depend on the Arctic Refuge and its resources to sustain their communities, culture and way of life. It is also home to all three species of North American bears, the Polar, the Black and the Grizzly. This is the only place in the entire U.S. where you can find all the three species living together (The Wilderness Society of the U.S.).

Did you know? More than 200 bird species from 50 states and six continents depend on the Arctic for their summer home (The Wilderness Society of the U.S.).

Did you know? Nearly 200,000 caribou march to their calving range on the Arctic Refuge's coastal plain each year to give birth to their young (the Wilderness Society of the U.S.).

Did you know? The state with the highest percentage of people who walk to work is Alaska.

Did you know? We toss more than 40 million tons of cracked phone cases and other electric waste each year. Much is shipped to developing countries, where workers strip precious bits-like rare -earth metals- and chuck the rest. This "recycling" leaves mountains of petrified, toxic chemicals and metal scraps.

Did you know? Humanity's legacy lies in our garbage. Trash offers archaeologists insight into the day-to day lifestyle of people long past. Even today, we are leaving future excavators plenty of specimens to ponder upon. Most Americans produce at least around 4.5 pounds of waste each day. The things we are tossing today will exist long after we are gone.

Did you know? The benefits of composting are that when organic matter is diverted from landfills, it reduces methane and carbon emissions. It also increases carbon in the soil, keeping carbon out of the atmosphere. In addition, it improves soil quality (Practice Composting Booklet by Sierra Club, p.24).

Did you know that **we are running out of elements?** We use in the world about 17 different rare earth minerals to produce the new technology that exist today in the world. Europium and Indium are crucial elements in order to produce televisions and touch screens. Rhenium is necessary in the production of fighter plane engines. We need Lithium and Cobalt for electric vehicle batteries, Tellurium for solar panels and Dysprosium for wind turbines. In addition, Dysprosium, as well as Terbium strengthen magnets and give screens color, and Palladium is essential for catalytic converters and fuel cells. Yet, we cannot make these elements - they formed, along with Earth, billions of years ago. To replenish our dwindling stores, and keep up with a growing demand, we must mine for more in remote areas that are hard to reach such as: the Arctic Circle, the deep sea, in Russia's tundra, and even in the asteroids nearest to Earth. Today 80% of the rare earth minerals come from China until they will run out of them in the near future (Discover Magazine, June 2020, pp.32-34).

Did you know? In general, a single tree can intercept 760 gallons of rainwater in its crown, reducing runoff and flooding.

Did you know? Trees that are properly placed around buildings and houses can reduce air-conditioning needs by about 30% and save 20% - 50% in energy used for heating (www.ameicanforests.org).

Did you know? More than 180 million Americans depend on drinking water that originates in forests (www.americanforests.org).

Did you know? Particulate matter in pollution kills. Harvard University scientists including Francesca Dominic, a senior author and biostatistician at the Harvard T.H. Chan School of Public Health, and her colleagues, found out after extensive research, that tightening annual EPA air quality standards for fine-particulate matter by about 17% - from 12 micrograms to 10 micrograms per cubic meter of air - would save about 143,257 lives in one decade. However, NAAQS standards for this pollutant are too loose. Another study in 2020 found out that a 25% decrease of dust particulate matter in West Africa would decrease infant mortality rates in the region by about 18%. In general researchers claim that air pollution is widespread in the world and can affect people's health even at low levels (Discover Magazine, January/February 2021, p.60).

Did you know? A study led by Harvard researchers found a significant link between air pollution and an increased risk of hospitalization for patients with several neurological disorders including Parkinson's Disease, Alzheimer's Disease and Dementia. They also stress that the air pollution standards that we have now are not protecting the aging American population (Newsmax, May 2021, p.90).

Did you know? One acre of forest can consume all the pollution produced by one car that is driven 26,000 miles in one year (www. americanforests.org).

Did you know? Chicago's urban forest of more than 3.5 million trees removes every year about 888 tons of pollution (www. americanforest.org).

Did you know? Giant Sequoia trees are the largest in volume and hardiest in the world. They can grow to about 30 feet (9 meters) in diameter and more than 275 feet (84 meters) tall, has a 102 – foot (31meters) circumference, and weighs about 2.5 million lbs. (1.2 million kilograms). Their thick bark makes them flame resistant as well as resistant to fungal rot and wood-boring beetles. Some of them can surpass 3,000 years of age. The biggest of these is known by the name of General Sherman, a giant Sequoia in Sequoia National Park in Northern California (Discover Magazine, January/ February 2021, p.74).

Did you know? Redwood trees are known to be the world's tallest trees and they can be found in a very narrow strip along the coast of California from the extreme southwestern corner of Oregon to 150 miles south of San Francisco the Soda Springs drainage of Big Sur. This area is about 500 miles long and about 20 or 30 miles wide. These trees can get as high as more than 350 feet (107meters) and live up to about 2,000 years (bigsurcalifornia.org).

Did you know? In 1931 the first ever Christmas tree went up in New York City's Rockefeller Plaza, and it was only 20 feet tall (Consumer Report On Health, December 2020, p.16).

Did you know? A giant 32-foot 4,000-pound menorah near Central Park in Manhattan is proclaimed the largest in the world by Guinness World Records.

Did you Know? Every 200,000 to 300,000 years, with some exceptions, the magnetic poles of the Earth shift polarity, Magnetic north will appear on the compass at the South Pole and Magnetic south will appear at the North Pole. The latest reversal occurred around 780,000 year ago, so technically, we are long overdue for a switch (Popular Mechanics, September/October 2020, p.29).

Did you know? The magnetic North Pole of Earth is not where it used to be, since James Clark Ross first identified it in Canada's Nunavut territory in 1831.The pole used to move at an average of about 9 miles annually, but since 1990 it has been racing at 37 miles per year toward Siberia The magnetic poles of the Earth naturally undergo precession, as in that the axis of rotation of the Earth itself rotates around over time, shifting the location of the axis and also the tilt of the Earth as well (Popular Mechanics, September/ October 2020, p.29).

Did you know? The shore of the Dead Sea is the lowest point on the Earth's land surface at about 1,300 feet below sea level.

Did you know? The Dead Sea is in fact not "dead". It is the saltiest body of water in the world. It is landlocked Salt Lake between Israel and Jordan. Its name goes back to about 323 B.C.E. While no fish can survive in it, the Dead Sea contains salt-loving microorganism that thrives in it. In addition, salt and other minerals are extracted from it in vast quantities for use in the chemical industry.

Did you know why Judea-Samaria region is also called the "West Bank"? The "West Bank" was the name concocted by King Abdullah I of Trans-Jordan and his British advisors, allowing the King to annex land outside of his artificially "created" kingdom (Middle East Rules of Thumb, p.170).

Did you know? The Islamic culture contributed significantly to the development of Western perfumery. In Islamic culture, perfume usage has been documented as far back as the 6th century, and its usage is considered a religious duty.

Did you know? The knowledge of how to make perfume came to Europe as early as the 14th century due to Arab influences and knowledge. However, the Hungarians were the ones who introduced the first modern perfume to Europe by the orders of Queen Elizabeth, the queen of England at the time.

Did you know? The word UP has more meanings than any other two-letter words in the English language. It can be a noun, verb, adjective, adverb and preposition. Here are some examples: We can look UP, wake UP, a topic comes UP, speak UP, you are UP for election, it is UP to you, call UP your friends, brighten UP the room, polish UP your shoes, warm UP the leftover, lock UP the house, do not stir UP trouble, work UP an appetite, don't think UP an excuse, dress UP for the occasion, open UP your business, close UP the store, are you UP to the task of looking UP the word UP in the dictionary? If so, you will find out that it takes UP about ¼ of a page and can add UP to about thirty definitions.

Did you know? Some English words are actually Arabic words that entered the English language such as: lilac, magic, orange, sofa, spinach, tariffs, tulip, elixir, and zenith to mention a few.

Did you know? Dubai built the world's first under water tennis stadium.

Did you know? Some English words are actually Turkish words that entered our language such as: gazelle, hazard, horde and ghoul- a legendary evil being that robs graves and feeds on corpses, to mention a few.

Did you know? "Dreamt" is the only English word that ends in the letters "mt".

Did you know? No word in the English language rhymes with month, orange, silver, or purple.

Did you know? "Stewardesses" is the longest word typed with only the left hand and "lollipop" only with the right.

Did you know? The word "racecar," "kayak" and "level" are the same whether they are read left to right or right to left (palindromes).

Did you know? There are only two words in the English language that have all five vowels in order: "abstemious" and "facetious" (a-e-i-o-u).

Did you know? There are only four words in the English language which ends in "dous": tremendous, horrendous, stupendous, and hazardous.

Did you know? TYPEWRITER is the longest word that can be made using the letters only on one row of the keyboard.

Did you know? The first novel ever written on a typewriter was *Tom Sawyer.*

Did you know? The sentence: "The quick brown fox jumps over the lazy dog" uses every letter of the alphabet.

Did you know? In 499 B.C. Histiaelus, tyrant of Miletus, sent a secret military dispatch by tattooing it on the head of his most trusted slave. The recipient then shaved the slave's head to read the message.

Did you know? Ancient sailors, before the inventions of maps or the compass, navigated the seas by keeping in sight of land, and observing the positions of the Sun and the stars. If clouds rolled in, they would pull down their sails and wait for better visibility (Popular Mechanics, July/August 2020 p.36).

Did you know? Geographia, an eight-volume atlas that was compiled by Ptolemy, a Greek-Egyptian astronomer, helped Columbus's voyage to the Americas as well as helped Ferdinand Magellan's expedition around the globe. This eight-volume atlas later disappeared with the fall of the Roman Empire and reemerged about 800 years later. Around the 9th Century it was discovered and translated to Arabic by Islamic cartographers. They ended up correcting errors made by Ptolemy, such as, that they accurately drew the Indian Ocean as open body of water and connected it to the Pacific Ocean, instead of a land-locked sea according to Ptolemy's drawings.

Did you know? Christopher Columbus believed that the world was round. However, he did not think that the Earth was a perfect sphere but rather has the shape of a pear. In addition, on his fourth voyage to the new world, he was able to save his life and the lives of his crew by convincing Jamaican natives, that he was a very powerful man that can hurt them, if they were to hurt his crew, by making the moon disappear (it took place during the lunar eclipse in 1504).

Did you know? Our Moon moves two inches away from the Earth each year.

Did you know? Scientists found out that radiation levels on the Moon are 200 times higher than on Earth and therefore astronauts can end up be affected by it and end up having cataracts, cancer and other diseases down the road.

Did you know? February 1865 is the only month in recorded history not to have a full moon.

Did you know? Due to Earth's gravity, it is impossible for mountains to be higher than 15,000 meters.

Did you know? The Earth gets 100 tons heavier every day due to falling space dust.

Did you know? Everything weighs one percent less at the equator.

Did you know? The letter J does not appear anywhere on the periodic table of the elements.

Did you know? A comet can have two tails, ore of dust and one of gas. The gas one always points away from the sun but the dust one can points anywhere and is dependent on the comet's trajectory.

Did you know? If you happen to get to the bottom of a well or a tall chimney and look up you will be able to see stars, even in the middle of the day.

Did you know? For every extra kilogram carried on a space flight, 530 kg of excess fuel is needed at lift-off.

Did you know? Soldiers do not march in step when going across bridges because they could set up a resonance which could be sufficient to knock the bridge down.

Did you know? After the Battle of Shiloh in 1862, many Civil War soldiers' lives were saved by a phenomenon called 'Angel's Glow'. The soldiers, who lay in the mud for two rainy days had wounds that began to glow in the dark and heal unusually fast. In 2001, two teens won an international science fair by discovering why it all happened. They found out that because the soldiers were very cold their bodies created the perfect conditions for growing a bioluminescent bacterium, which ultimately destroyed the bad bacteria that could have killed them (Blowing facts .org).

Did you know? The Civil War claimed 620,000 soldiers' lives, the most of any conflict in American history. That ended up necessitating the establishment of the country's first national cemeteries.

Did you know? Kites were used in the American Civil War to deliver letters and newspapers.

Did you know? When the Confederate general Robert E. Lee joined the Confederacy, his farm was taken and later became Arlington National Cemetery.

Did you know? The Memorial Day holiday started after the Civil War ended, on the last Monday of May, and it has continued to be celebrated each year. However, it has morphed over time and expanded to include and honor all who have died in all American wars. Only in 1971 did Memorial Day became an official national holiday by an act of Congress.

Did you know? The reason why the holiday falls in May has to do with Maj. Gen. John A. Logan, who was the head of the Grand Army of the Republic, an organization of Union vets. He is the one who declared that the holiday should be observed at the end of May because it did not fall on the same day as the anniversary of any particular battle, and the flowers would be blooming all around America and be abundantly available for people to purchase and decorate the soldiers' graves (VA.gov).

Did you know? Memorial Day was not always called this way. It was originally known as Decoration Day. That is because it was originally celebrated by decorating the graves of soldiers who lost their lives with flowers and flags.

Did you know? More than two dozen locations in both the north and south claim to have hosted the first Memorial Day. However, in 1966, the U.S. Federal Government headed by Lyndon Johnson proclaimed Waterloo, New York as the holiday's official birthplace. It was there, a century earlier, that a celebration to honor Civil War vets first took place and went on to become an annual tradition.

Did you know? Modern Memorial Day follows a specific Federal timeline. First, flags on the holiday be flown at half -staff, but only until noon. Secondly, the official time to remember the fallen soldiers each year takes place at 3:00 pm local time around the country (VA.gov).

Did you know? Most glass takes one million years to decompose, so it can be recycled an infinite amount of times.

Did you know? Gold is a metal that does not rust, even if it is buried in the ground for thousands of years.

Did you know? You can make paper easily by mixing wood pulp with saliva to form a paste, which dries stiff.

Did you know? The roar that we hear when we place a seashell next to our ear is not the ocean, but rather the sound of blood surging through the veins in our ear.

Did you know? Airports at higher altitudes require a longer airstrip due to lower air density.

Did you know? India's "Go Air" airlines only hires female flight attendants, because they are lighter, so they save up to $500,000 per year in fuel.

Did you know? Finish and British scientists found more traces of flu and other viruses in the trays in the security areas of airports, than in any other location in the airport, even the toilets. Why? This is because these trays are handled by nearly all embarking passengers and are not disinfected routinely after each usage at every airport.

Did you know? The song *Auld Lang Syne* is sung at the stroke of midnight in almost every English-speaking country in the world to bring in the new year.

Did you know? The world's first speeding ticket was written in 1896 in the village of Paddock Wood, England. The violator was caught driving eight-mph through a two-mph zone and fined 10 shillings (Reader's Digest, February 2020, p.81).

Did you know? In 1959, a coffee maker was an optional extra in Volkswagen cars.

Did you know? About 20% of fires of unknown origin in the U.S. are believed to be caused by mice and rats chewing on electric wires.

Did you know? Unlike people, wildfires move uphill much more quickly than downhill. Why? because fire needs air (oxygen) to burn, and steep hills allows more air to come from below the blaze than from above it, which in turn encourages the fire to climb.

Did you know? The lit end of a cigarette reaches approximately 1,292 degrees Fahrenheit when the smoker inhales.

Did you know? Cigarette butts are the most littered item in the world, with an estimated 4.5 trillion littered annually. Each butt can take 5 to 400 years to completely break down.

Did you know? The longest word in the English language has 189,819 letters. It would take you about three and half hours to say it out loud. It is basically the technical name of a protein.

Did you know? There are exactly 46,783,665,034,756,288,456,012 ,645 move possibilities in a game of Chess.

Did you know? The most common used letter in the English language is "e", and the most common second letter is "h". In addition, the most common consonant is "t". So, can you then guess what is the most popular word in the English language? It is "the."

Did you know? The first non-human to win an Oscar was Mickey Mouse.

Did you know? The first transcontinental telephone line was completed in 1914 on January 25, 1915. The first call was made by Alexander Graham Bell in New York to Thomas A. Watson in San Francisco.

Did you know? The San Francisco cable cars are the only mobile National Monuments.

Did you know? The bikini swimsuit was named after the American detonation of an atomic bomb at Bikini Atoll, in the South Pacific on July1, 1946. The designer, Lois Read, hoped his swimsuit design would make a similar explosion in the fashion world.

Did you know? Voting on Tuesdays started in the 19th century because farmers often had to travel long distances to the nearest polling places. They did not want to travel on Sunday, and they needed to be back home for market day on Wednesday. In addition, farmers also voted in the month of November, because by then the harvest was over (Reader's Digest, November 2020, pp.24-25).

Did you know? A 100-pound woman in high heels exerts more pressure per square inch (psi) when walking than a 6,000-pound elephant. The elephant clocks in at around 75 psi pressure, but a woman can apply about 1,500 psi (one pound per square inch) to the heel point of her shoe.

Did you know? When humans began to settle in Australia during the Last Glacial Period, 65,000 years ago, sea levels were at least 260 feet lower than they are today (Archaeology, September/ October 2020, p.23).

Did you know how Australia got its name? Ancient geographers believed that there should be a great continent in the Southern Hemisphere to balance the land masses of the Northern Hemisphere. Therefore, they named it Terral Austalis Incognita, meaning "undiscovered land of the South." Terra means land, Australis means South, and Incognita means undiscovered.

Did you know? The rise of acidity as well as temperatures in the oceans is destroying the coral reefs in Australia. In addition, changes in water temperature cause algae to leave coral reefs, turning them white and making them vulnerable to disease and death, a phenomenon known as coral bleaching (worldwildlife.org).

Did you know? In Australia lake Hillier has naturally pink water.

Did you know that the boomerang did not originate in Australia? The Australians, however, can be credited with bringing the boomerang to the attention of the modern world and giving it its name. The boomerang was used as a weapon of war and especially as a tool for hunting small game for nearly 10,000 years. Evidence of the use of boomerangs can be found all the way to the Neolithic -era in France, Spain, Poland, Crete and in Africa, from Sudan to Nigeria and Cameroon to Morocco. It was also used by tribes in southern India, the American southwest, Mexico and Java. In addition, King Tutankhamun, ruler of ancient Egypt around 1350 B.C., had a large collection of boomerangs, several of which were found when his tomb was discovered in the late 1920s. Furthermore, boomerangs were used in ancient Greece and Rome as well as by the Germanic Tribes.

Did you know how Scandinavia got its name? Its name came from the word *Skadino*, meaning "dark." Thus, the name means land of darkness. Indeed, the northern part of the peninsula does have six months of short days every year culminating in winter.

Did you know how Crimea got its name? The name comes from the Russian word *Kremnoi* which means rocky cliffs. This indeed describes the area well. By the way the peninsula is located between the Black Sea and the Sea of Azov.

Did you know how the Volga River in Russia got its name? Russia has many large rivers, but the greatest of all of them is the Volga, and the Russians recognized it in its name. Volga comes from a Slavonic word **wolkoi** which means "great".

Did you know how Sardinia got its name? The island of Sardinia is named for its first inhabitants, the Sardi. However, their name comes from the Phoenicians term *Sarado*, which means "footprint".

Did you know how Brazil got its name? In Portuguese, "live coal" (red) is *braza.* When the Portuguese explorers landed on the eastern bulge of South America, they found a wood that produced a bright red dye. So, they called the wood Brazil wood and the country that grew it Brazil.

Did you know how Venezuela got its name? Venezuela in Spanish means "little Venice." The Italian city of Venice was first built on posts in a swamp. When the European explorers of South America first came to the cost of where today Venezuela is, they saw Indian villages built on posts over the water. So, they ended up calling the place "little Venice" hence, Venezuela.

Did you know how Argentina got its name? Its name is associated with the Latin word *argentum* "silver". Why? This is because the early Europeans mistakenly believed that the area had a lot of silver. The mistake was made because the early Europeans saw the natives bringing silver down river. However, in fact, the silver came from the mountains of Bolivia, far in the north.

Did you know? The Influenza Pandemic of 1918, known also as the Spanish Flu, took the life of 500,000 Americans and about 50 million people worldwide. The pandemic was brought by Chinese laborers who were brought to Europe. The Influenza Pandemic killed nearly twice as many people as those who died in WWI. The Spanish Flu, unlike most flu outbreaks, did not kill, in most cases, young children, but it did kill those in poor health and the elderly. The flu invaded the body's strong immune system and caused it to attack its victim's lungs. As a result, more people with strong immune system survived and those with a weak one ended up dying. Historians believe today that it may have been originated in China and was brought out of China, to the Americas in 1917, by some of the 96,000 Chinese laborers that were transported across Canada to the U.S. and Europe. Some on the other hand point out that it was spread to Europe by infected U.S. soldiers who brought it overseas. Today, many scientists still do not know for sure where the flu originated. So, today the theories still point to China, France, Britain and the United States.

Did you know why the Spanish Flu is called this way even though it did not originate in Spain? It is because during World War I, Spain was a neutral country with a free press that covered the flu outbreak from the very beginning. The first reporting of the flu outbreak took place in Madrid, Spain in late May of 1918. The Allied countries as well as the Central Powers had wartime censors who covered it up and did not report it to the public, to keep the morale high. Only the Spanish news sources reported it, so people thought that it originated there. On the other hand, the Spanish believed, wrongly, that it originated from France and called it the "French Flu."

Did you know? The Swine Flu vaccine in 1976 actually caused more death and illness than the disease it was intended to prevent.

Did you know? The flu in general tends to put stress on the heart. So, if you have underlying heart disease it is crucial that you get the flu vaccine annually to prevent health complications. According to a recent study, people were six times more likely to suffer a heart attack within one week of getting the flu. Furthermore, a recent larger study showed that 1 in 8 patients who were hospitalized with the flu ended up suffering from cardiovascular disease a CVD event (AARP, February/March 2021, p.25).

Did you know? The word vaccination comes from the Latin word *vacc*, meaning "cow." The first European vaccinations infected people with cowpox, a disease that is less severe than smallpox. By doing so people ended up being immune to cowpox and smallpox.

Did you know? Vaccines are one of the greatest inventions in history for the most part. The smallpox vaccine campaign conducted by the World Health Organization eradicated the disease from the face of the earth by 1980. Before the invention of this vaccine, from 1900 to 1980, more than 300 million people died around the world from smallpox. However, since 1980 people in the world are no longer dying from this disease.

Did you know? Unlike other vaccines, annual seasonal influenza vaccines are developed within about six months. That is because the only vaccine ingredient that changes each year is the antigen. All other ingredients can remain intact, eliminating the need for additional research and lengthy clinical trials. This also allows for speedy production since the manufacturing process does not need to be updated each year (*healthafter50*, University of California, Berkeley, September 2020 p.3).

Did you know? The city of Sochi, Russia erected a fish statue costing about $3,800 in honor of Gambusia (aka the "mosquito fish"). In early 1900's the fish species were purposefully introduced to the area to fight the infestation of Malaria mosquitos, and it worked. There have been no cases of Malaria there for over 60 years (Blowingfacts.com).

Did you know? The winter of 1932 was so cold that the Niagara Falls froze completely solid.

Did you know? Brides have not always worn white dresses. They used to wear their finest dress of any color. However, since the wedding of Queen Victoria and Prince Albert of England in 1840 white wedding dress became the norm in the Western World.

Did you know that there are many wedding superstitions that we still believe in today? For example: some tie tin cans to the bride and groom's car to frighten away the evil spirits, or after toasting, it is a good luck for the bride and groom to smash their glasses (that ensure the glasses will never be used for a better reasons), another superstition belief is that the bridesmaids dress like the bride to confuse the evil spirits, we also do not let the groom see the bride in her wedding dress before the ceremony. Furthermore, in Mexico, it is bad luck for the bride to wear pearls, because it signifies the tears she will cry in her marriage.

Did you know that the lighter was invented before the match? In 1823 a German chemist invented the lighter, and only three years later in 1826 an English chemist invented the first friction match.

Did you know? The early matches were called "Lucifers" because they would burst into flame when jostled.

Did you know why statues of famous leaders who fought in wars have their horses poses in a different way? The artists that created the statues were trying to tell us the faith of the leader riding their horses. Here are few examples: if a statue with a person riding a horse with two front legs in the air, the person died in battle, if the horse has one front leg in the air, the person died because of wounds received in battle. If the horse's all four legs are on the ground, the person died of natural causes.

Did you know that the face of the Statue of Liberty was modeled after the face of Frederic Auguste Bartholdi's mother, Charlotte?

The statue was completed in Paris in June 1884 and was given to the American people on July 4, 1884. The statue has 25 windows and 7 spikes in Lady Liberty's crown. It symbolizes the seven seas of Planet Earth. The Statue of Liberty was functioned as an actual lighthouse from 1886-1902 and could be seen 24 miles away. More than 4 million people visit it every year.

Did you know? Christmas was not declared a national holiday in the United States until 1890.

Did you know? In 1814, the original Library of Congress was burned down by the British along with the Capital. To replace it, Congress bought Thomas Jefferson's personal book collection, which consisted of approximately 6,500 volumes.

Did you know? George Washington was a distant relation to King Edward I, Queen Elizabeth II, Sir Winston Churchill, and Robert E. Lee.

Did you know? The Liberty Bell was last rung on George Washington's birthday in 1846.

Did you know? Only two people signed the Declaration of Independence on July 4, 1776. It was John Hancock and Charles Thomson. Most of the rest signed it on August 2, but the last signature was not added until 5 years later.

Did you know? Rivals John Adams and Thomas Jefferson died on the same day, July 4, 1826 - the 50th anniversary of the signing of the Declaration of Independence.

Did you know why we have the saying:" I gave them the whole nine yards"? It originated during WWII when airplanes were armed with belts of bullets which they would shoot during dogfights. These bullet belts were folded into the wing compartments that fed the machine guns. These belts measured 27 feet and contained hundreds of rounds of bullets. Often, the pilots who returned from their missions and used all their ammunition tend to state that they gave the enemy "the whole nine yards."

Did you know that the saying "God willing, and the creek don't rise" was in reference to the Creek Indians and not a body of water? It was written by Benjamin Hawkins in the late 18th century. He was a politician and an Indian diplomat. While in the south, Hawkins was requested by the President of the U.S. to return to Washington, in his response, he was said to write, "God willing, and the Creek don't rise." Since he capitalized the word "Creek", he was referring to the Creek Indian tribe and not to a body of water.

Did you know that the Lakota (Sioux) people, a Native American tribe, consider the medicine wheel a sacred symbol with much meaning? The circular shape represents the continuous cycle of life and death. The horizontal and vertical lines represent the sun and man's sacred paths. The center of the Earth (indicated where the lines intersect) is where one stands when praying. The four colors: red, black, white and yellow are sacred to the Lakota people.

Did you know? In 499 B.C., Histiaeus, tyrant of Miletus, sent a secret military dispatch by tattooing it on the head of his most trusted slave. The recipient then saves the slave's head to read the message.

Did you know? Genghis Khan, a famous and powerful Mongol leader, slept with so many women that about 1 in 200 people today are related to him.

Did you know that the city of Chicago is called the Windy City not because of its weather? It is called so because journalists used to criticize Chicago's elites for being "full of hot air" (Reader's Digest, Feb. 2019, p.61).

Did you know? The town of Quincy, Massachusetts is known as the Birthplace of the American Dream. It was the original home for two fast-food icons: Howard Johnsons' and Dunkin' Donuts.

Did you know that Betty Crocker was a fiction character? That did not stop anyone from considering her the second-most-popular woman in the nation in 1945, right behind Eleanor Roosevelt.

Did you know that the famous palace of Versailles took 50 years to build? It is the size of 7 football fields, and it has 1,300 rooms. During the reign of Luis XIV 10,000 servants worked there. In addition, the Treaty of Versailles, that ended WWI was signed there on June 28, 1919, in the Hall of Mirrors. Its provisions were primarily drawn up by US President W. Wilson, British Prime Minister D. Lloyd-George, French Premier G. Clemenceau, and Italian Prime Minister V. Orlando. Germany was not consulted. The US did not ratify the treaty, but its provisions were implemented and helped to cause the early rise of A Hitler and Nazism. (World History compiled by Bruce Wetterau, p.820).

Did You know? There is a road in France that can only be used twice a day, for a few hours. Then it disappears under 13 feet of water.

Did you know? Neuschwanstein Castle that was built for "mad" King Ludwig, is one of Germany's most popular sites that inspired the design for Disneyland's Sleeping Beauty Castle.

Did you know who and why the organization called the "March of Dimes" was created? Franklin Delano, Roosevelt, the thirty-second U.S. President, started it. Why? He was sickened with Polio at the age of 39 and understood how it can devastate the life of many people. Therefore, he founded the organization called the Infantile Paralyses Foundation that later will be known as the "March of Dimes." The comedian Eddie Cantor was the one who came up with the name and ask people to mail a dime to the White House. They were soon overwhelmed with 2,680,000 dimes mailed to them, literally truckloads, mostly from children. These dimes went directly to research in order to find a cure for Polio, and in 1955 Jonas Salk discovered the Polio Vaccine. As a gesture of thank you for the founder of this organization you can find today on a Dime, the face of FDR.

Did you know how we got the expression 'crack a smile' or 'losing face'? It originated in the past when women and men ended up developing acne scars by adulthood, because no medicine existed to remedy it. So, women ended up spreading bee's wax over their faces to smooth out their complexions. If the women ended up smiling at one point, the wax would crack, hence the term 'crack a smile.' Furthermore, when they sat too close to the fire, the wax would melt, hence the expression 'losing face.'

Did you know how we got the saying "Okay, but it will cost you an arm and a leg"? In George Washington's days, there were no cameras. One's image was either painted or sculpted. Some paintings of George Washington showed him standing behind a desk with one arm behind his back while others showed both arms and both legs. Prices for painting were based on how many limbs the painter was asked to paint, and not on how many people were to be painted. Hence the expression, "Okay, but it will cost you an arm and a leg."

Did you know how we got the expression "Big Wig? In the past, people took baths only twice a year, in May and October. Since there was a lot of lice and bugs, men ended up shaving their heads and wore wigs. Wealthy men were able to afford to buy good wigs made of wool. They could not wash the wigs, so to clean them they carved out a loaf of bread, put the wig in the shell of the bread, and baked it for 30 minutes in the oven. The heat would make the wig big and fluffy, hence the term 'big wig'. Today we often use the term "here comes the Big Wig" to indicate how powerful and wealthy a person is.

Did you know how we got the title" Chairman' or 'Chairman of the Board'? In the late 1700's, many houses had a large room with only one chair. The head of the household always sat in the chair while everyone else ate sitting on the floor. Occasionally, a guest, who was usually a man, would be invited to sit in this chair during a meal. To sit in the chair meant that you were important and in charge. They called the one sitting in the chair the 'chairman.'

Did you know that each king in the deck of playing cards represents a great king from the past? Spades - King David, Hearts – Charlemagne, Clubs - Alexander the Great, and Diamonds – Julius Caesar.

Did you know how we got the saying "you are not playing with a full deck"? It originated in the past when people's common entertainment included playing cards. When people purchased playing cards, they had to pay tax on only the 'Ace of Spades card'. People who could not afford to pay the tax, ended up purchasing only 51 cards. However, since card gams requires 52 cards, these people were thought to be stupid or dumb because they did not play with a full deck of cards.

Did you know? Games have been a part of the human experience since the beginning after the advent of spoken language. Tombs dating from pre-historic Egypt have been found to contain *Senet* board games from 3,500 B.C., as well as multi-thousand-year-old games from Africa and Asia that are still widely played to this day including Mancala, Chess, Go, and Backgammon. While some are abstract, some are actually tell a story just like in the case of the Chess game that has its intrigue and leaping knights ending in the capture of a king (Casual Game Insider, Fall 2020, p.33).

Did you know how we got the term 'gossip'? In the old days there were no phones, radios, or TVs, so politicians end up sending their assistants to get feedback from the public, about different issues of the day. The best places to gather public opinion were in taverns, bars, and pubs. So, the assistants went there to 'sip some ale' and listen to the people. Thus 'go sip' ended up becoming 'gossip'.

Did you know how the word GOLF enter the English language?
Many years ago, in Scotland, a new game was invented. It was ruled 'Gentlemen Only...Ladies Forbidden'...and thus, that is how the word GOLF came about.

Did you know how we got the saying "Goodnight, sleep tight"?
In Shakespeare's time, mattresses were secured on bed frames by ropes. When you pulled on the ropes, the mattress tightened, making the bed firmer to sleep on. Hence the phrase... 'Goodnight, sleep tight.'

Did you know how the word gibberish came about? It is associated with the alchemist Abu Musa Jabir ibn Hayyan (c.721-c.815), known to the West as "Geber". He lived in what is now Iraq. His writings attracted a great number of followers. His followers' work was often written in such a way that it was impossible to decipher their writings, that is how the word gibberish came about.

Did you know? A knocker-upper was someone whose purpose was to wake people up during a time when alarm clocks were too expensive and not very reliable. They earned about six pence a week using a pea shooter to shoot dried peas at the windows of sleeping workers in East London, in the 1930's. She would not leave a window until she was sure that the workers had woken up.

Did you know? The U.S. Army in 1836 considered using camels as a pack animal, instead of mules and horses. The reason was because camels are used to desert like weather. They are therefore requiring less water and forage than mules and horses. In addition, the camels can move faster than mules and carry more supplies, in Southwest climate of Texas, which is desert like weather. The first caravan left Texas in June 1857 and made its way to California. The camels carried up to 800 pounds each and traveled an average of 25 to 30 miles a day. The caravan made it to California and back successfully. However, this successful experiment was cast aside as the Civil War came about in April 12, 1861.

Did you know? 8 million horses, donkeys and mules lost their lives during World War I, 1914-1918.

Did you know how we end up using the blockbuster word to refer to a successful movie? During WWII, the word "blockbuster" was a nickname used by the Royal Air force for large bombs that could "bust" an entire city block.

Did you know how we ended up with the saying "Push the envelope"? In WWII test pilots listed a plane's abilities – speed, engine power, and maneuverability on its flight envelope and then did their best to get the plane to outperform its pre-determined limits.

Did you know who came up with the Zumba Dance? In the 1990's Alberto Perez, an aerobics dance instructor in Columbia, forgot to bring his usual aerobics music to his class he was teaching. So instead, he had to improvise and end up using salsa and merengue music. His students loved the change and his classed became extremely popular. In 2001, he joined Alberto Perlman and Alberto Aghion to trademark and market the Zumba Fitness regimen. Today more than 15 million people enjoy weekly Zumba classes in the world, and it is growing by the day. The Zumba Fitness incorporates squats and lunges, which improve functional strength, and it has been shown to burn 600 calories in an hour, increase aerobic fitness, build endurance, and improve mood. (Diabetes Self-Management Magazine, March/April 2019, p.59).

Did you know that Super Mario is named after a real-life businessman Mario Segale? He rented a warehouse to Nintendo. After Nintendo fell far behind on rent, Segale did not evict them but gave them a second chance to come up with the money. Nintendo eventually succeeded and named their main character after him.

Did you know? John Harvey Kellogg was the king of cornflakes, but he was almost famous for his Michigan-based sanitarium and health spa. Among its patients: Henry Ford, Thomas Edison, and President William Howard Taft.

Did you know? Lewis Carroll is best known as the author of Alice's Adventures in Wonderland, but very few people if any, know that he was also gifted mathematician who developed games of logic that combined his analytical skills.

Did you know? Mark Twain tried his hand at developing a board game of historical trivia called Mark Twain's Memory Builder. It did not sell anywhere near as well as *The Adventures of Huckleberry Finn*, but you can visit <u>timeonline.uoregon.edu/twain/index.php</u> to try it.

Did you know? The first crossword puzzle was printed in the *New York World* on December 21, 1913, but many people did not care much for it. In 1924, the *New York Times* considered crosswords to be "sinful waste in the utterly futile finding of words....". *The Times* did not publish its first crossword until 1942.

Did you know if you were to spell out numbers, how far would you have to go until you would find the letter 'A'? Until you would spell *One Thousand.*

Did you know why we have an Electoral College System? The Founding Fathers of the United States were brilliant scholars. They came up with the Electoral College System for an incredibly good reason. They created it to ensure that the states will be fairly represented, small and big. Otherwise, if it were to be based on population only, the most populated states will have all the say for the entire country. In other words, with the current Electoral College System 319 sqm (two very populated states) will not be able to represent 3,478 sqm (US 3,797 minus 319 sqm) which is the rest of us.

Did you know? Rainbows appear as full circles when you are in the sky. They only appear as half circles from the ground because there is no rain below the person viewing it.

Did you know? Rainbows can appear at night, and they are called "Moonbows".

Did you know? Since 1787, more than 300 billion pennies have been produced. Today, there are about 150 billion pennies in circulation, enough to circle the Earth 137 times or more.

Did you know? Since 1909, Abraham Lincoln's image has been on the penny. However, it was not always that way. There have been 11 different designs, including the popular Indian Head penny, which was introduced in 1859.

Did you know? The princess on the Indian Head penny was neither a Native American nor a princess. She was, in fact, Sarah Longacre, the sculptor's daughter.

Did you know? The word Bluetooth predated that technology by 1,000 years. The engineers who developed the wireless connection in the 1990's named it after King Harald Bluetooth, who united and ruled Denmark and Norway in the 10ᵗʰ century.

Did you know why the color Ultramarine was as valuable as gold for a millennium? For more than a thousand years, a single region in Afghanistan was the only source of Lapis Lazuli, the blue mineral we refine into Ultramarine. Scarcity and a supposed resistance to fading made it unbelievably valuable.

Did you know how the Scheele's Green color came about? Carl Wilhelm Scheele came up in his lab with a color derived from Copper Arsenate tincture. Even though he was worried that it will be toxic, many companies used it on everything from wallpaper to dresses. Only after some people started to die from it, did the companies stop using it.

Did you know how the Perkin's Mauve color came about? The Chemist William Perkin accidentally invented his eponymous purple while trying to synthesize the malaria treatment quinine from coal tar in 1856. Victorians adored it, but what we call "mauve" today is a demurer shade.

Did you know what causes leaves to change color? Notably not all leaves will change color in the fall. Only a few deciduous species of trees usually will do so, such as: maple, aspen and oak. Several factors contribute to the fall color of leaves including temperature, precipitation, soil moisture and reduced daylight. The reduced daylight triggers chemical changes in deciduous plants causing a corky wall or "abscission layer" to form between the twig and the leaf stalk. This layer prevents the leaf from getting water, and nutrients as well as trapping simple sugars in the leaf. This will lead to the death of the Chlorophyll pigment the "green" in leaves. Once the green is gone, two other pigments show their bright faces. These pigments, Carotene (yellow) and Anthocyanin (red), exist in the leaf all summer but are masked by the Chlorophyll. The browns in the autumn leaves are the result of Tannin, a chemical that exist in many leaves, especially oaks. The sugar that is trapped in autumn leaves by the abscission layer is largely responsible for the vivid color. However, if freezing temperatures and a hard frost come too early in the fall it will harm the process within the leaf and lead to poor fall colors. Usually, North America tends to have the most beautiful autumn foliage color show (The Old Farmer's Almanac, Fall/Winter 2020, p.11).

Did you know why our calendar has 365 days in a year? The Western world uses the 365-day calendar called the Gregorian calendar named after Pope Gregory XIII, who introduced it in October 1582. It is based on Earth's orbit of the Sun, so the Sun appears to be in the same place in the sky on the same date each year. However, the traditional Chinese, Hindu Jewish, and Muslim calendars are based on the Moon's cycles. The ancient Aztec calendar was solar, like the Gregorian, but consisted of 18 months of 20 days and five extra days that were considered lucky.

Did you know? 400 million years ago, there were 22 hours in a day and 400 days in a year.

Did you know? Iceland has one of the largest gun ownership rates in the world, and yet it has one of the lowest crime rates in the world.

Did you know? The internet speed at NASA in 2020 is 91 Gb per second. Making it 2,000 times faster than the average household connection speed of 50 Mb.

Did you know? When the world's largest cut diamond was transported to England, an elaborate and secure journey by sea was arranged with a fake diamond. However, the real diamond was simply posted by mail.

Did you know? The cruise liner, QE 2, moves only six inches for each gallon of diesel that it burns.

Did you know? Nauru, a country in Africa, has the most overweight population in the world. Ninety five percent of its population is overweight because Western fast food was introduced to it, and the population seems to like to eat it a lot.

Did you know? Canada has the most lakes in the world totaling 3,000,000 lakes which equal to about 60% of the lakes in the world.

Did you know? Canada has the most literate people in the world constituting 50% of its population follow by Israel 45% and Japan 44%.

Did you know? Israel became a cyber superpower in 2021. It is all due to the fact that its enemies keep on cyber attacking it with no mercy. Therefore, the enemy indirectly forced it to develop the greatest protection against these attacks. Today many countries are purchasing the most advanced and sophisticated cyber security systems in the world, from Israel.

Did you know? The Falkland Islands have more sheep than people. The population of the islands consists of 3,594 people in 2019, while they have ½ a million sheep. So, there are 139 sheep for every person on the island. Therefore, their major export is wool.

Did you know? Saudi Arabia has no rivers or fresh surface water. So, it gets its water from desalinization plants that use sea water, or from underground reservoirs.

Did you Know? You can save money per year by setting your water heater temperature between 110 and 120 degrees.

Did you know? You can save money per year by running full loads of laundry instead of smaller loads.

Did you know? You can save money per year by cooking in a microwave than cooking in an oven.

Did you know? In order to double the life of fresh flowers you need to add 1xTbs. of sugar and 1xTbs. of vinegar to the vase before adding the flowers. Sugar provides nourishment while vinegar kills bacteria that could cause the blooms to wilt (*First for women,* June 15, 2020, p.77).

Did you know? Dry tea leaves absorb odors as well as baking soda does. Leave a few bags in the fridge, or drop some into shoes, pocketbooks, and cars.

Did you know? The astringent substances in tea called Tnnins make it a natural skin toner, as well as can help reduce acne. In addition, when used as a final rinse it will condition and restore shine to hair. Furthermore, cooled tea when applied to skin can give relief from poison ivy, hives, or insect bites (The Book of Home Remedies, The Old Farmer's Almanac, Boys Town 2020, p.13).

Did you know? Strong tea extract left in cooking pots overnight will remove burnt-on food and stains.

Did you know? If you are looking to get rid of bathroom mirror fogging, you may want to try to rub a cucumber slice along the mirror. It will eliminate the fog.

Did you know? If you want to get rid of grubs and slugs that are ruining your planting beds it is a good idea to place a few slices of cucumber in a small aluminum container. The chemicals in the cucumber react with the aluminum to give off a scent undetectable to humans but it drives the garden pests crazy and make them live your planting beds alone to thrive.

Did you know? You can polish your shoes with a fresh cut of cucumber. The chemicals in the cucumber will provide a quick and durable shine that looks great and also repels water.

Did you know? If you have a squeaky hinge and you ran out of WD 40, you can use a cucumber slice and rub it along the squeaky hinge, it will work like as if you used WD 40.

Did you know? If you want to clean your faucets, sinks or stainless steel without using harsh chemicals, use a slice of cucumber and rub it on the surface that you want to clean. It will remove years of tarnish and bring back the shine and won't harm your hands and fingernails while using it.

Did you know? Compact fluorescent light bulbs last 10x longer than incandescent bulbs, and light emitting diode based light bulbs last even longer.

Did you know? Your freezer will run more efficiently if you keep it full.

Did you know? If you have never experienced the solitude of prison, the horror of war, or were not close to death from starvation, then you are much better off than about 500 million people in the world.

Did you know? If you can go to your place of worship, church, synagogue, temple or a mosque, without fear that someone or somebody will assault or kill you, then you are luckier than about 3 billion people in the world.

Did you know? If you have clothes on you back, a roof over your head, a place to sleep and a refrigerator full of food, you are considered to be wealthier than about 75% of the world's population.

Did you know? If you have money in the bank and money right now in your wallet, you are considered to be one of the eight privileged few per 100 people in the world.

Did you know? Electricity has to be one of the least efficient ways to power things, despite the fact that we are told otherwise. We are told that electric cars for example are good to own. Yet, a home charging system for an electric car requires 75-amp service. However, the average house is equipped only with 100-amp service. Keep in mind that our residential electrical infrastructure is not able to bear the load if all of us were to have electric cars. In addition, we would not be able to reduce pollution in the world on a large scale if we were all to own eco-friendly electric cars. Why? This is because we will still need to consume a lot of electricity for the cars that will be produced by coal and fuel for the most part. Not to speak that it takes about 10 hours to charge the one drained electric car battery. In addition, we will end up paying twice as much for an electric car, and it will cost us more than about seven times as much to run it.

Did you know? The headrest of car seats is deliberately kept detachable and sharp so that it could be used to break open the glass of car in case of fire and emergency. The car's glass too is kept easily breakable from inside. Very few people know about it and thus cannot save themselves in case of emergencies.

Did you know? In order to find out if you really need to purchase new tires for your care you need to use the "Honest Abe" method. This method requires you to slide a penny upside down into various parts of the tread. If you can see any of Lincoln's head, the tread is too worn and the tires do in fact need to be replaced (Reader's Digest, December 2020/January 2021, p.38).

Did you know? A petrol/diesel engine has 20,000 individual parts, while an electrical motor has only 20. So, it takes only 10 minutes to remove and replace an electric motor in a car.

Did you know? Employees of Ferrari are not allowed to buy Ferrari cars.

Did you know? If you were to fit the entire world population into one village that consist of 100 people, that village would consist of: 57 Asians, 21 Europeans, 14 Americans (north, Central and south) and 8 Africans. In addition, there would be: 52 women and 48 men, 30 Caucasians and 70 non-Caucasians, 30 Christians and 70 non-Christians, 89 heterosexuals and 11 homosexuals.

Furthered more 6 people would possess 59% of the wealth in the world and they all would come from the USA, 80 would live in poverty, 70 would be illiterate, 50 would suffer from hunger and malnutrition, 1 would be dying, 1 would be being born, 1 would own a computer, and 1 (yes, only one) would have a university degree.

Some Bad Manners That Are Seen as Good, in Some Cultures Around the World

Did you know? Belching is considered a compliment to the chef in China, Taiwan and much of the Far East.

Did you Know? In most Asian countries, a business card is seen as an extension of the person it represents. Therefore, folding a card, writing on it, or shoving it into your pocket without looking at it, is considered disrespectful to the person who gave it to you.

Did you know? When dining in China, you should leave some food on your plate at each course as an acknowledgement of your host's generosity. However, in the Western World it will look like that the food was not that great.

Did You know? In Japan and Korea, a tip is considered an insult rather than a compliment. However, this tradition is beginning to change with more and more Westerners coming to visit these countries.

Did you know? The "okay" sign is not okay in much of the world. In Germany and most of South America, it is an insult, like giving the someone the middle figure in the United States. While in Turkey it is a gesture that implies that someone is homosexual.

Did you know? In the United Kingdom, when the two fingers "V for victory" or "peace" salute is given with the hand turned so that the palm faces inward, it is considered extremely rude, as it has a meaning similar to raising the middle figure to someone in the United States.

Did you know? In the Middle East and the Far East, it is considered an insult to point the soles of your shoes at another person or resting with your feet up.

Did you know? A bone-crushing handshake is seen today as manly and admirable in the U.S. and the U.K., but in much of the East, particularly the Philippines, it is seen as a sign of aggression.

Did you know? Orthodox Jews will not shake hands with someone of the opposite sex.

Did you know? A strict Muslim woman will not shake hands with a Muslim man. However, a Muslim man will shake hands with a non-Muslim woman. People in these cultures generally avoid touching people of the opposite sex who are not family members.

Unexpected Hobbies of Some U.S. Presidents

Did you know? **Thomas Jefferson** was the 3rd U.S. president who also was a great architect. His designs included his famed home, Monticello, and the Virginia State Capitol building. In addition, he was also a fairly good cook.

Did you know? **Theodore Roosevelt** was the 26th U.S. president that also had more hobbies than any president before or since. He liked to explore, hunt, read, write, and Ornithology (the branch of science devoted to birds). He also was an avid poker player.

Did you know? **Franklin Delano Roosevelt** was the 32nd U.S. president who also liked to collect stamps, and by the way, helped oversee the design and promotion of about 200 stamps. In addition, he was an avid poker player too.

Did you know? **Dwight D. Eisenhower** was the 34th U.S. president who also loved to play golf.

Did you know? **Bill Clinton** was the 42nd president who also loves to play the saxophone and enjoys doing crossword puzzles.

Did you know? **Barack Obama** was the 44th president who loves to play basketball.

Little-Known Tidbits About Some Animals and Insects

Did you know? About 285 land animals are killed every second of every day in the United States. Plant-base meals will reduce the meat productions' impact. Just ONE day a week of not eating meat can make a world of difference for your health, animals, and the environment.

Did you know? Animal play is not just for fun. It is also a means to allow youngsters to practice skills they will need to use later on in life. It includes evading predators, forging alliances and competing for mates in a safe environment (Scientific American, August 2021, p.1).

Did you know? The only two animals that can see behind themselves without turning their heads are rabbit and parrot.

Bald Eagles

Did you know? All raptors, including the Bald Eagle, hawks, Condors, and Golden Eagle remain faithful until their mate dies. In addition, when it loses a feather on one side, it will automatically shed the same feather on its other side to maintain balance.

Eagles

Did you know? Eagles have the longest life span of its species. It can live up to nearly 70 years. However, in order for it to reach this old age it has to make a tough choice when it enters its 40th year of life. It needs to get rid of its beak, talons and feathers that got old and useless. The process is very painful for the eagle and will take about 150 days to complete. When completed the eagle in a way is reborn again and can live for up to 30 more years.

Parrots

Did you know? It is rare for wild parrots to mimic sounds made by other species. In the wild, parrots live in large cohesive groups and squawk constantly, updating one another on where the best seeds are and which direction to search next for food. However, in captivity, they will mimic barking dogs, car alarms, and human speech in an attempt to bond with their human flock. Furthermore, a large parrot's beak can exert 500 pounds of pressure per square inch, enabling the bird to feast on Brazil nuts and other nuts at ease (Reader's Digest, February 2020, p.68).

Birds

Did you know? Falling air pressure causes pain in bird's ears. So, if birds are flying low to the ground it almost always means a thunderstorm is coming (1000LifeHacks.com).

Ravens

Did you know? Ravens can spot a cheater. They will shun one another for being unfair. The birds work together to gain equal amount of food, but if they notice another raven taking more than its fair share, they immediately lose trust and would not cooperate with it in the future (Bolowingfacts.org).

Chickens

Did you know? There are more chickens than people in the world. In addition, chickens are not stupide but rather very smart. They have different vocalizations for different objects, they see more colors than people can, they can differentiate human faces, they can plan for the future, and they can count to ten. They have complex social structure, hence comes the term "pecking order". Chickens have extensive communication skills. Before they hatch, chicks start peeping to their mothers, who respond with soothing sounds. The Chicks learn from watching their moms and other chickens. They learn to steer away from unhealthy or poisonous food, as well as, to avoid predators and other dangers. Roosters keep watch over chickens and have different calls to let their ladies know where the best food is. In addition, they alert them when danger is present or tell them when it is time to return to the coop for the night. You can have chickens as pets and teach them to even play a simple melody on a small keyboard (The Humane League).

Ducks

Did you know? Ducks are constantly at risk of being attacked by predator. Therefore, they keep half of their brain awake while they sleep.

Did you know? A duck's quack doesn't echo, and no one knows why. In addition, never feed bread to ducks. The reason is that they cannot digest it properly and it could kill them (1000LifeHacks. come).

Turkeys

Did you know? A male turkey is called a tom, a female is a hen and a younger is a poult. Turkeys are the true original native bird to America. It can purr when they snuggle and when they are content, just like cats do. Did you also know that their snoods- the flaps of skin that hang down over their foreheads- will change colors from white, to red, to blue depending on how they feel? The color change is common among males during courtship dances. Only male turkeys, or toms, can gobble, and they mostly do it in the spring and fall. It is a mating call and attracts the hens. Wild turkeys gobble at loud sounds and when they settle in for the night. Furthermore, the wild turkey is one of the more difficult birds to hunt. It would not be flushed out of the brush with a dog. Instead, hunters must try to attract it with different calls. Even with two seasons a year, only one in six hunters will get a wild turkey. Moreover, a wild turkey can fly, however it usually prefers to walk or run. On the other hand, domestic turkeys are not agile flyer, though the birds will perch to stay safe from predators in trees. The average life span of a domestic turkey, from birth to freezer, is 26 weeks. On the other hand, the average life span of a wild turkey is three to four years. In general, the average person in the United States will tend to eat about 15 pounds of turkey a year.

Ostriches

Did you know? An ostrich's eye is bigger than its brain.

In addition, the real reason that they stick their head in the sand is to search for water.

Cows

Did you know? In a natural environment, a cow can live for over 20 years. Cows have a memory of three years, are pregnant for nine months and cannot see red or green. They also share child-care duties. They are sensitive animals who withdraw from humans or other animals who have treated them badly. They like to groom one another to help reduce tension and increase bonding. Cows also work in groups to care for calves. When the herd need to graze, rest, or take a dip in the water, one or two cows are left to watch over the calves. Cows develop strong bonds with their offspring. When separated, mother cows and calves will cry out for one another. In addition, cows love to play and have best friends and get stressed when they are separated. Cows are not all that environmentally friendly. They burp and fart up to twice as much methane as conventionally reared cattle. Methane gas is 20 times more powerful greenhouse gas than CO_2. (Nutrition Action Health Letter, November 2020, p.11 & The Humane League).

Did you know? 2,500 dairy cows produce as much waste as a city of 400,000 people. However, it was found lately that if you add lemon grass to the livestock feed the cows will have less flatulence and will burp less. This will cut methane production (CH4) by 30%. Burger King introduced it to their cows' diet in order to reduce climate change. (Nutrition Action Health Letter, November 2020, p.11 & The Humane League).

Did you know? It is possible to lead a cow upstairs but not downstairs.

Goats

Did you know? Goats are very curious animals. They like to investigate anything new in their environment. They are very cleaver at planning how to escape in case of danger. They have been known to hop on the backs of their taller animal friends, such as donkeys, and leap over fences. They are also very social. They like to play, cuddle, fight and even make up. Goats can also be more optimistic based on studies done by scientists.

Sheep

Did you know? Sheep remember one another, and they are intelligent too. They can recognize the faces of at least 50 other sheep and remember them for several years. Sheep are also excellent problem-solvers. On one farm in England that had installed hoof-proof metal grids, to keep them from grazing in local gardens, the sheep figured out how to overcome the challenge by laying down and roll over the grids.

Pigs

Did you know? Pigs are highly intelligent, and they like to cuddle and snuggle up. They are smarter than dogs. They can learn their own names quickly at just two weeks old, respond to simple voice commands and even play simple video games. Researchers can teach pigs to use joysticks to direct cursor to its targets on a screen. A complex process for an animal. Pigs are family oriented. They also love belly rubs. They can run up to 11 mph. Piglets like to stay close to their mother and siblings until they mature enough to be on their own. Piglets that are weaned abruptly will often eat less, lose weight, and become more aggressive and reckless (NRDC – Natural Resources Defense Council & The Humane League).

Pronghorn Antelopes

Did you know? Pronghorn antelopes have 10 x vision, which means that on a clear night they can see the rings of Saturn.

Horses

Did you know? The horse's evolution started about 55 million years ago. The early horse, "dawn horse" was a forest forager that stood as tall as a beagle. Archaeological evidence suggests that the early horse went from wild to mild about 5,500 years ago. The first horses originated in North America and then spread to Asia and Europe. The horses that were left in North America became extinct about 10,000 years ago and were re-introduced by colonizing Europeans. According to a 2016 *Biology Letters* paper, horses respond differently to unfamiliar humans as well as can sense if a human is happy or angry. Only dogs previously were known to demonstrate this kind of interspecies perception. That responsiveness to human cues may explain why equine- assisted therapy (EAT) has shown wide-ranging, positive results for people with conditions ranging from Cerebral Palsy to Multiple Sclerosis (Reader's Digest, February 2020, pp.68-69).

Elephants

Did you know? Elephants stand while they are dozing in non-REM sleep, but once REM sleep kicks in, they lie down. In addition, just as humans are either right-or left -handed, so are elephants are either right-or left-tusked. In addition, adults' elephants cannot jump. Furthermore, they "hug" by wrapping their trunks together as a way of greeting one another. Baby elephants are known to suck their trunks for comfort – sort of human babies suck on their thumbs. Elephants have trunks because their necks are truly short, so they are not able to reach the ground. The trunks allow them to eat from the ground as well as the treetops. Additionally, an elephant's trunk is comprising of 150,000 different muscle fibers, and it weighs about 400 pounds while the average weight of an elephant is between 10,000 to 12,000 pounds. Furthermore, a female elephant usually can be pregnant for 22 months - almost two years. Elephants, especially the African elephants that has the longest tusk are the most sensitive to scent and can smell water from 12 miles away (Reader's Digest, June 2021, p.46).

Koalas

Did you know? The Koala is not actually a bear but a marsupial. It gets all the liquid it needs from licking dew off tree leaves.

Polar bears

Did you know? Polar bears are not actually white. They appear white because their fur is made up of hollow, transparent, pigment-free hairs, which scatter and reflect visible light. The bear actually under its fur has black skin.

Emperor Penguins of the Antarctic

Did you know? A pair of Emperor Penguins share responsibilities of raising the young. The female lays the eggs, but the male protects the eggs and keep them still for two months until they hatch, and the female returns to feed the chicks.

Kangaroos

Did you know? A mother kangaroo can have two babies of different ages in her pouch at the same time. She produces different milk for each of them, depending on their age and nutritional needs.

Giraffes

Did you know? Giraffes will spend about 70% of their day eating. In addition, they can survive on less than an hour of sleep each day (Reader's Digest, June 2021, p.117).

Lions and Tigers

Did you know? Currently, India is the only country in the world confirmed to have both lions and tigers in its wilderness.

Did you know? Tiger cubs will stay with their mother until approximately the age of 2 years. After that they will leave or are chased away by their mother in order to start to form their own territory.

Cats

Did you know? Cats have over one hundred vocal sounds. Their taste buds cannot detect sweetness. A cat has 32 muscles in each ear. In order to protect your vegetable garden from cats you need to place lemon and Thyme intermittently around the perimeter of your garden. Cats detest the scent of citrus and Thyme.

Did you know? Cats will sleep anywhere from 16 to even 20 hours a day, more than dogs or humans. In addition, cats as well as dogs do tend to dream when they sleep (Health, May 2021, p.74).

Did you know? Do not forget to close the dryer door as soon as you take out the laundry, because a warm dryer is an invitation for a cat nap (Better Homes & Gardens, May 2021, p.118).

Did you know? In order to keep your cat from getting an electric shock, because some cats like to gnaw on electrical cables, you need to dab the cords with Grannick's Bitter Apple, a flavor that cats hate, or another deterrent spray for pets In addition,

33% of cats taken in by shelters are black (Reader's Digest, March 2020 p.33 & Reader's Digest, June 2020, p.43).

Did you know? If you want your cat to eat more slowly so it will not throw up the food after it eats it, you need to put its food in a clean, carboard egg carton. Simply distribute a few bits of kibble between the wells of the carton (*First for Women,* April 2021, p.90).

Did you know? Cats tend to purr not only when they are content but also when they are sick or injured. They also do it to communicate with other cats. The kitten purrs to let its mother know that it is getting enough milk, they also purr when they are frightened, ill or injured. They even purr while giving birth. They also purr to comfort themselves during stressful situations and to let other cats know how they feel (Reader's Digest, February 2020, p.65).

Did you know? Cats do not forgive, and once they realize that a particular person causing them anxiety or harm, they will keep away (Reader's Digest, February 2020, p.66).

Did you know? Once cats master an essential skill such as hunting, they will remember it for the rest of their lives (Reader's Digest, February 2020, p. 66).

Did you know? If you do not want your cat to sleep or lie down in a particular place, cover the surface with aluminum foil or sticky paper and they will find another place to be (Reader's Digest, November 2020, p.35).

Did you know? Napoleon Bonaparte suffered from Ailurophobia, which is the fear of cats.

Did you know? Belgium once experimented with using cats to deliver mail.

Did you know? Ancient Egyptians used to mourn the death of a pet cat by shaving off their eyebrows (*First for Women*, June 15, 2020, p. 86).

Dogs

Did you know? Dogs can read human facial expressions as well as tell based on the ton of their voices whether they are happy or mad (Reader's Digest, February 2020, p.69).

Did you know? Dogs have 10 vocal sounds, unlike cats that have one hundred. The Bible contains 32 references to dogs, but none to cats. Humans have more empathy for dogs than they do for other humans.

Did you Know? Foods and medicines that make us feel better can make our pets sick. Among the top **11 toxins for pets** are some of our favorite foods and drinks. They include **chocolate**, **coffee**, **caffeinated products**, **alcoholic beverages**, **citrus fruits**, **grapes**, **raisins**, **onions**, **garlic**, a c**hives** and **Xylitol that is found in sugar free products, like gum, candy, toothpaste and peanut butter.** Don't also forget to keep pets out of rooms and yards were **chemicals or fertilizers** were used, because pets will walk through the chemicals and later, they will lick them off their paws (Better Homes & Gardens, May 2021, p.118).

Did you know? If a dog ends up nibbling on something it shouldn't they may end up with an upset stomach, passing gas and have gurgling sounds coming from their tummy. If so, it is a good idea to let it **lick a tablespoon of honey**. Enzymes in the honey will settle its stomach in no time. Long walks or rides in the car during hot summer days can quickly overheat your dog. Since dogs do not sweat through their fur, wetting their coat can help cool them down. (*First for Women,* June 15, 2020, p.86).

Did you know? The cost of raising a medium-size dog to the age of eleven is about $16,400.

Did you know? Approximately 3.3 million dogs enter U.S. animal shelters nationwide every year. Approximately half of those will be adopted into forever homes and about 620,000 dogs who enter shelters as strays are returned to their owners.

Did you know? Three dogs from first class cabins survived the sinking of the Titanic – two Pomeranians and one Pekingese.

Did you know? Toronto researchers found out that people with a canine companion have a 31% lower risk of death from cardiovascular disease than those who do not. Being around dogs can reduce blood pressure, depression, and stress. In addition, Caroline K. Kramer, M.D. found out that having a dog tends to reduce the risk of overall mortality by about 24% (Health, September 2020, p.48).

Did you know? Researchers found out that dogs can detect whether a person has certain types of cancer, including breast, colorectal, lung, ovarian, prostate and skin cancer. How? They can detect abnormalities by sniffing a person's breath, urine or blood (Reader's Digest, February 2020, p.62).

Did you know? The average dog has a mind that is equivalent to a 2 to 2 ½ year old human. In addition, take also into consideration that dog's emotional maturity is similar to that of toddlers, and they can also be jealous if you end up petting another dog. On average, dogs comprehend about 165 words, so they can follow a bit more than just simple commands. They tend to learn words associated with objects or activities rather than with words that associated with emotions. Once in a blue moon you can find dogs that have minds of a 3-year-old that can understand more than 250 to about 1,000 words (Reader Digest, February 2020, pp.61-63).

Did you know? Dogs that have predominantly white coat have higher chance of being born deaf in at least one ear. In fact, about 30% of dalmatian are born with this condition. Why? This is because the gene that cause a dog to have a white coat just happens to be associated with deafness as well as with blue eyes (Reader's Digest, February 2020, p.63).

Did you know? Dogs will typically sleep anywhere from 12 to 14 hours a day (Health, May 2021, p.74).

Did you know? Little dogs have shorter dreams than big dogs. Researchers know it because they can scan dog's brains just as they can ours. A pug for example might have five or six one-minute dreams every 90 minutes, and a Saint Bernard can have a four-minute dream every 45 minutes (Reader's Digest, February 2020, p.63).

Did you know? If you are tense and upset, your dog will start to act tense and upset too (Reader Digest, 2020, p.62).

Did you know? Sergeant Stubby (1916-1917) – April 4, 1926), was the most decorated war dog of World War I and the only dog to be promoted to sergeant through combat. America's first war dog, Stubby, served 18 months and participated in seventeen battles on the Western Front. He saved his regiment from surprise mustard gas attacks, found and comforted the wounded, and even once caught a German spy by the seat of his pants (holding him there till Americans Soldiers found him).

Opossums

Did you know? The opossum is the oldest surviving mammal family on Earth, dating back to the dinosaurs and the Cretaceous Period, some 70 million years ago.

Chipmunks

Did you know? A single chipmunk can gather and store up to 165 acorns a day (All Animals, The Humane Society of the United States, Winter 2021, p.28).

Horned Lizards

Did you know? They are also known as Horney Toads even though they are not amphibians. They can squirt blood from their eyeballs to attack predators. They can shoot it up to three feet. This however only happens in extreme cases.

Rodents

Did you know? Nearly half of all mammal species on Earth are rodents. A group of rats is called a 'mischief.' Rats are color blinded and cannot vomit or burp. The average life span of a rat is less than three years, but a pair of mice can produce in one year 2,000 offspring. Rats use their tails to regulate their body temperatures, to communicate and to balance. They can fall 50 feet without injury and jump 36 inches vertically and 48 inches horizontally. In addition, according to the Center of Disease Control and Prevention, more than 45,000 Americans are bitten by rats each year. Also, rodents in the US spread many diseases such as the Bubonic Plague, Murine Typhus, Salmonellosis, Trichinosis and Hantavirus. Furthermore, each year, rats cause more than $1 billion in damages in the United States alone (The Book of Unusual Knowledge, p.175).

Snakes

Did you know? There are 3,000 known snake species on the planet, but only 450 of them are venomous. Snake attacks account for close to 125,000 deaths per year in the world, making them the deadliest reptiles on the planet.

Did you know? Snakes have no eyelids, and their eyes turn a milky white just before they shed their old skin.

Did you know? Boomslang snake venom can cause a person to bleed out from every hole in their body.

Chameleons

Did you know? Chameleons have tongues that are longer than their bodies. It can also focus its eyes separately to watch two objects at once.

Turtles

Did you know? Turtles can breathe through their butts.

In addition, the Golden Turtle often rides on the tops of jellyfish to conserve energy when traveling throughout the ocean (Weird World 1.pdf).

Pacific Leatherback Sea Turtles

Did you know? They are the largest turtles in the world. Each year they migrate about 7,000 miles from Indonesia, Papua New Guinea and the Solomon Islands to their foraging grounds on the U.S. West Coast and back (Nature Conservancy, Summer 2021. P.58).

Sea Turtles

Did you know? About one out of a thousand baby sea turtles survive after hatching. In addition, sea turtles absorb a lot of salt from the sea water in which they live. They excrete excess salt from their eyes, so it often looks as though they are crying.

Frogs

Did you know? Frogs typically eat their old skin once it has been shed. While swallowing, a frog eyeballs retreat into its head, applying pressure that helps push food down its throat. In addition, a frog's ear is connected to its lungs. This keeps the frog from hurting itself when it blasts loud mating calls. In addition, it is interesting to note that archaeologist discovered the earliest known frog fossils in Arizona that are about 190 million years old.

Crocodiles

Did you know? Crocodiles have no lips and can hold their breath for an hour. They also can not stick out their tongues. The Nile crocodiles are the most dangerous to humans.

Octopuses

Did you know? The suction cups on an octopus tentacle have tastes buds. In addition, it has 6 arms and 2 legs, not 8 legs.

Sharks

Did you know? Sharks are the only animals that never get sick. They are even immune to every known disease including cancer. In addition, they are the only fish that can blink with both eyes.

Blue Whales

Did you know? A Blue Whale's tongue outweighs the average adult elephant. It is estimated that there are approximately 2,000 Blue Whales off the coast of California. They are the world's largest creatures ever. An average size of a Blue Whale can weigh 440,000 pounds. Its tongue outweighs the average adult elephant, and its heart weigh about the weight of an average car. Pregnancy will take about 11 months and the newborn can weigh about 5,952.481 lbs.

Pilot Whales

Did you know? They are in fact one of the largest members of the dolphin family, but they are treated as whales for the Marines Mammals Protection Regulations of 1992. They were named so because it is thought that each pod, of about 1,000 pilot whales, follows a 'pilot' in the group. They are long-lived and live together in multi-generational, tight-knit stable pods. They also have very sociable and inquisitive nature.

Bowhead Whales

Did you know? A Bowhead Whale can live for longer than two centuries, making it the oldest mammal to survive in the world.

Dolphins

Did you know? There are pink dolphins in the Amazon River.

Risso's Dolphins

Did you know? They are squid-and-octopus-hunting specialists that are usually found over the continental shelf and slope. Its distinctive blunt heads often scarred by the beaks and tentacles of its prey. Some 11,000 to 16,000 Risso's dolphins live along the U.S. West Cost (Nature Conservancy Magazine Summer 2021, p.58).

Long-Beaked Common Dolphins

Did you know? They are social creatures that commonly travels in groups of between 100 and 500 animals but sometimes in herds numbering into the thousands. They feed primarily on anchovies, hake, pilchards, sardines and other small fish (Nature Conservancy Magazine, Summer 2021, p.58).

Goldfish

Did you know? The average lifespan of a goldfish living in the wild is about 25 years. In addition, it has a memory span of three seconds.

Fangtooth & black swallower fish

Did you know? They are some of the 16 species of ultra-black fish that reflects as little as 0.04 percent of light. They were discovered in the deep sea by marine biologists in the waters of Monterey Bay and the Gulf of Mexico. They evolved this way to stay hidden from many predators or prey (The Week, August 7, 2020, p.17).

Parrotfish

Did you know? Scientists from the Australian Institute of Marine Science (AIMS) made surprising discoveries in 2020. First, they found out that the Parrotfish flourish in the wake of severe coral bleaching caused by prolonged exposure to high sea-surface temperatures. Usually, this fish eats organisms off the coral, but after coral bleaching take place, they enjoy eating the microorganism that colonizes the newly barren surface of the coral reef. Secondly, they discovered that this fish became 20% larger than those living in unbleached areas. Thirdly, they found out that the attendance of Parrotfish in the area suppress the spread of algae and cleared the way for new coral growth and reef vegetation to take place. Lastly, they found out that as the reef begins to return to health, the Parrotfish populations tend to decline.

Tuna Fish

Did you know? There are actually seven species of Tuna fish. In general, Tuna fish is one of the ocean's fastest fish. It can grow to be 1,500 pounds of pure muscle. It is high in protein and low on fat. It can fetch millions of dollars at Japanese fish markets. Paintings of Tuna fish can be found in caves dating back 3,000 years ago. Phoenicians' coins from 2000 B.C. feature Hercules on one side and Tuna fish on the other. In 2015 modern Navy scientists modeled their new underwater spy drone, the Ghost Swimmer, after the Tuna fish body features (Reader Digest, June 2020, pp.40-43).

Bluefin Tuna Fish

Did you know? It is the largest type of a Tuna Fish. It is as long as a BMW sedan and can be found at the top of the food chain. A single Bluefin Tuna can sale for $3 million dollars.

Frogs

Did you know? Some types of frogs vomit their entire stomach. The frogs then clean out the contents of the stomach and then swallow the empty stomach.

Hummingbirds

Did you know? Hummingbirds can zip around at over 34 mph (54 km/h) while flapping their wings at over 80 times per second. Their wings can create a prism-like effect when sunlight passes through them, causing rainbow colors to appear.

Did you know? The **Bee Hummingbird** is the smallest bird in the world that can be found in Zapata, Cuba. It tends to flap its tiny wings over 80 times per second.

The American Robin

Did you know? The American Robin once used to return from wintering in Florida and Mexico as a harbinger of spring across the continental U.S. However, now robins are spotted as far north as Alaska and New England all winter long. It all means that indeed climate change is taking place in the world. According to the National Audubon Society two-thirds of America's birds are threatened with extinction from climate change and that we should realize that it is actually "the fifth alarm in a five-alarm fire" (AARP Bulletin, June 2021, p.20).

Bats

Did you know? Bats make up a quarter of all mammals. There are more than 1,100 species of bats in the world. Some types of brown bats can live to be 30 years old. Bats are the only mammals that can fly. In addition, a single brown bat can catch around 1,200 mosquito-size insects in an hour. So, if you were to install bat houses on your property you will have fewer bugs than your neighbor (The Book of Unusual Knowledge, p.134 & How You Can Help Save Animals, The Humane Society International p.4).

Vampire Bats

Did you know? There are only three species of Vampire Bats in the whole world. They can be found in Central and South America. They do not suck blood, instead they bite and then lick blood from the wound, no sucking involved (The Book of Unusual Knowledge, p.134).

Butterflies

Did you know? A butterfly's taste buds are located on its feet and tongue, and they smell with their antennas. In order to drink nectar from flowers, they uncoil a long proboscis and use it as a straw.

Monarch Butterflies
(Dananus Plexippus)

Did you know? They are the best known and the most beloved of North America butterflies. The Monarch migrates up to 4,000 miles round-trip each year, because they cannot survive the cold northern winters. So, they spend the winter in milder climates. Its large winter gatherings are among the greatest natural spectacles on Earth. But their numbers have dropped dramatically lately with 80% fewer Monarchs wintering in Mexico, and the California's winter population is down by 99%. Monarchs lay their eggs on milkweed plants, that are the only source of food for the caterpillars (larvae) once they emerge, and they eat the leaves voraciously. Without milkweed habitat, there will be no Monarchs alive in the world. Even though the milkweed plants produce toxins to deter animals from eating it, the Monarchs have developed immunity to these toxins. As they feed, the caterpillars store up the toxins in their body, making them taste bad, which in turns deters their predators. In addition, the toxins remain in their system even after metamorphosis so, the adult butterflies are protected as well. Most adult Monarchs only live for a few weeks, searching for food, for mates, and for milkweeds on which to lay their eggs. However, the generation of Monarchs that hatches in late summer delays finding a mate and undertakes a fall migration. This migratory generation can live upward of 8 months (National Wildlife Federation, NRDC-Natural Resources Defense Council & EDF – Environmental Defense Fund & nwf.org/milkweeds).

Did you know? Small aggregations of monarch butterflies spend the winter in the greater Phoenix area especially along the Salt River, Tucson and along the Colorado River in Parker and Lake Havasu (https://www.swmonarch.org).

Did you know? The toxic chemical 2,4-D – found in the pesticide Enlist Duo – poses risks to the Monarch butterflies (NRDC- Natural Resources Defense Council).

Housefly

Did you know? The average housefly lives only for about one month.

Mayflies

Did you know? The eggs of some mayflies take three years to hatch, yet the insect lives only for six hours.

Caterpillars

Did you know? A caterpillar has five to six times as many muscles in its body than a human. In addition, many caterpillars of many species of moths will use camouflage to look like bird droppings to protect themselves from predators.

Shipworms

Did you know? Researchers, to their surprise, found a new-to-science shipworms. It is a kind of clam in the Abatan River on the Philippines' Bohol Island. It is unlike any other shipworms, both in appearance and in its unusual habits. Shipworms got their name because they bore through wood that is in contact with water eating the woods of ship and boat bottoms. Shipworms have been a maritime plague for millennia. However, the new shipworm called in technical term *Lithoredo abatanica* actually eats rock and not wood (Discover Magazine, January/February 2020, p.90).

Spiders

Did you know? Spider silk is five times stronger than steel, but it is also highly elastic. The silk can stretch 30% farther than the most elastic nylon.

Snails

Did you know? The average snail can sleep for three years and lives for six years.

Ants

Did you know? Ants stretch when they wake up. They also appear to yawn in very human manner before taking up the tasks of the day.

Did you know? Do not use chemicals to kill ants. Instead fill a spray bottle with water and 25% salt. Shake it well and spray it on the ants and they will die before you know it (1000LifeHacks.com).

Tree Crickets

Did you know? They sing in exact mathematic ration to the temperature of the air. No need for a thermometer. On a summer night just count the number of chirps a cricket makes in 15 seconds, add 40 and the result will be the current temperature in Fahrenheit degrees.

Cockroaches

Did you know? Fossil records indicate to us that the modern cockroach evolved about three hundred million years ago. They have spent millions of years surviving every calamity the earth could throw at them. They are indeed very resilient and probably be able to survive a nuclear catastrophe on Earth, as long as they are stationed at least two miles away from ground zero. The cockroaches' chief advantage has to do with the fact that they can withstand up to 6,400 rads (accepted measurement for radiation exposure). On the other hand, this amount of radiation will be indeed fatal for humanity and to most of all other Earth's organism. The organism that will be able however to survive this calamity include the Parasitoid Wasp that can take more than 100,000 rads and still sting the heck out us. Also, some forms of bacteria can handle one million rads and keep doing whatever it is that bacteria like to do. Clearly, the cockroach will not be the only specie to survive it (The Book of Strange but True Science, Publications International, Ltd. 2019 p. 371

Scorpions

Did you know? There are 1,500 species of scorpions in the world of which only 25 species are deadly to humans, and they can be found in Africa, the Americas, and Central Asia. In addition, the most lethal scorpions are the fat-tailed once that live in North Africa (The Book of Unusual Knowledge, p.165).

Arizona Bark Scorpions

Did you know? They are the most common scorpion in the Phoenix area out of more than 45 species of scorpions found in Arizona. However, they are the most venomous and the only lethal scorpions in Arizona. The female gives birth during the summer months to about 25-35 baby scorpions. The mother carries them on her back, and they stay there for up to three weeks. She will end up protecting them until their first molt (when they shed their exoskeleton for the first time, in order to grow larger in size). By the way, the life span of an adult scorpion is about 6 years.

Honeybees / Bumblebees & Honey

Did you know? Fallout from nuclear bomb tests in the 1950's and s1960's is showing up in U.S. honey today (2021), decades after the bomb tests. Scientists even suspect that the level of radiation has been 10 times higher in the 1970's and 80's. However, according to the Food and Drug Administration the levels of radioactivity are not dangerous for our health today. The scientists came to this conclusion by measuring the radio-Cesium levels in honey and found out that it is well below 1200 becquerels per kilogram – the cutoff for any food safety concerns. So even though the new study does not raise any alarm bells over today's honey, one needs to understand how nuclear contaminants can affect agriculture and the planet ecosystems for many years to come. Furthermore, we know that bumble bees are wiped out from pesticides but scientist also suspect today that they could have been effected by the nuclear fallout of half century ago (http://sciencemag.org/news.2021/04/ nuclear-fallout-showing-us-honey-decades-after-bomb-tests).

Did you know? Honeybees are critical to U.S. food supplies. 1/3 of the food we eat are pollinated by honeybees, especially the good food that we like to eat that contains vitamins and nutrients. The bees are like the tiny forces behind more than $20 billion worth of U.S. crops every year (NRDC- Natural Resources Defense Council Earthjustice Organization).

Did you Know? It takes two hives, or 60,000 bees to pollinate one acre of an orchard. Each spring bees pollinate almonds, apples, apricots, squash, zucchini, and dozens of other fruits and vegetables (earthjustice.org).

Did you Know? Seventy out of 100 major crops are pollinated by bees. However, bees are in a crisis. Forty-three percent of America's bee colonies collapsed in 2020. The reason has to do with the fact that farmers use pesticides called Neonicotinoid short for "neonics" that are bee toxic. These pesticides tend to change a bee's life and impact the entire colony. It makes it hard for bees to groom themselves, making them susceptible to disease and mites and weakening their immunes systems. Furthermore, the neonics affect the bees' ability to navigate back to the hive. Unable to find their way home, they die. Worker bees supply the colony's food. So, if they do not come back to their hives the entire colony can starve (NRDC- Natural Resources Defense Council & Earthjustice Organization).

Did you know? Researchers discovered that bees love Cannabis, so, Hemp can help restore bee populations in the world. In addition, according to a study published in the journal *Precision Oncology* that was conducted by England, Ireland and Perth, Western Australia, it was found that venom from honeybees and bumblebees can rapidly destroy triple-negative breast cancer, a type of cancer that has limited treatment options.

The African honeybees / killer bees

Did you know? As the name applies, the sting of Killer Bees can be fatal. Killer bees are easy to provoke and hard to escape. Do not stay still and never jump into water. Bees are smart enough to know that you will have to come up for air as soon as possible. Instead, you will need to run away from them and find a dark place indoors. They will chase you farther than the regular common honeybees, up to 600 yards. While doing so keep your hands over your eyes, nose and mouth, because they tend to go after the face and head of a person. They can also stay angry for up to a full 24 hours.

Murder Hornets

Did you know? They are native to Asia, but they invaded in 2019 the U.S. Pacific Northwest. They probably made their way to the U.S. via shipping containers from East Asia. They tend to kill the honeybees by decapitating them and feed the carcasses to their larvae. Their sting is very painful like as if a hot nail was driven into your skin and the venom can hurt your kidneys and liver. In addition, they fly extremely fast, and the queen hornet can fly 20 miles an hour and can grow up to 2 inches long. (Discover Magazine, January/ February 2021, pp.62-63).

Wasps

Did you know? Not only bees are great pollinators, but wasps are too. There are about 33,000 wasp species that pollinate at least 960 different kind of plants, and 164 plants are completely dependent on them. Wasps not only pollinate but they also kill and eat crop-damaging insects like Aphids. Unfortunately, hatred for wasps run deep because of widespread ignorance of their positive role to the environment (Defenders Magazine, Summer 2021, p.6).

Did you know? Wasp venom and saliva have antibiotic properties, and yellow jacket venom has shown promise in treating cancer (Defenders Magazine, Summer 2021, p.6).

Mosquitos

Did you know? There are 3,500 different species of Mosquitoes in the world, but only a handful carry diseases, such as Malaria and the West Nile virus to mention a few. The species that live in Africa, Asia and the Americas are the deadliest. Mosquitoes bite about 270 million people each year in the world, killing as many as 2 million. They are not just annoying but can be dangerous for some people with inflammatory arthritis and Rheumatoid Arthritis. This is because people that take an immune-suppressing medication have a greater risk of having that bug bite become infected. It tends to happen when they scratch the bite area and then bacteria from their own skin enters the wound and infect. In addition, keep in mind that mosquitoes tend to develop resistance to a specific repellent over time. So, it is hard to find a repellent that will keep them away for a long time, it (The Book of Unusual Knowledge, p.165 & Scientific American, August 2021, p.23).

Beetles of the Genus Melanophila

Did you know? These beetles are actually attracted to fires; hence they are sometimes called fire chaser. They prefer to lay their eggs in freshly burned (or still smoldering wood), according to the American Museum of Natural History. It turns out that their eggs are safer from predators in a just burned landscape.

Fruit Flies

Did you know? Researchers discovered that blue light damaged the brain cells, and in a way accelerated aging and shortened the life of fruit flies by about 10 percent (Reader's Digest, March 2020, p.54).

Dragonfly

Did you know? The eyes of a dragonfly are bigger than its brain and it has a life span of 24 hours.

Praying Mantis

Did you know? The praying mantis is the only insect that can turn its head 360 degrees.

Farming / Plants

Did you know? Potatoes are not native to the state of Idaho. They originally were cultivated by the Incas in Peru. A missionary by the name Henry Harmon Spalding brought them in 1836 to the city of Lapwai, Idaho and taught members of the Nez Perce tribe living there how to cultivate them. They learned how to store them by dehydrating and meshing them into a substance called **chunu** and they were able to store it for up to 10 years. Eventually the potatoes travelled to Europe by way of the Spanish Conquistadors. In the 1600s the potatoes spread to Spain, Italy, Belgium, Holland, Switzerland Austria, France Germany Ireland, and Portugal and were almost exclusively fed to animals. It all had to do with the fact that the Europeans population was suspicious of potatoes, because of their resemblance to plants in the nightshade family. Some people even thought that they were crafted by witches. Eventually down the road potatoes became one of the top 5 most important crops in the world (littlepotatoes.com).

Did you know? One acre of seagrass can produce 50,000 liter of Oxygen per day, absorb 3,500 miles worth of Carbon emitted by an average car each year, support 40,00 fish and 50 million invertebrates, as well as absorb enough nutrients to treat the amount of sewage created by 100 people annually. In addition, it can also generate $35,000 in ecological services every year (Defenders Magazine, Summer2021, p.8).

Did you know? About 850 pesticide ingredients were approved by the U.S. government but they are destroying our soils. They harm worms, ground beetles, ground-nesting bees as well as thousands of other vital subterranean species. In a scoop of healthy soil, you will likely be holding more living organisms than there are people on Earth. It will include subterranean species of invertebrates, nematodes, bacteria and fungi that are all constantly filtering our water, recycling nutrients and helping to regulate the planet's temperature. Currently, in 2021, the regulations ignore pesticides' harm to soil species (Scientific American, August 2021, p.12).

Did you know? Tulips are native to the mountain regions of Central Asia and not Holland, in the Netherlands. They were brought to Holland by plant bulb collectors and breeders centuries ago (Better Homes & Gardens, March 2021, p.52 & p.55).

Did you know? From environmental standpoint, rotational grazing of beef, bison, and lamb is the #1 most environmentally sustainable and beneficial form of farming there is, and it is also one of the best solutions for climate change. This method protects the soil from erosion, as well as the groundwater and surface water. By doing so the ecological diversity remains high in areas that are grazed by cattle and other ruminants. In addition, soil scientists claim that grass-fed beef is generally carbon negative in most cases, even after factoring in the methane produced by cattle. It all has to do with the way ruminant animals indirectly improving the growth and decay cycles of grasslands by root shedding, keeping bacteria and fungi intact in the soil and that in turn create stable soil carbon that was pulled from the atmosphere. It should also be noted that most ruminant animals are raised on land that cannot be used for crops, because either it is too steep, dry or rocky. So, cattle produce very nutritious food for people on mostly land that cannot be used to grow crops anyway (help-desk@truthablutabs.com & Mike Geary's Nutrition Watchdog Ezine Newsletter).

Did you know? The media as well as vegan activists and filmmakers, are not soil scientist nor do they have environmental education, so they are actually misleading the vegan population and the rest of us. They do not understand that most plant farming is actually very destructive to soil, groundwater, surface water and the environment in general. In order to grow corn, soy, wheat and beans one needs to plow the earth and use thousands of acres of land as well as pesticides, and herbicides. By doing so these chemicals are effecting the ecosystems. Birds, rodents and other wildlife has been harmed or pushed out of their habitats because of it, as well as it also harms significantly the bacteria and fungi in the soil (help-desk@truthaboutabs.com).

Did you know? Hydrologists estimate that if all the water on Earth filled a 5-gallon bucket, just one drop of it would represent the clean, fresh water accessible to humans.

Did you know? The United Nations predicts that the human population of the world will need 70 percent more food by the year 2050. However, only 10 percent of the Earth's surface is suitable for agriculture, and one third of it is used to grow livestock feed (Popular Mechanics, November/December 2020 p.46).

Did you know? Richard Ballard and his friend Steve Dring, from Great Britain, came up with a brilliant idea about how to solve the water and food shortages in the world. They came up with a high-tech commercial undergrown farming system using old, abandoned, bomb shelters from World War II to grow their crops. Their farm is known as Growing Undergrown (GU), and its located 108 feet below the main street, in Clapham, a south London suburb. They are growing plants from seeds without soil or sunlight and are using special lights called Spectrum AP673L LED from Valoya of Finland. Three LEDS utilize a red; far-red (R;Fr) spectrum ratio that targets the red and far-red light, absorbing photoreceptors on the plant leaf. The light resembles sunlight at its peak level, which delays flowering of herbs and allows the plant to focus its energy into fast biomass development. These farms are using 70 percent less water than conventional field farming. Every year they are able to grow 100 tons of pea shoots, garlic, chives, cilantro, broccoli, wasabi mustard, arugula, fennel, red mustard, pink stem radishes, watercress, sunflower shoots, and salad leaves. Most of the GU's crops are micro herbs. The only two that are larger crops are pea shoots and sunflower shoots. These farms are not susceptible to weather, and crops can be protected from food contamination and grown without herbicides and pesticides. In addition, harvesting is often automated, and much of the water used to grow the crops can be recycled. In addition, these farms do not need to be underground They can be in grown in abandoned factory buildings, or warehouses etc. (Popular Mechanics, November/December 2020, pp.48-51).

Did you know? The British GU's (Growing Underground) farms inspired South Koreans to have their own farms in underground stations on the Seoul Metro thanks to a start-up called Farm 8. In addition, in Tokyo, Japan, abandoned utility tunnels that were previously built to form the basis for the foundation of a skyscraper city that never materialized, have also been converted into GU-style farms. Furthermore, in Hamburg, Germany, one can also find GU's farms that grow salad crops using just 5,920 square feet of indoor space that would require otherwise 161,458 square feet of open fields (Popular Mechanics, November/December 2020, p.51).

Did you know? About 30 million acres of U.S. farmland are owned by investors from Canada, Germany, China, and other foreign countries. Foreign ownership is expected to increase in the future, because many American farmers who are approaching retirement age have no family members that are willing to take over their farms (The Week, June 14, 2019, p.14).

Did you know? In Indonesia, farmers introduce fish into their water-laden rice fields. The method is called Rice-Fish Culture. The fish droppings act as fertilizer, while the fish eat any insect pests and improve oxygen circulation around the field. This method increases the rice yields by up to 10 percent. Sometimes this kind of method is also used to combat mosquito larvae as well.

Did you know? Some crops are thirstier than others and irrigated, processed, crops use the most water. Even so, most plant-based foods use less water than is needed to raise animals. Thus, the tea plant, for example, requires 7.9 gallons of water to grow, which is less than is required to grow coffee, which needs 37 gallons of water. Polyester creating requires 92 gallons of water per one unit of fiber, while cotton requires 713 gallons to develop an analogous amount. Pizza requires 333 gallons of water, while a cheeseburger requires 660 gallons, and cola requires 46 gallons of water, while milk needs 54.9 gallons.

Did you know? There are some plants that do not play well with one another. The garlic plant in general tends to hinder many other plants. Do not grow beans and members of the onion family in the same area. The onion family includes vegetables such as onions, leeks, chives, and garlic. However, beans and carrots complement each other, giving each other nutrients that encourage growth. Carrots also help beans by attracting ladybugs that keep aphids from damaging leaves.

Did you know? Celery and carrots are not compatible. They both need water and shade. Instead, plant celery with Thyme plants.

Did you know? Tomatoes and corn fight each other for soil nutrients if planted too close together. Tomatoes also do not like cabbage or potatoes. Instead, pair tomatoes with lettuce, which will shade the soil and keep it moist for the water-loving tomatoes.

Did you know? Italians have been making lasagna since ancient Rome but without the tomatoes. Why? Tomatoes originated in the Andes, in South America and the Europeans of the era of the Roman Empire had no knowledge nor contact with the Americas until hundreds of years later during the Age of Explorations. Tomatoes first appeared in Italian records by 1548 as an ornamental plant not to be eaten. It was not until 1692 that cookbooks featured it as edible ingredient. Only by the 19th century, did tomatoes become part of the lasagna recipe that we enjoy today.

Did you know? Tomatoes belong to the nightshade family and are considered a health food by many. They contain rich supplies of antioxidants like Lycopene, Beta-Carotene, Folate, Potassium, Vitamin C, other flavonoids and other nutrients. Lycopene in particular is a well-known as cancer-fighting substance, and especially combats prostate cancer in men. Lycopene is also scientifically shown to stop or slow cancerous tumor growth as well as helping to fight lung, stomach, colon, breast, oral and cervical cancers too. In addition, tomatoes also contain other antioxidants such as Beta-Carotene, Phytoene and Phytofluene, that fight inflammation and diseases like heart disease, cancer, Diabetes, Arthritis and Dementia. This powerful antioxidants also protects against high blood pressure, and helps to lower cholesterol, improving blood vessel health, as well as protects against Macular Degeneration. On the other hand, tomatoes can be bad for you if you are sensitive to nightshades or if you suffer from Arthritis since it can increase your joints pain.

Did you know? Potatoes and sunflowers do not get along because sunflower seeds contain toxic ingredients that prevent potatoes from growing to the fullest. Instead, grow spinach with potatoes.

Did you know? Eggplant and fennel are not compatible either. Eggplant is a member of the nightshade family, and fennel produces a chemical that slows nightshade growth. Instead, choose beans as eggplant's companion. Eggplants love the nitrogen that the bush beans add to the soil. Beans also repels the Colorado Potato Beetle, which has a taste for eggplant.

Did you know? Parsnips and carrots are root crops that like the same growing conditions. Both are susceptible to the Carrot Root Fly. So, it is best to give them their own space.

Did you know? Pumpkins and Summer Squash should not grow close to one another. This is because the pumpkin plants are aggressive, and they can choke out the Summer Squash such as zucchini. Both plants need a lot of water and space to grow. Corn however, will grow well next to the pumpkin plants.

Did you know? Asparagus and garlic are incompatible plants because they share the same need for nutrients in the soil. Instead try parsley or dill.

Did you know? The banana plant was domesticated in Southeast Asia 7,000 years ago.

Did you know? The type of banana that we eat today cannot reproduce itself. It can be propagated only by the hand of man.

Did you know? The bananas were introduced to the Americas during the Centennial Exploration in 1876, where vendors sold bananas peeled and wrapped in foil for a dime (Popular Science, Spring 2020, p.15).

Did you know? Bananas are curved because they grow against the pull of gravity. They start off hanging downwards, but as they get bigger, they start trying to grow upwards to get more sun and end up having a curved shape.

Did you know? When you peel a banana from the bottom, you won't have to pick the little "string things" off of it (1000LifeHacks.com).

Did you know? Cassava root provides food for 500 million Africans. In countries like Ghana, a doughy mush of cassava is called Fufu. The cassava plant was actually introduced to Africa by Portuguese sailors and slave traders in the 16th century. The cassava root does well in Africa because it can survive the intense rain and drought that occurs in the African continent and therefore it is an indispensable food source there.

Did you know? Almonds are a member of the peach family.

Did you Know? Half of the world's present calorie consumption by humans comes from a small variety of wheat and barley grains, first cultivated in the Middle East around 8,000 B.C.

Did you know? Strawberries and cashews are the only fruits whose seeds grow on the outside.

Did you know? Yuma County in Arizona is America's second-largest producer of lettuce, behind California.

Did you know? Georgia is the number two producer of Kale, after California and is also the birthplace of the growing health-food chain Kale Me Crazy.

Did you know? Mulberry is the self-proclaimed Edamame (immature soybeans in the pods) capital of the world.

Did you know? Steaming eggs - not boiling them – is the secret to "hard-boiled" eggs that are consistently perfect.

Did you know? Hawaii used to be famous for growing pineapples. However, in the 1980's the pineapple manufacturers, including Dole, relocated their operations from Hawaii because of rising costs, to Ecuador, Honduras and Costa Rica.

Did you know? Making one cotton shirt takes 2,700 liters of water? (Health Magazine, April 2020, p.75).

Did you know? The first American Hemp farmers were the founding fathers of the U.S., George Washington, and Thomas Jefferson. They grew it mainly on their farms. Benjamin Franklin owned a paper mill that uses the Hemp plants to make paper.

Did you know? During the time of the Founding Fathers, bibles, charts, maps, and Betsy Ross's flag were all made of Hemp.

Did you know? It was against the law in the 17th and 18th centuries to refuse to grow Hemp in the U.S. In Virginia, for example, you could be jailed if you were to refuse to grow Hemp from 1763-1769.

Did you know? The 1st draft of the Declaration of Independence and the Constitution were made of Hemp too.

Did you know? In 1631 until about the early 1800's it was legal to pay taxes with Hemp in the U.S.

Did you know? Eighty percent of all textiles were made from Hemp until the 1820's when the Cotton Gin was introduced.

Did you know? CBD products for sale nationwide in the US are made from Hemp, which is a type of Cannabis that is a botanical cousin to Marijuana. CBD will not make you high. Tetrahydrocannabinol (THC) is the substance that does that, and there is little if any of it in Hemp. (The maximum amount of THC legally allowed in CBD products is 0.3 percent).

Did you know? There was no need for labels saying "certified organic" before the mid-20th century because organic was the only way to farm. However, in the 1940's, after World War II, Nitrate factories that had been making bombs, switched to producing synthetic fertilizers. The era of mass-scale chemical fertilizer and pesticides dramatically increased crop yields worldwide. For example, the yield of rice grown in India increased by 164% from the 1950s to the 1990s.

Did you Know? Nearly half of organic farmers are women, even though women make up only 29% of all American farmers, according to the USDA.

Did you know? The biggest organic retailer in the country is not Whole Foods. It is Costco, which sold about $4 billion in organic products in 2017, compared with $3.6 billion at Whole Foods.

Did you know? 76% of the US grown, organic spinach contains 33 different pesticides. In order to pick the safest produce, you need to check CR.org/pesticides1220 (Consumer Report On Health, December 2020, p.8).

Did you know? The top pork producing state in the United States, is the state of Iowa. It is the home to nearly eight times as many pigs (23.5 million 2019) as people (3.1 million residents).

Did you know? Do not wash raw chicken before cooking. Why? This is because raw chicken tends to be contaminated with harmful bacteria and when washed, it can splash all over the kitchen without you noticing it.

Did you know? Great amounts of plant protein can be found in nuts, blackberries, avocado, lentils, mushrooms and broccoli. By the way, avocados have the highest calories of any fruit at 167 calories per one hundred grams. In addition, avocados are nutrient-dense, containing an amazing 20 vitamins and minerals and have anti-inflammatory properties too (Newsmax Magazine, Natural Cures 2021, p.41).

Did you know? Every year, farmers in Kansas typically grow enough wheat to make 36 billion loaves of bread.

Did you know? The cocoa bean emerged in Mesoamerica, where the indigenous people used it in religious ceremonies, traded it as currency, and fermented it into alcohol. Europeans did not like the bitter taste, so they added sugar, honey, and vanilla (another New World contribution) to it. In the early 1800's Swiss chocolatiers made it smoother and mixed it with condensed milk, creating a creamy milk chocolate (Popular Mechanic, Spring 2020, p.14).

Did you know the difference between Cacao and Cocoa? Cacao beans are dried, fermented and heated at low temperatures. The heat separates the fatty part of the beans from the rest of it and it is not as sweet as Cocoa, however, it contains more antioxidants. Even though Cocoa is harvested the same way as Cacao, it is heated at high temperature and the final product is much sweeter than Cacao. Therefore, because Cocoa is more processed than Cacao it ends up containing less antioxidants.

Did you know? Many Alaskans wear "bear bells" when they go picking berries, to avoid surprising the bears who love them too.

Did you know? There is only one type of corn that will pop. The scientific name of it is *Zea mays everta*.

Did you know? The Wampanoag Native Americans tribes brought popcorn to the colonists for the first Thanksgiving in Plymouth, Massachusetts.

Did you know what really makes the popcorn pop? Each kernel contains a small amount of moisture. When the kernel is heated, the moisture form into steam. Pressure builds up in the kernel until it explodes, turning inside out.

Did you know? Allegedly Christopher Columbus introduced popcorn to Europe in the late 15th Century.

Did you know? In 1885 Charles Cretors introduced the first commercial popcorn machine in Chicago, Illinois.

Did you know? A native of Brazil, Indiana, Orville Redenbacher started producing his own popcorn when he was 12. His special hybrid – where only one kernel in every 45 does not pop – helped build an empire.

Did you know? Nebraska produces more popcorn than any other state in the U.S.- around 250 million pounds per year.

Did you know? Americans consume 17 billion quarts of popcorn each year. That is enough to fill the Empire State Building 18 times.

Did you know? Walnuts, chestnuts, and hazelnuts are not nuts at all, nor are pistachios or cashews. The soft flesh that we eat are the seeds inside the pits.

Did you know? If you want to add raw onion to your food but want to make sure that it adds a milder flavor, you need to cut the onion with the grain and use the outer layers. This is best when you use it in salads or sandwiches. If, however you want to add a stronger flavor to your food you need to cook the onion and cut it against its grain and use the inner layers. This is best when you use it in rice pilaf or French onion soup.

Did you know that we still do not know who came up with the birthday cake tradition? Some scholars believe that the ancient Greeks came up with it. While others believe that it was the ancient Romans. Others, however, believe that it was started in the Middle Ages in Germany.

Did you know? A "bride's pie" (not cake) was served at most weddings up until the early 19th century.

Did you know? Sponge cake was first created in the mid-16th century by an Italian pastry chef for a Spanish lord.

Did you know who were the first people that started to chew gum? It is believed that the ancient Greeks were the first people to chew gum. Thousands of years ago, they were chewing Mastic. Mastic is a rubbery resin from the Mastic tree. People chew it to clean and freshen their teeth. Hippocrates, the famous Greek father of medicine, recommended Mastic as a remedy for chronic coughs, liver problems and upset stomachs. At the time of explorations, the Native American tribes introduced it to European settlers in the Americas. The Native American tribes made the gum from spruce-tree resin. Later, in the mid-nineteenth century, the Americans added to it sweetened paraffin wax. However, neither one was popular at that time. The Maya of the Yucatan Peninsula had been chewing Chicle for ages. They probably used it to reduce thirst during long journeys. The practice of chewing gum helped them produce more saliva, which in turn, reduced their thirst. General Santa Anna, yes the one who attacked the Alamo, brought Chicle - a latex product extracted from the Sapodilla tree to the U.S. in the late 1860's. He is also believed that Chicle could be used as a rubber substitute in making tires. So later, he introduced his idea to Thomas Adams. However, Thomas Adams soon realized that Chicle is not useful for making tires, so instead he discovered an effective way to make chewing gum. Adams came up with flavored chewing gum, the gumball, and the gumball machine (The Book of Amazing Curiosities pp. 36-37).

Did you know? In a 2013 study in the British *Journal of Psychology*, researchers wrote that gum chewing increases the flow of Oxygen to regions of the brain responsible for attention.

Did you know? In Luxemburg, Switzerland and France, public chewing of gum is considered vulgar, while in Singapore most types of gum have been illegal since 1992, after residents got tired of scraping the sticky stuff off their sidewalks.

Did you know? Researchers have found that enjoying a stick of gum instead of snacking is proven to curb cravings and help you avoid packing on extra unneeded pounds.

Did you know? The pretzel was invented about 1,400 years ago in A.D.610 by an Italian monk who wanted to reward his students for being good. At the time it was called "pretiola" – Latin for "little reward". When it reached Germany, the name changed to "pretzel".

Did you know? The holes in crackers are called Docker Holes and exist to prevent large air pockets from forming while baking.

Did you know? In 1953, in Omaha, Nebraska, the company C.A. Swanson and Sons overestimated the demand for Thanksgiving turkey and found itself with 260 extra tons of frozen Turkeys. That led to the creation of the first TV dinners, complete with corn bread dressing, gravy, peas, and sweet potatoes.

Did you know? Sweet potatoes originated in Central and South America and eventually they were introduced to North America during the Age of Exploration. Today North Carolina produces more sweet potatoes than the other 49 U.S. states combined. In fact, many North Carolinians insist that sweet potato pie is the true Thanksgiving dessert and not pumpkin pie.

Did you know? About 60 percent of the 75 million bushels of Durum wheat which is produced annually in North Dakota, is used to make pasta.

Did you know? We need to consume more plant protein because it is much healthier for us than animal protein, but we need both to stay healthy.

Did you know why do bagels have holes? They have holes so that the immigrants (who sold the yeasty rolls in New York City's Lower East Side at the turn of the 20th century) could stack them up on sticks to take to customers.

Did you know? Saltwater Taffy was invented in 1883 in Atlantic City, New Jersey. The business became so competitive that a patent dispute over taffy-making machines ended up in the U.S. Supreme Court in 1921.

Did you know? Virginia and Georgia both lay claims to inventing the Brunswick Stew. Why? This is because both have locations named Brunswick. The Virginians use chicken in their stew, while the Georgians use pork and beef with hotter spices in their stew.

Did you Know? Wyoming is a fisherman's paradise, because it has more than 70 species of fish, including the state fish, the Cutthroat Trout.

Did you know? In 1923, brothers Thomas and Walter Belshaw invented an automated doughnut maker in Seattle, Washington

State. Today, Krispy Kreme and Dunkin' Donuts still use their invention successfully.

Did you know? Wisconsin is not only America's leading producer of cow's milk, but also is a leading producer of goat milk and cheese.

Did you know? Researchers at the University of St. Andrews in Scotland studied 13 common beverages to see how much water the body retained two hours after they were ingested. To their surprise, they found out that plain water was near the bottom of the list. The winner was skim milk. Its sugar, protein, and fat, slow the emptying of fluid from the stomach, and its Sodium acts as a sponge, keeping fluid in the body.

Did you know? There is really no difference between brown or white eggs. However, the brown eggs cost more than the white eggs because the farmer needs to spend more money feeding the chickens that lay brown eggs since they are bigger in size than the white egg laying chickens who eat much less food.

Did you know? Americans refrigerate their eggs because they wash them before they send them to market. However, other countries in the world do not do so. The European Union for example insists on not washing the eggs, because they are naturally covered with kind of wax called Cuticle that protect them from being spoiled, and therefore they do not need to be refrigerated. However, unwashed eggs can look very dirty and not pleasing to the eye of the buyer.

Did you know? The pilot and co-pilot of a flight never eat the same kind of meals in case one causes food poisoning.

Signature Dishes of the Fifty States of the US

Did you know what the signature dish of Alabama is? It is chicken in white sauce.

Did you know what the signature dish of Alaska is? It is King Crab legs.

Did you know what the signature dish of Arizona is? It is Posole, which is a stew made from pork shoulder and hominy (coarsely ground corn).

Did you know what the signature dish of Arkansas is? It is the barbecue sandwich.

Did you know what the signature dish of California is? It is the fish taco.

Did you know what the signature dish of Colorado is? It is green chili pork.

Did you know what the signature dish of Connecticut is? It is clam pie.

Did you know what the signature dish of Delaware is? It is Scrapple (pork scraps, cornmeal, flour, and spices).

Did you know what the signature dish of Florida is? It is the Cuban sandwich.

Did you know what the signature dish of Georgia is? It is peach cobbler.

Did you know what the signature dish of Hawaii is? It is Kalua pig (pork butt).

Did you know what the signature dish of Idaho is? It is fried Trout.

Did you know what the signature dish of Illinois is? It is deep-dish pizza.

Did you know what the signature dish of Indiana is? It is Hoosier Pie or sugar cream pie.

Did you know what the signature dish of Iowa is?

It is the breaded pork tenderloin sandwich.

Did you know what the signature dish of Kansas is? It is Bierocks (German pastries stuffed with ground beef, cabbage, onions, and spices).

Did you know what the signature dish of Kentucky is? It is Hot Brown, which is an open-faced turkey and tomato sandwich doused in Mornay sauce, sprinkled with cheese, broiled, and topped with bacon.

Did you know what the signature dish of Louisiana is? It is Gumbo soup. The soup is made of a strongly flavored stock, meat or shellfish, a thickener, and vegetables, namely celery, bell peppers, and onions.

Did you know what the signature dish of Maine is? It is the lobster roll – with a toasted, buttered, split-top bun.

Did you know what the signature dish of Maryland is? It is the Crab Cake.

Did you know what the signature dish of Massachusetts is? It is Boston baked beans.

Did you know what the signature dish of Michigan is? It is meat pasties (a folded pastry case with meat filling).

Did you know what the signature dish of Minnesota is? It is a Hotdish, which is a casserole made with cream of mushroom soup, vegetables, meat, and Tater Tots (grated and deep-fried potatoes).

Did you know what the signature dish of Mississippi is? It is Catfish.

Did you know what the signature dish of Missouri is? It is barbecue.

Did you know what the signature dish of Montana is? It is the chicken-fried steak.

Did you know what the signature dish of Nebraska is? It is Runza, a pocket sandwich like Kansas's Bierocks, with extra cabbage.

Did you know what the signature dish of Nevada is? It is the shrimp cocktail.

Did you know what the signature dish of New Hampshire is? It is Poutine, cheese curds, French fries, and gravy.

Did you know what the signature dish of New Jersey is? It is Taylor Ham or also called Pork roll.

Did you know what the signature dish of New Mexico is? It is pork Tamales.

Did you know what the signature dish of New York is? It is Buffalo wings.

Did you know what the signature dish of North Carolina is? It is barbecue.

Did you know what the signature dish of North Dakota is? It is Knoephla soup, made with chicken, potatoes, and dumplings.

Did you know what the signature dish of Ohio is?
It is Cincinnati chili.

Did you know what the signature dish of Oklahoma is? It is a whole meal that includes chicken-fried steak, sausage with biscuits and gravy, corn bread, corn fried okra, black-eyed peas, barbecued pork, squash, grits, and strawberries, topped off with a piece of pecan pie.

Did you know what the signature dish of Oregon is? It is Tofurky. A football-sized turkey substitute.

Did you know what the signature dish of Pennsylvania is? It is the Philly cheesesteak.

Did you know what the signature dish of Rhode Island is? It is doughnuts.

Did you know what the signature dish of South Carolina is? It is shrimp and grits.

Did you know what the signature dish of South Dakota is? It is Chislic, which are bite-size portions of beef, lamb venison, or mutton that are grilled or deep-fried and served on a stick.

Did you know what the signature dish of Tennessee is? It is Nashville hot chicken. It is fried chicken prepared with plenty of cayenne pepper.

Did you know what the signature dish of Texas is? It is the Pecan pie.

Did you know what the signature dish of Utah is?

It is Fry Sauce, which is one part ketchup, two parts mayonnaise, some lemon or pickle juice, and onion seasoning.

Did you know what the signature dish of Vermont is? It is Ben & Jerry's Ice Cream.

Did you know what the signature dish of Virginia is? It is Ham biscuits-rolls filled with Virginia ham, mustard, and other seasonings.

Did you know what the signature dish of the state of Washington is? It is grilled wild salmon.

Did you know what the signature dish of West Virginia is? It is Pepperoni rolls.

Did you know what the signature dish of Wisconsin is? It is cheese curds.

Did you know what the signature dish of Wyoming is? It is Bison or beef jerky.

Famous Personalities That Never Attended or Dropped Out of School/College, or Did Not Have Much Schooling

Did you know? Some incredibly famous personalities, that we are familiar with today, dropped out of school. The secret to their success has to do with their exceptional great talents, otherwise they could have been great losers.

Did you know? **John Peake Knight** was an English railway manager and inventor, credited with inventing the traffic light in 1868 despite the fact that at the age of 12 he dropped out of school to work in the parcel room of the Derby railway station in the UK. In addition, he also did a great deal to improve the quality of railway travel by introducing the Westinghouse Air Brake, safer carriages with communication cords, electric lighting, and the Pullman Cars to the English railway (http://en.m.wikipedia.org).

Did you know? **Philo T. Farnsworth** was a self-taught, inventor from Utah, who came up with the first electronic television system.

Did you know? **Thomas Edison** invented the lightbulb, phonograph, and the motion picture camera from among 1000 other inventions which he created.

Did you know? **Benjamin Franklin** was a politician, diplomat, author, printer, publisher, scientist, inventor, Founding Father of the U.S.A., and both coauthor and cosigner of the Declaration of Independence.

Did you know? **Albert Einstein** was a Nobel Prize -winning physicist, famous for his theory of relativity and contributed to quantum theory and statistical mechanics.

Did you know? **"Big Cheeks"** was also known as Louis "Satchmo" Armstrong – 'Satchmo' means, in the Yiddish language, "Big Cheeks." He was a grandson of black slaves. He was born in a poor neighborhood of New Orleans known as the "Back of Town." His father abandoned the family when he was an infant, and his mother became a prostitute, so he and his sister ended up living with his grandma. Early in life, he proved to be gifted for music and with three other kids he sang in the streets of New Orleans. A Jewish family, the Karnofskys, who had emigrated from Lithuania to the USA, had pity for him and brought him into their house to stay with them. For the first time in his life, he was treated with kindness and tenderness. The Karnofskys realized his great talent for music and gave him money to buy his first musical instrument. They sincerely admired his musical talent. Later when he became a professional musician and a composer, he used some Jewish melodies in his compositions, such as St. James Infirmary and Go Down Moses. When he grew up, he wrote a book about this Jewish family and until the end of his life, he wore the Star of David and said that in this family, he had learned "how to live real life and have determination." In addition, Louis Armstrong also spoke fluent Yiddish that he acquired living with the Jewish family.

Did you know? **Andrew Carnegie** was one of America's first multibillionaires.

Did you know? ***Vidal Sassoon*** made millions as the founder of Vidal Sassoon hairstyling salons and hair care products.

Did you know? **Bill Gates** is the cofounder of the software giant Microsoft and has been ranked the one of the richest persons in the world.

Did you know? Paul Allen made billions as one of the cofounders of Microsoft.

Did you know? **John D. Rockefeller** founded the Standard Oil Company in 1870 and was the first recorded billionaire in the U.S.A.

Did you know? **Walt Disney** founded the Walt Disney Company, a film making company, and became a multimillionaire.

***Did you know why was* Walt Disney's *classic movie Snow White banned in the Arab world*?** It was banned because it contained a horse named "Samson" – a Jewish name. Syria (a Moslem country) demanded the horse's name to be changed, but Disney refused to do so (Understanding the Volatile and Dangerous Middle East, Dr.Steven Carol, iUnivere 2015, p.504)

Did you know? **Frederick Henry Royce** made millions as the cofounder of Rolls-Royce.

Did you know? **Richard Branson** was a self-made British billionaire. He founded Virgin Atlantic Airways, Virgin Records, Virgin Mobile and a space tourism company to provide suborbital trips into space for anyone who can afford it.

Did you know? **Colonel Sanders** became a millionaire by founding the Kentucky Fried Chicken restaurant chains (now KFC).

Did you know? **Charles Dickens** was a famous author of numerous classics including Oliver Twist, A Tale of Two Cities, and A Christmas Carol.

Did you know? **Elton John** is a famous and successful musician who sold more than 250 million records and has more than 50 Top 40 hits.

Did you know? **Ray Kroc** was not the founder of the McDonald's restaurants, but he turned it into the world's largest fast-food chain. The 1st McDonald restaurant, in San Bernardino California, was opened in 1948 by the McDonald's brothers, Richard James and Maurice James McDonald. In 1956 they opened the 1st McDonald restaurant in Chicago, Il. They were the first to invent the "Speedee Service System" known today as "fast food". Ray Kroc bought them out in 1961 for $2.7 million and ended up earning $500 million doing so. Since then, the company has opened 700 restaurants nationwide.

Did you know? **Harry Houdini** was the most famous and brilliant magician of the 20th century. He invented the Challenge Act offering to escape from any pair of handcuffs produced by the audience. This act was a turning point for his career that made him a legend.

Did you know? **John Thomas Walton** was the son of Sam Walton, the founder of the Walmart chain of retail stores. After attending two years of college, he decided to drop out of college and join the military to fight in the Vietnam War, even though he did not have to. After all, he was the 11th richest man in the world (18.2 billion net worth) and could have bought his way out. He ended up serving in the MACV-SOG. It was a unit involved in covert operations in Laos, Cambodia, and North Vietnam. During the war, his six-man reconnaissance unit was surrounded and overran by the enemy. Many soldiers in the group including the leader were wounded. He took upon himself, despite the grave danger, to rescue them and moved them away from harm's way. His act earned him the Silver Star, the United States Army's third highest award for valor. His famous quote was: "I figured if you are going to do something, you should do it the best you can". Despite his wealth and great courage, he was always humble and modest in his behavior. After the Vietnam War, he learned to become a pilot, and flew merchandise for his family business across the country. He was also a strong proponent of education and school vouchers and helped to establish the Children's Scholarship Fund. His goal was to send low-income children to private schools. Thanks to John, advocacy the Walton's family ended up donating about $700 million for the public good.

Unfortunately, John Walton died on June 27, 2005, when his plane crashed in Grand Teton National Park, Wyoming. He was only 58 years old at that time and still had a good deal of his life ahead of him. The cause for the fatal crash were loose flight control components. He left behind a wife Christy, and a son, Lukas.

Did you know? **Jim Carrey** was born in Canada and dropped out of school when he was sixteen years old. Yet, he ended up being one of the most gifted actors in Hollywood. He has the ability to switch between comedic and dramatic roles in no time. A rare talent indeed for any actor.

Did you know? **Annie Oakley** was a famous and highly skilled shooter. After her father died, she had to drop out of school and was sent to stay with an abusive, farm family. Shortly afterwards, she ran away from the abusive situation to her poor mother. Annie taught herself how to shoot, hunt, and helped her mother feed her eight siblings. After hunting for a while, she improved her skills of shooting to the point where she became a superb shooter. Later she became a star for 17 years in Buffalo Bill Cody's "Wild West" show. She did not just shoot a target, she could shoot glass balls while galloping around an arena on a horse with a gun in each hand, she could also hit two targets at once, and she could shoot upside down and backward while looking in a mirror. Later, in life she ended up in a train accident that left her with a slight paralysis in 1901. Despite it all, she continued to perform as a shooter for 20 more years in different venues. She used her fame to also teach young girls how to become self-reliant. Furthermore, she taught them to shoot, a skill that was still associated with men at that time. In addition, she used her wealth to support and educate 18 orphan girls.

Did you know? **Rush Limbaugh** was a brilliant American radio personality and a conservative political commentator, a television show host as well as a brilliant marketer and a businessman. He understood that his message could be sent throughout the country.

Most people probably do not know that he also was an author who wrote a series of children's books. Yet, he did not care much about school so after one year of attending Southeast Missouri State University he dropped out. However, he was truly knowledgeable about many complex issues and topics because he was his own self-taught man. He used to state that his "talent is on a loan from God." He had the courage to lead the conservative media revolution and was one of the most powerful voices of truth for the American right. In addition, he inspired many conservative commentators in the U.S. that became famous after following his footsteps. Among them are Mark Levin, Sean Hannity, Glen Beck, and Bill O'Reilly to name a few. In 2020, President Donald Trump awarded him, the Presidential Medal of Freedom, the nation highest civilian honor. Here are some of his famous quotes: "No nation has ever taxed itself into prosperity," and "You know why there is a Second Amendment? In case the government fails to follow the first one." Another quote "What about feeling sorry for those... who pay the taxes? Those are the people NO ONE ever feels sorry for. They are asked to give and give until they have no more to give, and when they say 'Enough!' they are called selfish." Another famous quote is that "the world's biggest problem is the unequal distribution of capitalism. If there were capitalism everywhere, you would not have food shortages."

Did you know? William Phelps Eno never learned how to drive but nevertheless he invented the stop sign, the pedestrian cross walk, the traffic circle, the one-way street, the taxi stand, and the pedestrian safety island.

Did you know? Robert B. Thomas was the founder of The Old Farmer's Almanac in 1792. He was also a bookseller, schoolteacher, and an amateur astronomer living near Boston, Massachusetts.

Did you know? Almost 14% of **Google Employees** have never attended college.

Women and Men That Deserve to be More Famous

Did you know? **Women** invented many useful things such as the bulletproof vests, fire escapes, life rafts, windshield wipers, dishwasher machine, and the laser printers among other things.

Did you know? **Deborah Sampson** was the first woman to serve in the U.S. Army. She posed as a man in order to enlist in 1781. She sustained multiple injuries in battle but often treated them herself to avoid detection, including a wound from a pistol ball in her own thigh (Reader's Digest, September 2020, p.36).

Did you know? **Patty S. and Mildred J. Hill** were two sisters who composed the song **Happy Birthday** in 1935. Later on, Warner Communications paid them 28 million for the copyright of their song.

Did you know? **Claudette Colvin** and not Rosa Parks was the first woman/ teenager to defy racist bus laws in Montgomery, Alabama in 1955. The 15-year-old was the first person arrested for protesting the Montgomery's racist bussing rule and her defiance eventually became the subject of international attention. However, she was too young to receive credit for it. So, during the same year Rosa Parks was the one who went down in history for defying the Jim Crow Laws in 1955 (Reader's Digest, September 2020, p.101).

Did you know? **Amy Johnson** was an English aviator 1903-1941 and one of the first women to earn a pilot's 1icense. Johnson won fame when she flew solo from Great Britain to Australia in 1930. Her dangerous flight took 17 days. Later she flew solo to India and Japan and became the first woman to fly across the Atlantic Ocean East to West. During WWII, she volunteered to fly for The Women's

Auxiliary Air Force, but her plane was shot down over the River Thames and she was killed.

Did you know? **The Nightwitches** were female Russian bomber crews who bombed Germany during WWII. They had old noisy planes and the engines used to conk out halfway through their missions, so they had to climb out on the wings mid-flight to restart the props, and then drop their bombs. Their leader flew 200+ missions and was never captured.

Did you know? **Maria Beasley** invented life rafts in 1882.

Did you know? **Nancy Johnson** invented the ice cream maker in 1843.

Did you know? **Margaret Knight** invented a machine that makes square bottomed paper bags in 1871. In addition, she invented a safety device for cotton mills and her invention is still being used today.

Did you know? **Anna Connelly** invented the fire escape in 1887.

Did you know? **Josephine Cochrane** invented the first dishwasher in 1887. In addition, she even marketed her machine to hotel owners and even opened her own factory without the help of a man.

Did you know? **Tabitha Babbitt** invented the circular saws.

Did you know? **Ada Lovelace** essentially was the first computer programmer, due to her work with Charles Babbage at the University of London in 1842. In fact, her notes were essential key to helping Alan Turing's work on the first modern computer in the 1940s.

Did you know? **Letitia Geer** came up with the medical syringes which could be operated with only one hand in 1899.

Did you know? **Sarah Mather** invented the underwater lamp and telescope.

Did you know? **Margaret A. Wilcox** invented the car heater in 1893.

Did you know? **Giuliana Tesoro** invented multiple things in the textile industry. She came up with flame-resistant fibers and permanent-press properties to fabric among many of her other inventions.

Did you know? **Mary Anderson** in 1903 invented, what later became known as, the windshield wiper, and by 1916 it became standard on most vehicles. Furthermore, she was also a movie actress.

Did you know? **Elizabeth Magie** invented, in 1904, the game called Landlord's Game. The purpose of this game was to expose the injustice of unchecked capitalism. Her game was ripped off by Charles Darrow who sold it to Parkers Brother's 30 years later. However, Parker's Brothers later paid Elizabeth $500 for her game that later became known as Monopoly.

Did you know? **Florence Parpart** invented the electric refrigerator in 1914. She also invented an improved street cleaning machine.

Did you know? **Dr. Grace Murray Hopper**

was a computer scientist that invented COBOL in the 1940's which was the first user-friendly business computer software system. She was also a rear admiral in the U.S. navy and was the first one to use the term "bug" in reference to a glitch in a computer system after she literally found a bug (moth) causing problems with her computer.

Did you know? **Alice Parker** invented in 1919 the gas-powered central heater but it was never manufactured. However, it inspired the central heater systems used today.

Did you know? **Julia Ward Howe** was an American abolitionist and suffragist who came up with the first unofficial Mother's Day holiday that was held in Boston in 1872. She was also a poet and an author who was known for writing the "Battle Hymn of the Republic".

Did you know? **Anna Jarvis** was the West Virginia woman who officially founded Mother's Day in the United States after her mother's death in 1905. Jarvis's mother used organized events called Mother's Friendship Day, which end up uniting West Virginian families that had been separated during the Civil War. Jarvis, in honor of her mother, ended up writing many letters to elected officials and newspaper editors urging them to promote an official holiday to honor all mothers. In 1914, president Woodrow Wilson signed congressional resolution that designated the Sunday in May as Mother's Day across the nation. Later, it second spread around the world to other countries. The white carnation, the favorite flower of Anna Jarvis's mother, was the original flower of Mother's Day. Anna Jarvis, the founder, was terribly upset with those who fundraised off the holiday. She did not trust fundraisers to deliver the money to the people it was supposed to help. She did not want the holiday to get commercialized. Sadly, she went broke using what monies she had battling the holiday's commercialization. She died penniless at the age of 84. (The Book of Amazing Curiosities, p.33).

Did you know? **Nancy Green** was also known as "Aunt Jemima." She was a freed slave who used her talent and created a cooking brand. Aunt Jemima Milling Company bought her likeness almost a hundred years ago. Her wealth allowed her to be an organizer of the Oliver Baptist Church. She also became an activist and engaged in anti-poverty programs. She was one of the first Black

American missionary workers. She was a leading advocate against poverty and favor equal rights for individuals in Chicago, Ill. She passed away in 1923 as one of America's first black millionaires. A century after her death she has a generational net worth of 19M. Her company is currently owned by the Quaker Oats Company.

Did you know? **Norma Talmage** was a silent film actress, who started the tradition of stars putting their footprints in the cement at Grauman's Chinese Theatre in Los Angeles, California. It all started after she accidentally stumbled onto the freshly laid sidewalk in front of the theatre in1927.

Did you know? **Madam C. J. Walker (Sarah Breedlove)** was a famous, self-made, African American millionaire who established beauty schools, salons, and training facilities across America. Today she is considered to be one of the founders of the African American hair care and cosmetic industry (http://www.mentalfloss.com).

Did you know? **Hedy Lamarr and composer George Antheil** were pioneers in the field of wireless communication. They developed a secret communications system to help the Allies in World War II. They created unbreakable codes of communications. Two decades later their encryption was used abroad naval vessels during the Cuban Missile Crisis. This development of wireless communications inspired the creation of cellular phones, and fax machines. In addition, this technology also paved the way for everything from WI-FI to GPS.

Did you know? **Irena Sendler** during WWII got permission to work in the Warsaw Ghetto, as Plumbing Sewer Specialist. As such, she was able to smuggle 2,500 Jewish infants and children out of the ghetto and brought them to safety.

Did you know? **Dr. Maria Telkes** was a psychiatrist, and by the way, she invented, in 1947, a solar heating system for residential housing.

Did you know? **Cecile Steele** of Ocean View, Delaware ordered 50 chicks for her backyard chicken flock. Until the 1920s, people raised chickens primarily for the eggs. However, instead of the 50 chicks she ordered she end up receiving 500 by mistake. So, she ended up selling the excess birds, effectively hatching the broiler chicken industry.

Did you know? **Marie Van Brittan** Brown was an African American nurse and an inventor who created a precursor to the modern home TV security system. She invented the CCTV (Closed Circuit Television) because of the slow response of the local police to the crimes that were committed in Brown's New York City neighborhood in the 1960's. Brown filed a patent for this invention in 1966 and it was approved on December 2, 1969. This invention influenced the modern CCTV systems used for home security and police work today (http://www.mentalfloss.com).

Did you know? **Stephanie Kwolek,** invented Kevlar in 1965, which is a life-saving material that is 5 times stronger than steel and used to make bulletproof vests for police and soldiers.

Did you know? **Carolyn Davidson** was a graphic design student at Portland State University in 1971, who designed the Nike Swoosh. She was only paid $35 for the famous trademark.

Did you know? **Dr. Patricia Bath** revolutionized the field of Ophthalmology when she invented a device that refined laser cataract surgery called the Laserphaco Probe. She patented the invention in 1988, and today she is recognized as the first female African American doctor to receive a medical patent. In addition, she was the first African American to finish a residency in Ophthalmology at New York University, and was the first women to chair an ophthalmology residency program in the U.S. Furthermore, she also co-founded the American Institute for Prevention of Blindness (http://www.mentalfloss.com).

Did you know? **Dr. Shirley Jackson** developed some telecommunication technology including the portable fax machine, touch tone telephone, solar cells, fiber optic cables, and the technology behind Caller ID and call waiting.

Did you know? **Dr. Maulana Karenga** came up with Kwanzas, an annual celebration of African American family, community, and culture (Consumer Report, On Health, December 2020, p.17).

Did you know? **Debbie Allen** was an African American and one of the three producers of the 1997 movie *Amistad* that was based on the true story of the slave ship La Amistad, which was captured by a mutiny in the Caribbean Sea by African tribesmen who were abducted into the U.S. slave trade in 1839. When she first brought the idea of making a film about this topic to Hollywood in 1984, every studio executive rejected it. But she never gave up on her idea. It took her 18 years to eventually have this movie produced. This movie was coproduced by Steven Spielberg and was nominated for four Oscars and four Golden Globe awards. The famous movie stars that appeared in this movie included Morgan Freeman, Anthony Hopkins, Djimon Hounsou and Matthew McConaughey. Debbie Allen also stared as a dance teacher Lydia Grant in the TV series *Fame*. What most people do not know is that as a Black dancer from Huston, Texas, in the segregated 1960s, she was overlooked and dismissed for not fitting society's dancer standards, despite the fact of her being a talented dancer. She ended up acting, producing and directing in hundreds of TV and film projects over nearly 50 years.

In 2000 she founded a nonprofit Debbie Alen Dance Academy (DADA). In the show ABC's Grey's Anatomy, she plays the fiery Dr. Catherine Fox. Her famous quote is: "All we need is a good spark to start a fire that can reshape things" (Renew, UnitedHealthcare pp.16-19).

Did you know? **Katherine Johnson** was an African American NASA mathematician who help to calculate rocket trajectory and Earth orbits for many space missions. In 2015 President B. Obama awarded her with the Medal of Freedom. Sadly, she passed away on February 24, 2020.

Did you know? **Bea Arthur** before she became a famous actress in classic sitcoms like Maude and The Golden Girls, she served as a truck driver in the United States Marine Corps Women's Reserve during World War II. She respectively also earned Honorable Discharge and was regarded as "One Hell of a Marine."

Did you know? **Lori Roman** is the founder and President of The Ann Children's Fund. She founded the organization in honor of her mother Ann who performed Girl Scout Troop leader duties for girls with Down Syndrome and translated children's books into braille for local children who were visually impaired. The mother also gave these children the help, hope and love that they needed to thrive despite their disabilities. This organization today provides emergency aid to adopted children with disabilities, and their families, and the contributions to this organization are tax- deductible.

Did you Know? **Thomas Rawlinson** was an Englishman who invented the kilt (plaid skirt for men). Before 1745, Scottish aristocrats did not wear it. The plaid skirts were considered to be a lower-class wardrobe. However, when the kilts were banned by the British Parliament suddenly Scottish men, of all classes, decided to wear it and it became extremely popular clothes to wear for men there.

Did you know? **Thomas L. Jennings** was the first African American (a free slave at that time) to receive a patent in the U.S. in 1821. He paved the way for future inventors of color to gain exclusive rights to their inventions. Born in 1791, Jennings lived and worked in New York City as a tailor and dry cleaner. He invented an early method of dry cleaning called "dry scouring," four years before Paris tailor Jean Baptiste Jolly-Bellin refined his own chemical technique and established what many people claim was history's first dry cleaning business. Jennings used the money from his inventions to free the rest of his family from slavery and donated his money to abolitionists causes (http://www.mentalfloss.co).

Did you know? **John Walker** was an English chemist and druggist from Stockton-on-Tees, County Durham, who invented the first friction match in 1826.

Did you know? **Cornelius Swartwout** received the first U.S. patent in 1869 for a waffle iron. But the first waffles originated in Western Europe in the Middle Ages. By the way there are three main types of breakfast waffles, Belgian or also known as Brussels waffle, American and Liege, also invented in Belgium (but predating the Belgian waffle).

Did you know? **Antonio Meucci** was a Florentine immigrant to New York who actually invented the 'Teletrofono.' Sixteen years later, in 1876 Alexander Graham Bell actually adopted it and patent it. Meucci sued Bell for fraud, and the case was nearing the Supreme Court when Meucci died in 1889. After his death, the Supreme Court passed a resolution acknowledging Meucci as the original inventor of the telephone (The Reader's Digest, September 2020, p.103).

Did you know? **Alexander Miles** was an African American, who invented, in Duluth, Minnesota, an important safety feature for elevators, the automatic doors, which he patented in 1887. This invention prevented people from forgetting to close the shaft door and accidentally fall down the long, vertical hole. Today's elevators still employ a similar technology (https://www.mentalfloss.com).

Did you know? **William Middlebrook** patented a clip-winding machine in 1899 and the American Clip Company ended up creating the world's first paperclips. Today, its factory is located in Mississippi, and they produce 1,600 paperclips every minute (Popular Science, Spring 2020, p.73).

Did you know? **Nikola Tesla** in 1900 predicted that in the future we will have the internet. He actually believed that in the future there will be a "World System" of wireless communications that could send telephone messages, news, music, and pictures to any part of the world (Weird World 1.psf).

Did you know? **Willis H. Carrier** was a young engineer who invented in 1914 the air-conditioning system in New York City, New York (at that time it was not called so). It all has to do with the fact that in New York in August, the concrete, asphalt and humidity keep things steamy hot there, even in the early hours of the day. The humidity and the heat were causing quite a problem for the printing businesses there. The printing paper ended up expanding and contracting causing the printing to become misaligned or out of register. That major problem inspired Willis H. Carrier, to invent a system that ended up stabilizing the air inside the New York City, New York printing plants.

Did you know? **Jan Ernst Matzeliger** was a black immigrant from Dutch Guiana (modern day Surinam) who worked as an apprentice in a Massachusetts shoe factory. Matzeliger invented an automated machine that attached a shoe's upper part to its sole. Once it was refined, the device could make about 700 pairs of shoes per day instead of 50 pairs sewed by hand. It is important to mention that in the 19th century, the average person could not afford to buy shoes. So, Matzeliger invention led to lower shoe prices and that in turn led to making shoes within the financial reach for the average American (https://www.metalfloss.com).

Did you know? **Elzie Crisler Segar** was the cartoonist who drew Popeye the Sailor Man. This cartoon was based on a real person named Frank "Rocky" Fiegel. He was born in Jan. 27, 1868, in Poland and died on March 24, 1947. He was a retired sailor that was hired by Wiebusch's tavern in the city of Chester, Illinois, to clean and maintain order. He ended up however having a reputation of being always a fighter and as result he ended up having a deformed eye ("Pop-eye"). In addition, he always smoked his pipe, so he ended up speaking only with one side of his mouth. The Segar, the cartoonist was born in Chester and met Frank when they were young men. Olive Oil also existed; her real name was Dora Paskel. She was the owner of a grocery store in Chester and was dressed up just like Olive Oil.

Did you know? **Charles Richard Drew** was an African American physician responsible for America's first major blood banks that ended up saving countless individual lives. While studying at Columbia University, he refined key methods of collecting, processing, and storing plasma. In 1943 he became the first African American doctor to be chosen as an examiner for the American Board of Surgery (http://www.mentalfloss.com).

Did you know? **Pavel Peter Gojdic** was a humble Catholic monk, in Slovakia who served as resident bishop during World War II and is credited with directly or indirectly saving as many as 1,500 Jews during the Holocaust.

Did you know? **Moritz Hochschild** was a German tin baron who saved ten times as many Jews during the Holocaust than Oskar Schindler.

Did you know? **Joseph Rochefort** in World War II was able to crack the Japanese Navy's JN25 code that helped to intercept plans to have an assault on Midway Atoll. Thanks to his great work the Allies won a crucial victory that shortened the war, saving countless lives.

Did you know? **Alan Turing** was able to crack the infamous Nazi Enigma code, which saved many lives. He also came up with the concept of modern computer hardware and software.

Did you know? **Dr. Mohamed** Helmy was an Egyptian physician who lived in Berlin, Germany and risked his life to help his Jewish friends. Despite being targeted and barred from practicing medicine in 1938, he also spoke out against Nazi policies. When deportation of Jews began, he hid a former patient in his home, and provided care and provisions for her family members (United States Holocaust Memorial Museum).

Did you know? **Eleanor and Gilbert Kraus** were an affluent Jewish American couple who rescued in the spring of 1939, 50 Jewish children trapped in Nazi-occupied Vienna, Austria. The couple endured a difficult journey back to the United States with the children, who then were placed in foster homes (United States Holocaust Memorial Museum).

Did you know? **Martha and Waitstill Sharp** a reverend and his social worker wife, traveled in February 1939 from the USA to aid refugees in Prague, Czechoslovakia. They were outraged at the situation there and ended up leaving behind, for half a year, their two small children in order to help and organize escape efforts. In July of 1939, the Gestapo shut down the Sharp's operation in Prague. In May of 1940, they ended up operating in other parts of Europe, facing grave danger. Despite it all, they were able to ultimately help to rescue 2,000 refugees from the Nazi hands (United States Holocaust Museum).

Did you know? **Percy Spencer** was so fascinated by the sinking of the Titanic in 1912 that he became a scientist. While serving in the Navy he was trained to be a radio electrician, and ultimately became a civilian expert on radar during WWII, earning the Distinguished Public Service Award for his work. He was doing it all without ever having graduated from high school. He is the one who stumbled upon, by accident, as to what radiation can do to food and got together with a company called Raytheon to market the idea of using radiation to cook food. In 1947 his microwave cooking idea was introduced to the market and the first microwave ovens were then called Radarange. The first food that he cooked in it was popcorn, and it was first sold to the public in 1946. These ovens were nearly six feet tall and weighed 750 pounds and they end up costing $3,000, then and today that will be roughly about $35,000. That creation eventually will lead to the advanced microwave ovens of today (Reader's Digest, February 2020, pp.102-104).

Did you know? **Bob Heft** was a high school student who designed our current American flag. He sewed the prototype for his history class project in 1958. His teacher gave him only a B- for his project (Reader's Digest, Feb. 2019 p.60).

Did you know? **Mark E. Dean** is an African American inventor and a computer engineer. He holds three of the nine PC patents for being the co-creator of the IBM personal computer released in 1981. He also led the team that designed the ISA bus - the hardware interface that allows multiple devices like printers, modems, and keyboards to be plugged into a computer. This innovation helped pave the way for the development of personal computers at work and at home. In addition, Dean also helped develop the first color computer monitor. Furthermore, in 1999 he and his team of programmers created the world's first gigahertz chip. In 1997 Dean was_inducted into the National Inventors Hall of Fame (http://www.mentalfloss.com).

Did you know? **Norman Borlaug** won the Nobel Peace Prize for developing high-yield varieties of grain crop. By doing so his invention helped to avert mass famine in developing nations, saving hundreds of millions of lives.

Did you know? **Steve Ditko** was the artist who created_the Spider-Man image. He came up with the outfit and web shooters, among other details. Yet, Stan lee often received the sole credit for Spider-Man.

Did you know? **William Marston** was a lawyer, a psychologist and an inventor who came up with the lie detector, the polygraph, as well as created the famous comic book character Wonder Woman.

Did you know? **Peter Buck** was a nuclear physicist who came up with a genius idea, to open in 1965 the first Subway sandwich shop. Today, Subway is one of the biggest fast-food franchise in the United States.

Did you know? **Frederick W.** Smith was the founder of Fed Ex. He saved his company from bankruptcy by going to Vegas, gambling the company's last $5,000 on blackjack and wone $27,000 enough to keep Fed Ex going for another week while securing additional funds.

Did you know? **Dr. Phil Birbara** was a NASA chemist who helped crack the code to create drinkable and breathable air to help humans survive in space. In addition, it is his knowledge of natural compounds found in plants that is making a big difference here on Earth. He discovered that Capsaicin, found in chili peppers, works amazingly well to relieve pain from aching muscles and joints. So, he came up with a formula that provide 24- hour joint relief to Arthritis sufferers called PainBloc24. (Arthritis Today, May/June 2020, p.8).

Did you know? **George Carruthers** was an African American astrophysicist who spent much of his career working with the Space Science Division of the Naval Research Laboratory (NRL) in Washington, D.C. He is most famous for creating the ultraviolet camera/ spectrograph, which NASA used when it launched Apollo 16 in 1972. It helped prove that molecular hydrogen existed in interstellar space, and in 1974, space scientists used a new model version of the camera to observe Halley's Comet and other celestial phenomena on the U.S.'s first space station, Skylab. In 2003 Carruthers was inducted into the National inventors Hall of fame (http://www.mentalfloss.com).

Did you know? **George de Menstral** was a Swiss engineer who invented Velcro. It happened after his dog was covered with spiky burs. He put the burs under a microscope and found tiny hooks at the ends of their bristles that latched onto most any kind of fur or clothing. That gave him the idea to mimic it with nylon, which was strong enough for the hooks to hold but also strong enough to be separated with the right tug (Reader's Digest, February 2020, p.108).

Did you know? **Lawrence G. Tesler** invented Copy and Paste (Weird World 1.pdf).

Unknown Little - Facts about Men & Women That Are Famous for Their Contributions

Did you know? **Leif Eriksson** was the Norwegian explorer who was the first European to set foot in North America 500 years before Columbus.

Did you know? **George Washington** won a seat in the Virginia House of Burgesses in 1758 after he spent his entire campaign budget on drinks for his supporters. Buying votes with booze was the norm until 1811. However, after 1811 Maryland passed the first campaign finance reform law that prohibited the purchase of alcohol for voters. Furthermore, George Washington's final military promotion, to General of the Armies of the United States, did not occur until 1976, 177 years after his death.

(Reader's Digest, November 2020, p.24)

Did you know? **Thomas Jefferson** got one of the first smallpox inoculations.

Did you know? **Benjamin Franklin** left $2,000 to the cities of Boston and Philadelphia in his will to help young tradesmen, but they could not draw the balance for 200 years. In 1990, it was worth $6.5 million. The money has been used to fund scholarships, women's health and help firefighters and disabled children.

Did you know? **Abraham Lincoln** before he became the16th President of the USA, he was a skilled wrestler in his youth. His famous sayings can still be applied to today's political situation:

"America will never be destroyed from the outside. If we falter and lose our freedoms, it will be because we destroyed ourselves".

Did you know? James Buchanan was the only president to remain a bachelor while in office in 1841.

Did you know? **William Henry Harrison** was the first U.S. president to die in office. He also holds the record for the shortest term in office of 32 days.

Did you know? **Winston Churchill** was born in a ladies' room during a dance.

Did you know? **Samuel Wilson** provided the U.S. Army with barrels of preserved meat during the War of 1812. The barrels were stamped U.S., short for Uncle Samuel Wilson. Today Uncle Same image stands for the United States.

Did you know? **Wolfgang A. Mozart** composed his first piece of music when he was only 5 years old.

Did you know? **George Washington**

We all know that George Washington was the leader of the Continental Army and the first president of the United States, as well as the one who presided over the convention that drafted the U.S. Constitution. However, what a few of us know is that George Washington never chopped down a cherry tree, nor were his dentures made out of wood. They were actually made of bone, hippopotamus ivory, human teeth (purchasing human teeth was a fairly common practice in the 18th century for affluent individuals), lead, brass screws, and gold metal wire. Throughout his life he had many sets of dentures. We also did not know that he was famous throughout his life for having a volcanic temper. We also did not know that he was working on developing his character from an early age. As a teenage boy, he admired and copied by hand the 110 Rules of Civility and Decent Behavior in Company and Conversation, which originated from a Jesuit textbook, and he ended up carrying it all through his life. In addition, Washington believed that it was not enough to be well-born, well-connected or well- educated, but rather one should be above all - a person of character. Washington was not without his faults. Like virtually all plantation owners of his day, he was a slaveholder. Yet, he was the only Founding Father to free his slaves upon his death. He also made military blunders and many errors of judgment, including trusting Benedict Arnold right up until he ran off with the enemy. His greatest act however was probably when he voluntarily resigned the presidency after his second term, leading the way for peaceful, orderly transfer of power in the future (The Oxford Communique by Alexander Green, April 2021, Volume 35, NO.4 pp.6-7 & skeptics.stackexchange.com).

Did you know? **Thomas Nast** was the one who invented the image of Santa Claus as we know it today, and he was also the one who came up with the elephant to represent the Republican Party, and the donkey to represent the Democratic Party. He was probably the most influential political cartoonists that ever lived. Not only because he was exceptionally good at it, but also because in those days very few people knew how to read and write, but they could understand the political points that he made. He was also an unrelenting foe of the political corruption at that time. In 1868, Nast drew cartoons in the *Harper's Weekly* paper that were critical of William Magear Tweed, known also as "Boss" Tweed, the corrupt leader of N.Y. City's Tammany Hall, the Democratic Party-political machine. Tweed was the worst kind of political crook. He stole about $200 million from the New York taxpayers through political corruption. After three years of unrelenting attack against Tweed by Nast's cartoons, he was removed from politics and sent to prison 1877. In 1902 Nast accepted an appointment from President Theodore Roosevelt as Counsel General to Ecuador. There, shortly afterward, he contracted Yellow Fever and died on December 7, 1902.

Did you know? **George Washington Carver** was an African American born into slavery in Missouri. When he was a boy, the Civil War ended allowing him the chance to receive an education. Even though opportunities for African Americans were limited at that time he was able to receive his undergraduate and master's degree in agricultural science at Iowa State Agricultural College. After graduation, Carver was hired by Booker T. Washington to run the Tuskegee Institute's Agricultural Department in Alabama. He ended up teaching poor farmers about fertilization and crop rotation. At that time, the region's primary crop was cotton, and cotton tends to drain nutrients from the soil. After carefully conducting studies to determine which crops naturally thrive in the region, he found out that legumes and sweet potatoes will be great crops to enrich the soil there. However, there was not much demand for either. So, he introduced to the region the peanut plant and discovered how to make 300 products from growing it. Things ranging from laundry soaps to plastics and diesel fuel can all be made from components of the peanut plant. By 1940, it became the South's second largest cash crop (http://www.mentalfloss.com).

Did you know? **Henry Ford** founded the Ford Motor Company and was the chief developer of the assembly line technique of mass production. He happened to also spend millions of dollars on trying to turn soybeans into textiles and paints (Reader's Digest, June 2021, p.117).

Did you Know? **Alexander Fleming** was a Scottish physician, who discovered, by an accident in 1928, a magic medicine, which was the first antibiotic called Penicillin (Reader's Digest, February 2020, p.107).

Did you know? **Jonas Salk** came up with the Polio Vaccine in 1955 and decided not to patent it so that it would be affordable for millions of people who could not afford it. As a result, he lost out on an estimated 7 billion dollars, but save humanity from a terrible disease.

Did you know? **Sam Philips** recorded and launched Elvis career as well as other famous singers such as, Johnny Cash, Roy Orbison, and Jerry Lee Lewis.

Did you know? **Thomas Edison** not only invented the incandescent light bulb, but he also invented in 1932, among other things, the motion picture camera.

Did you know? **Isaac Newton** is famous for his explanation of gravity, but very few people know that he was Warden of the mint. He used to disguise himself and made the rounds of London's taverns in search of counterfeiters.

Did you know? **E. Remington & Sons** were famous gunmakers, but very few people know that they invented the first typewriter in 1868. Later, Mark Twain, who was enthusiastic about publishing innovations, bought one of the first typewriter, and used it to write the book titled: *Life on the Mississippi.*

Did you know? **Dr. Thomas Sowell** is one of the greatest and successful African American economist-philosophers of our age (21's Century)). At the beginning of his college life, he considered himself to be a Marxist. However, after studying the effects of a variety of government regulations such as the minimum age law, Sowell concluded that free markets are the best alternative, particularly for disadvantaged people, like he was at the beginning of his life. Sowell ended up writing 56 books as well as numerous scholarly publications. He has also authored 72 essays in periodicals and books, as well as 32 book reviews and was a regular columnist for *Creators Syndicate* for 25 years, *Forbes* magazine for eight years, *Scripps Howard* news Service from 1984 to 1990, and *the Los Angeles Herald-Examiner* from 1978to 1980. Sowell also had occasional columns in *The Wall Street Journal, The New York Times, The Washington Post, the Los Angeles Times, Washington Star, Newsweek, The Times* (London), *Newsday* and *The Stanford Daily.*

Did you know? **Walt Disney** was afraid of mice.

Did you know? **Betsy Ross** was credited for sewing the first American flag in 1870. However, some people are not aware that she was a Quaker and that the Quakers were abolitionists who helped to ban slavery first in England and then in the USA. In addition, the Quakers were vital to the American Underground Railroad that worked on freeing the slaves. Today some people still think that the Betsy Ross flag symbolizes racism and slavery. That shows how ignorant they are of the United States past history.

Did you know? **Amelia Mary Earhart** was an American aviation pioneer and author. She was the first female aviator to fly solo across the Atlantic Ocean in 1932. In addition, she wrote best-selling book about her flying experiences. She was also instrumental in helping to form The Ninety-Nines, an organization for female pilots.

During an attempt at becoming the first female to complete a circumnavigational flight of the globe in 1937, she and navigator Fred Noonan disappeared over the central Pacific Ocean near Howland Island.

Did you know? **Eleanor Roosevelt** was a target of the FBI. The public did not find out about the extraordinary record that the FBI kept on her until 1982. To this day, November 17, 2020, 12 pages of the file are still classified. Eleanor was targeted by the FBI because she embraced liberal causes and civil rights activists, many of whom were suspected of being Communists.

Did you know? **Agatha Christie** indirectly, in 1977 saved a girl's life despite the fact that she was deceased at that time. Her novel *The Pale Horse* describes Thallium poisoning so well that a nurse, who had been reading the story, was able to suspect that a sick 1-year-old girl indeed suffered from this poison, even though the doctors at that time had no clue as to why she was so sick. When the girl was eventually tested it was found that she had traces of Thallium in her system, and so she ended up being treated for it. As you can see, she was saved by a murder mystery novel written years ago by Agatha Christie.

Printed in the United States
by Baker & Taylor Publisher Services